F R O S T B I T E

# FROSTBITE

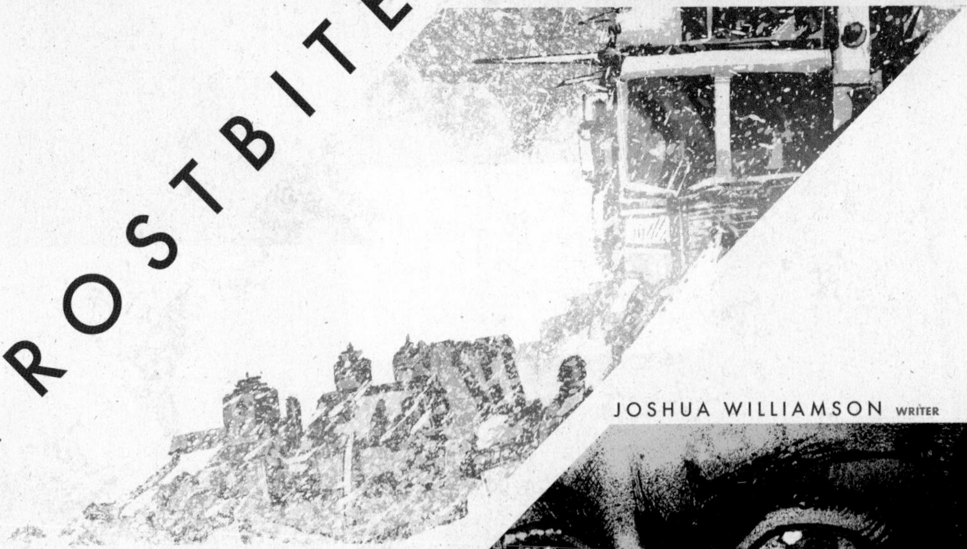

JOSHUA WILLIAMSON WRITER

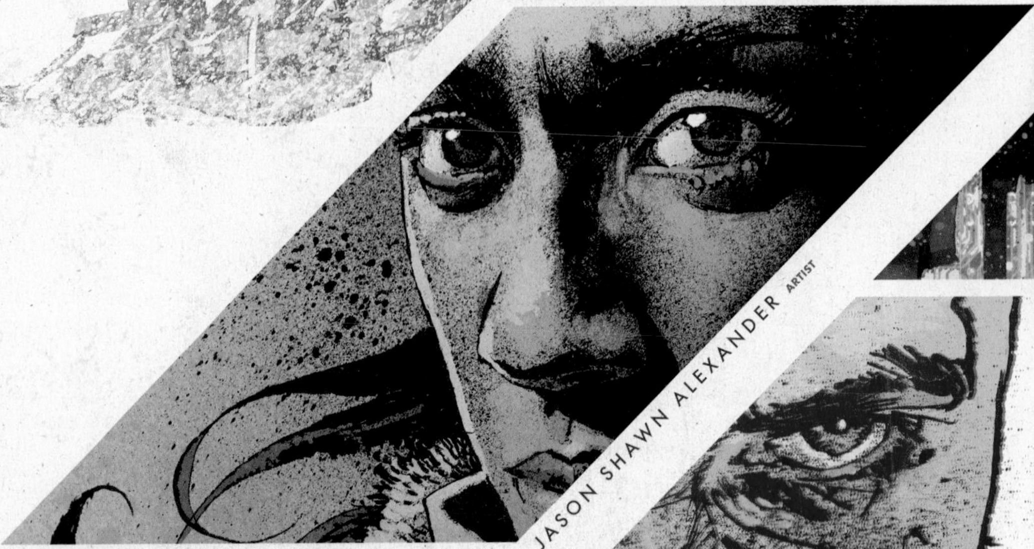

JASON SHAWN ALEXANDER ARTIST

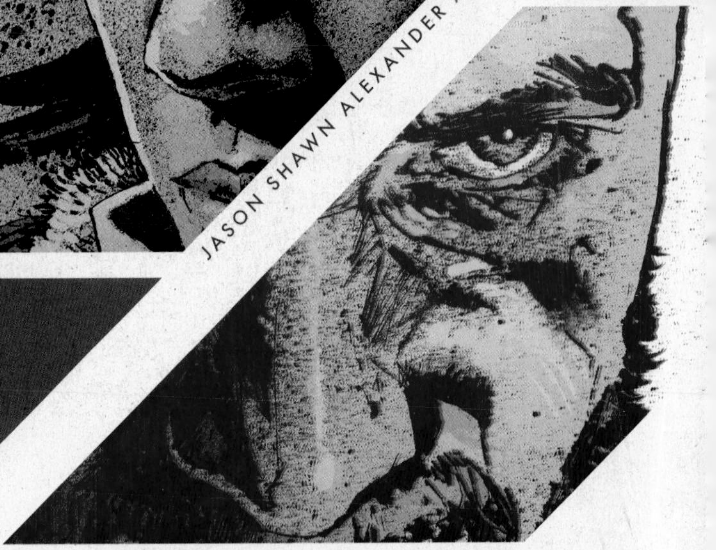

LUIS NCT COLORIST

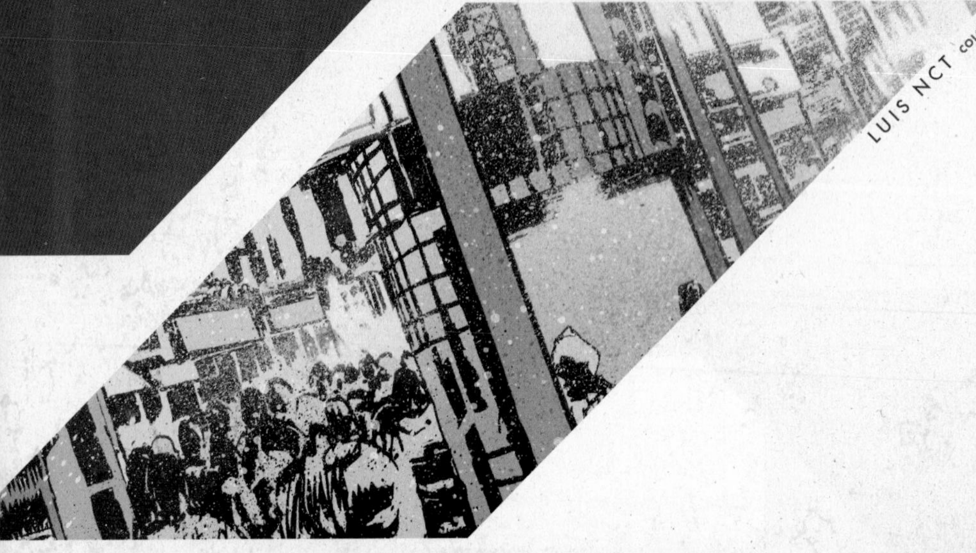

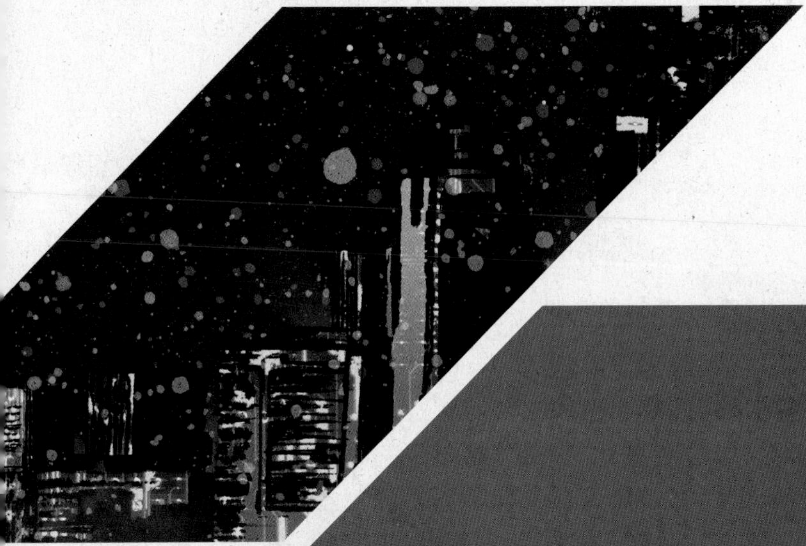

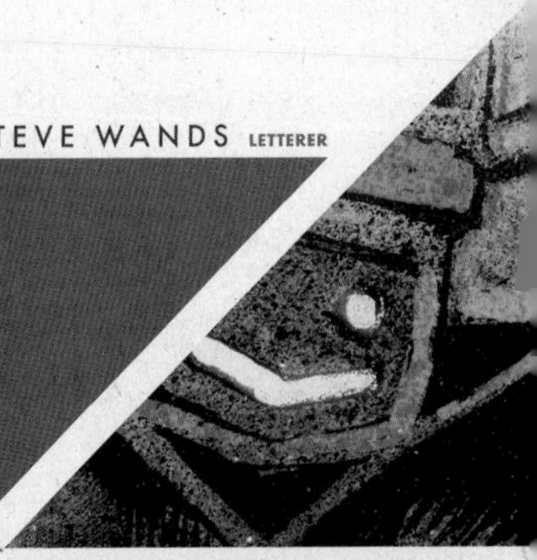

STEVE WANDS LETTERER

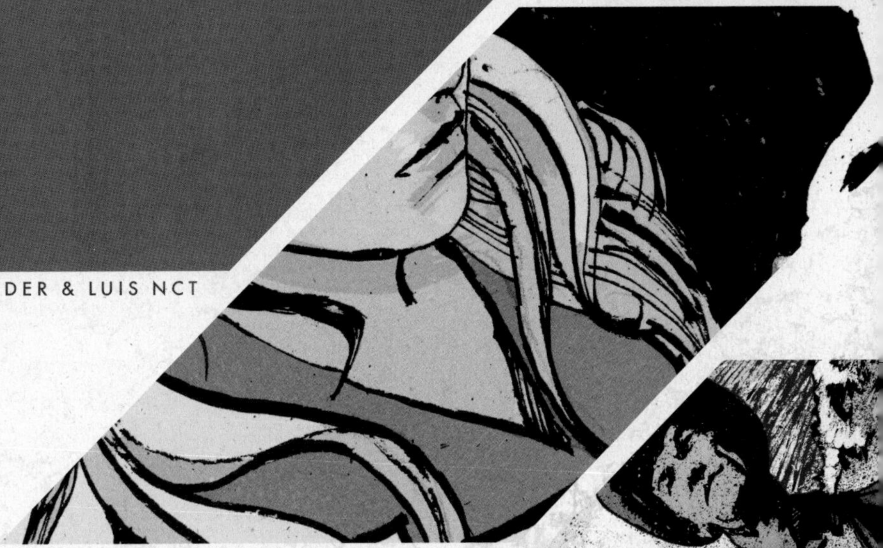

JASON SHAWN ALEXANDER & LUIS NCT
COVER ART

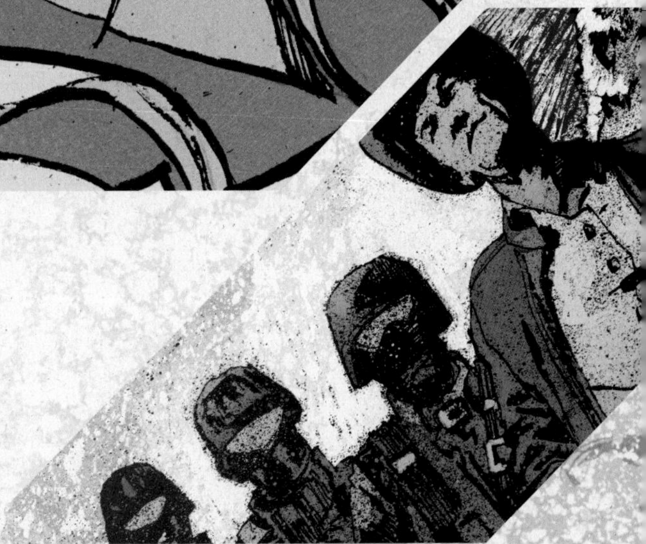

FROSTBITE CREATED BY JOSHUA WILLIAMSON AND JASON SHAWN ALEXANDER

**JAMIE S. RICH** EDITOR – ORIGINAL SERIES AND GROUP EDITOR – VERTIGO COMICS
**MAGGIE HOWELL** ASSISTANT EDITOR – ORIGINAL SERIES
**JEB WOODARD** GROUP EDITOR – COLLECTED EDITIONS
**SCOTT NYBAKKEN** EDITOR – COLLECTED EDITION
**STEVE COOK** DESIGN DIRECTOR – BOOKS
**MONIQUE GRUSPE** PUBLICATION DESIGN

**DIANE NELSON** PRESIDENT
**DAN DIDIO** PUBLISHER
**JIM LEE** PUBLISHER
**GEOFF JOHNS** PRESIDENT & CHIEF CREATIVE OFFICER
**AMIT DESAI** EXECUTIVE VP – BUSINESS & MARKETING STRATEGY,
DIRECT TO CONSUMER & GLOBAL FRANCHISE MANAGEMENT
**SAM ADES** SENIOR VP – DIRECT TO CONSUMER
**BOBBIE CHASE** VP – TALENT DEVELOPMENT
**MARK CHIARELLO** SENIOR VP – ART, DESIGN & COLLECTED EDITIONS
**JOHN CUNNINGHAM** SENIOR VP – SALES & TRADE MARKETING
**ANNE DEPIES** SENIOR VP – BUSINESS STRATEGY, FINANCE & ADMINISTRATION
**DON FALLETTI** VP – MANUFACTURING OPERATIONS
**LAWRENCE GANEM** VP – EDITORIAL ADMINISTRATION & TALENT RELATIONS
**ALISON GILL** SENIOR VP – MANUFACTURING & OPERATIONS
**HANK KANALZ** SENIOR VP – EDITORIAL STRATEGY & ADMINISTRATION
**JAY KOGAN** VP – LEGAL AFFAIRS
**THOMAS LOFTUS** VP – BUSINESS AFFAIRS
**JACK MAHAN** VP – BUSINESS AFFAIRS
**NICK J. NAPOLITANO** VP – MANUFACTURING ADMINISTRATION
**EDDIE SCANNELL** VP – CONSUMER MARKETING
**COURTNEY SIMMONS** SENIOR VP – PUBLICITY & COMMUNICATIONS
**JIM (SKI) SOKOLOWSKI** VP – COMIC BOOK SPECIALTY SALES & TRADE MARKETING
**NANCY SPEARS** VP – MASS, BOOK, DIGITAL SALES & TRADE MARKETING

**LOGO DESIGN BY NESSIM HIGSON & JASON HAMMEL**

FROSTBITE

DC COMICS
2900 WEST ALAMEDA AVENUE
BURBANK, CA 91505
PRINTED IN CANADA. FIRST PRINTING.
ISBN: 978-1-4012-7134-3

LIBRARY OF CONGRESS CATALOGING-IN-PUBLICATION DATA IS AVAILABLE.

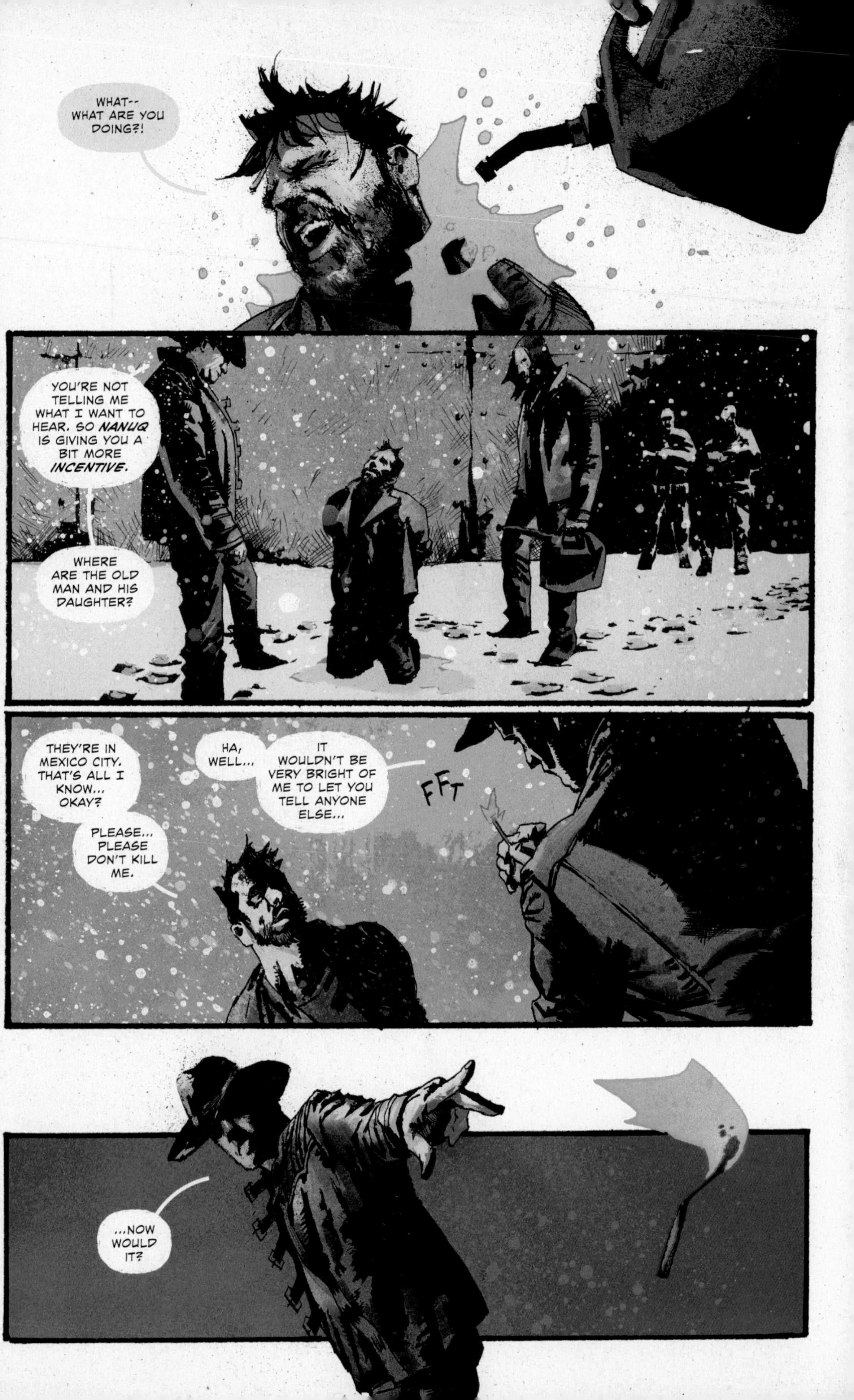
WHAT-- WHAT ARE YOU DOING?!
YOU'RE NOT TELLING ME WHAT I WANT TO HEAR. SO NANUQ IS GIVING YOU A BIT MORE INCENTIVE.
WHERE ARE THE OLD MAN AND HIS DAUGHTER?
THEY'RE IN MEXICO CITY. THAT'S ALL I KNOW... OKAY?
PLEASE... PLEASE DON'T KILL ME.
HA, WELL...
IT WOULDN'T BE VERY BRIGHT OF ME TO LET YOU TELL ANYONE ELSE...
FFT
...NOW WOULD IT?

LOS ANGELES.
FIFTY-SEVEN YEARS INTO THE NEW ICE AGE.
12°F.
SO I TAKE IT I'M GOING TO MEXICO CITY, FUEGO?
BINGO.
GRAB THE GOOD DOCTORS AND BRING THEM WHERE THEY ARE NEEDED.
AAAHHH!

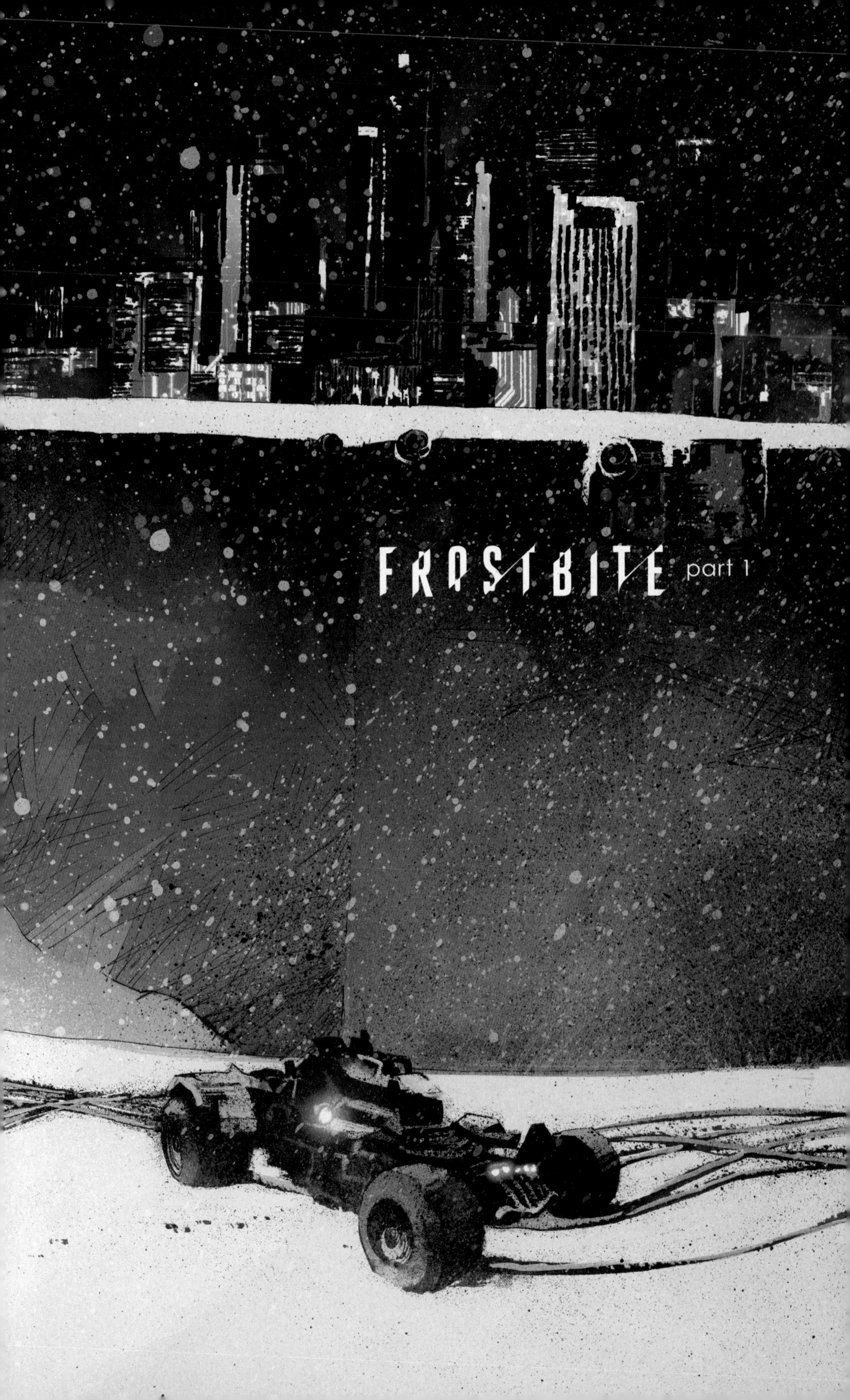
FROSTBITE part 1

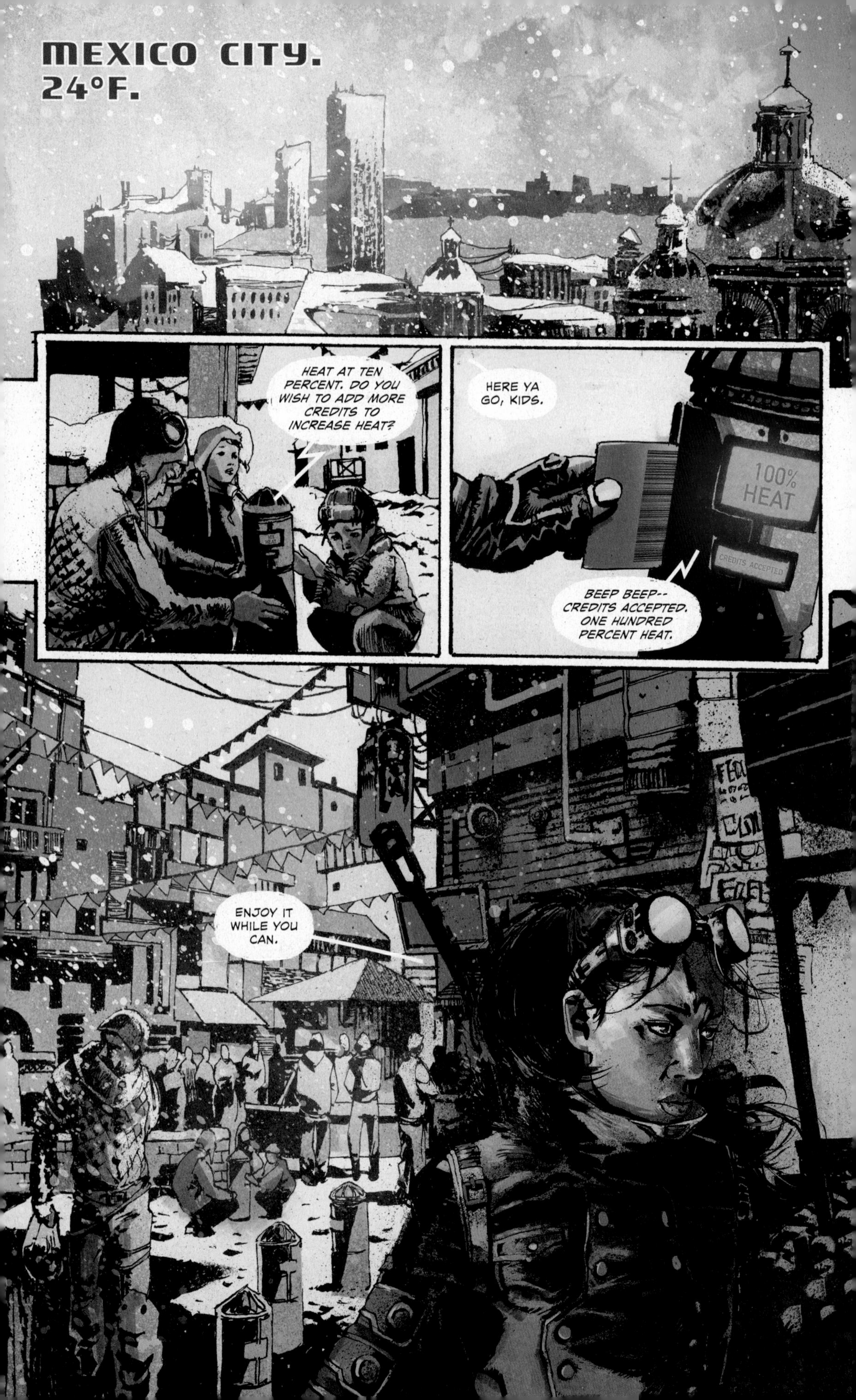
MEXICO CITY.
24°F.
HEAT AT TEN PERCENT. DO YOU WISH TO ADD MORE CREDITS TO INCREASE HEAT?
HERE YA GO, KIDS.
100% HEAT
CREDITS ACCEPTED
BEEP BEEP-- CREDITS ACCEPTED. ONE HUNDRED PERCENT HEAT.
ENJOY IT WHILE YOU CAN.

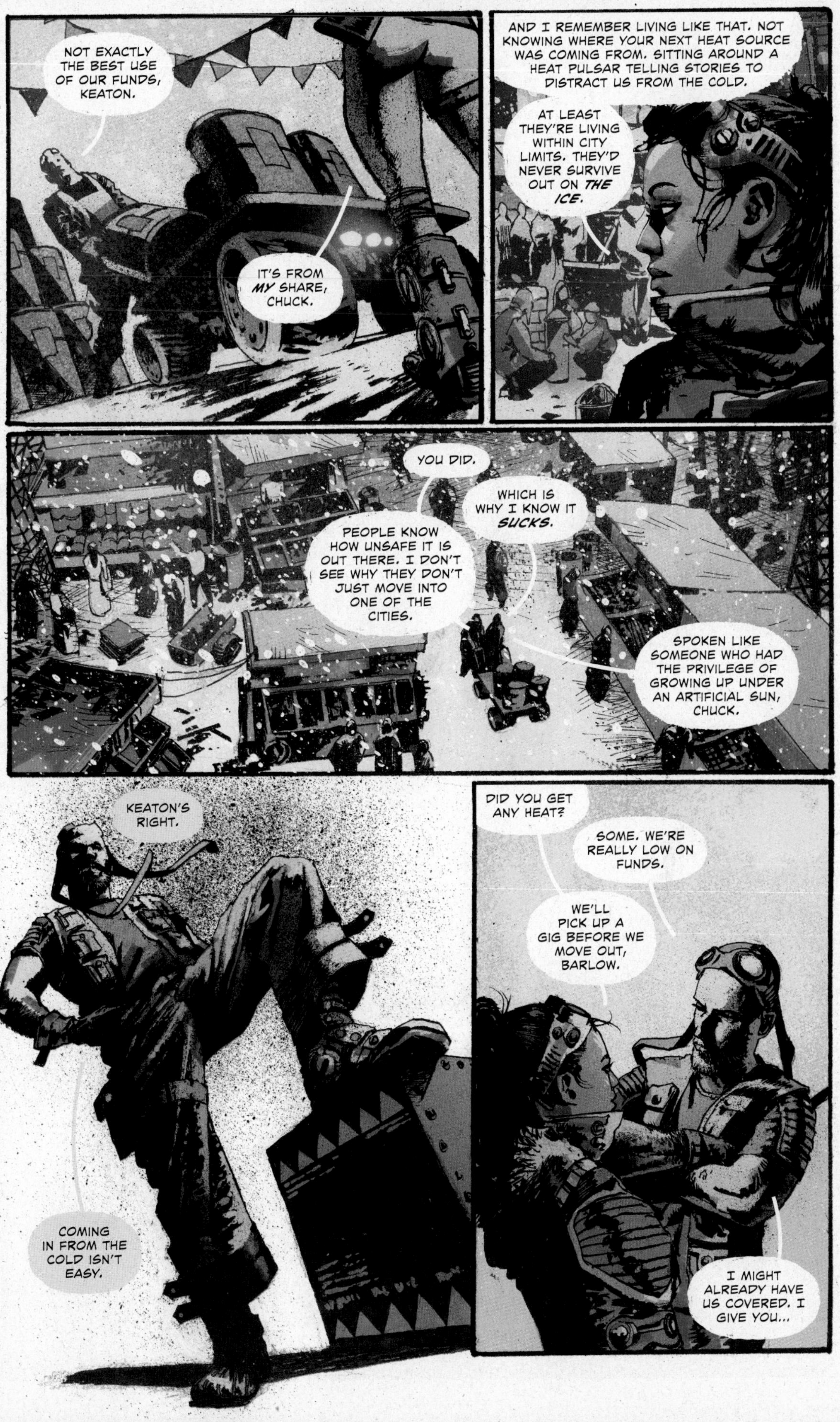
NOT EXACTLY THE BEST USE OF OUR FUNDS, KEATON.
IT'S FROM *MY* SHARE, CHUCK.
AND I REMEMBER LIVING LIKE THAT. NOT KNOWING WHERE YOUR NEXT HEAT SOURCE WAS COMING FROM. SITTING AROUND A HEAT PULSAR TELLING STORIES TO DISTRACT US FROM THE COLD.
AT LEAST THEY'RE LIVING WITHIN CITY LIMITS. THEY'D NEVER SURVIVE OUT ON *THE ICE.*
PEOPLE KNOW HOW UNSAFE IT IS OUT THERE. I DON'T SEE WHY THEY DON'T JUST MOVE INTO ONE OF THE CITIES.
YOU DID.
WHICH IS WHY I KNOW IT *SUCKS.*
SPOKEN LIKE SOMEONE WHO HAD THE PRIVILEGE OF GROWING UP UNDER AN ARTIFICIAL SUN, CHUCK.
KEATON'S RIGHT.
COMING IN FROM THE COLD ISN'T EASY.
DID YOU GET ANY HEAT?
SOME. WE'RE REALLY LOW ON FUNDS.
WE'LL PICK UP A GIG BEFORE WE MOVE OUT, BARLOW.
I MIGHT ALREADY HAVE US COVERED. I GIVE YOU...

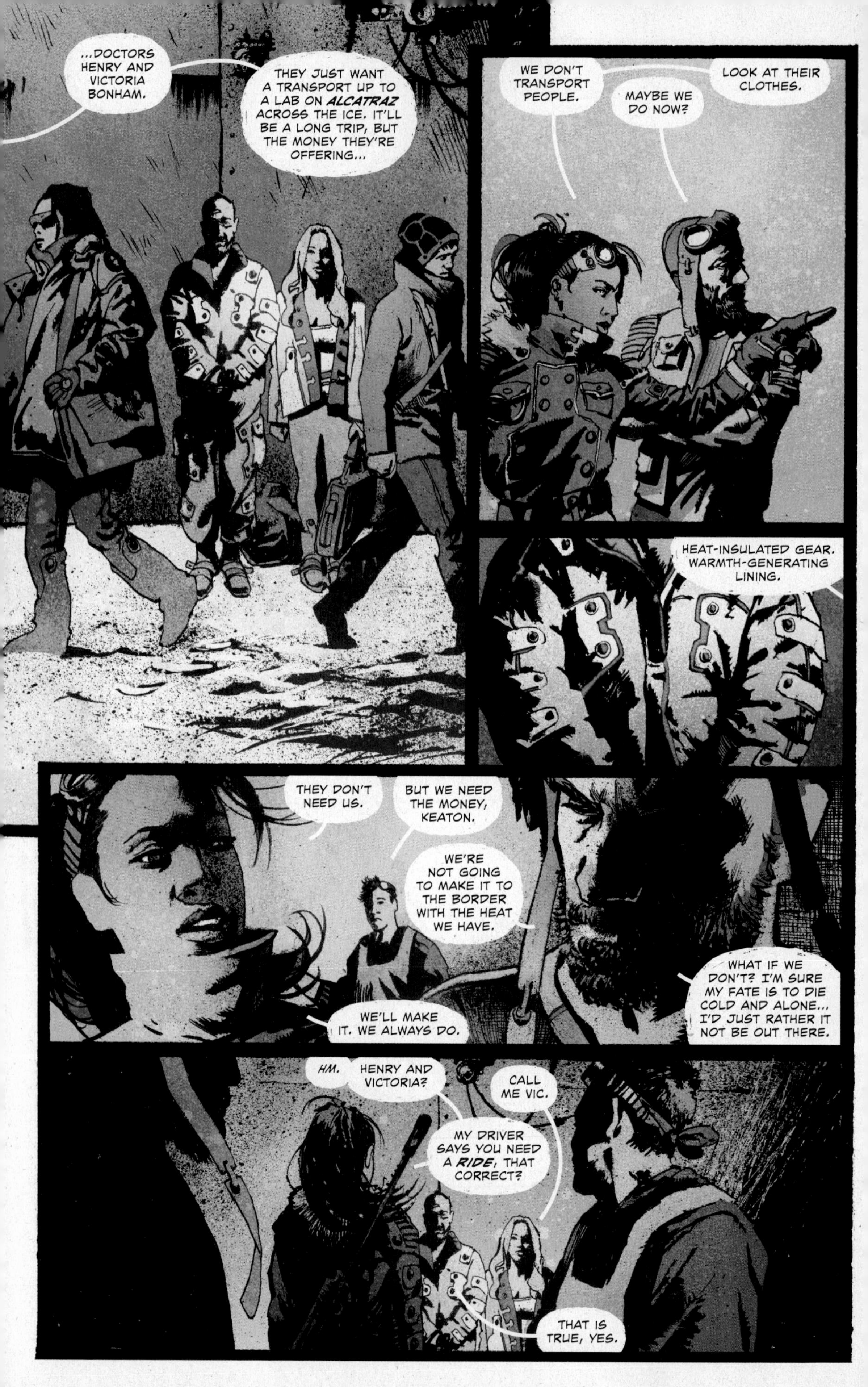
...DOCTORS HENRY AND VICTORIA BONHAM.
THEY JUST WANT A TRANSPORT UP TO A LAB ON *ALCATRAZ* ACROSS THE ICE. IT'LL BE A LONG TRIP, BUT THE MONEY THEY'RE OFFERING...
WE DON'T TRANSPORT PEOPLE.
LOOK AT THEIR CLOTHES.
MAYBE WE DO NOW?
HEAT-INSULATED GEAR. WARMTH-GENERATING LINING.
THEY DON'T NEED US.
BUT WE NEED THE MONEY, KEATON.
WE'RE NOT GOING TO MAKE IT TO THE BORDER WITH THE HEAT WE HAVE.
WE'LL MAKE IT. WE ALWAYS DO.
WHAT IF WE DON'T? I'M SURE MY FATE IS TO DIE COLD AND ALONE... I'D JUST RATHER IT NOT BE OUT THERE.
*HM.*
HENRY AND VICTORIA?
CALL ME VIC.
MY DRIVER SAYS YOU NEED A *RIDE*; THAT CORRECT?
THAT IS TRUE, YES.

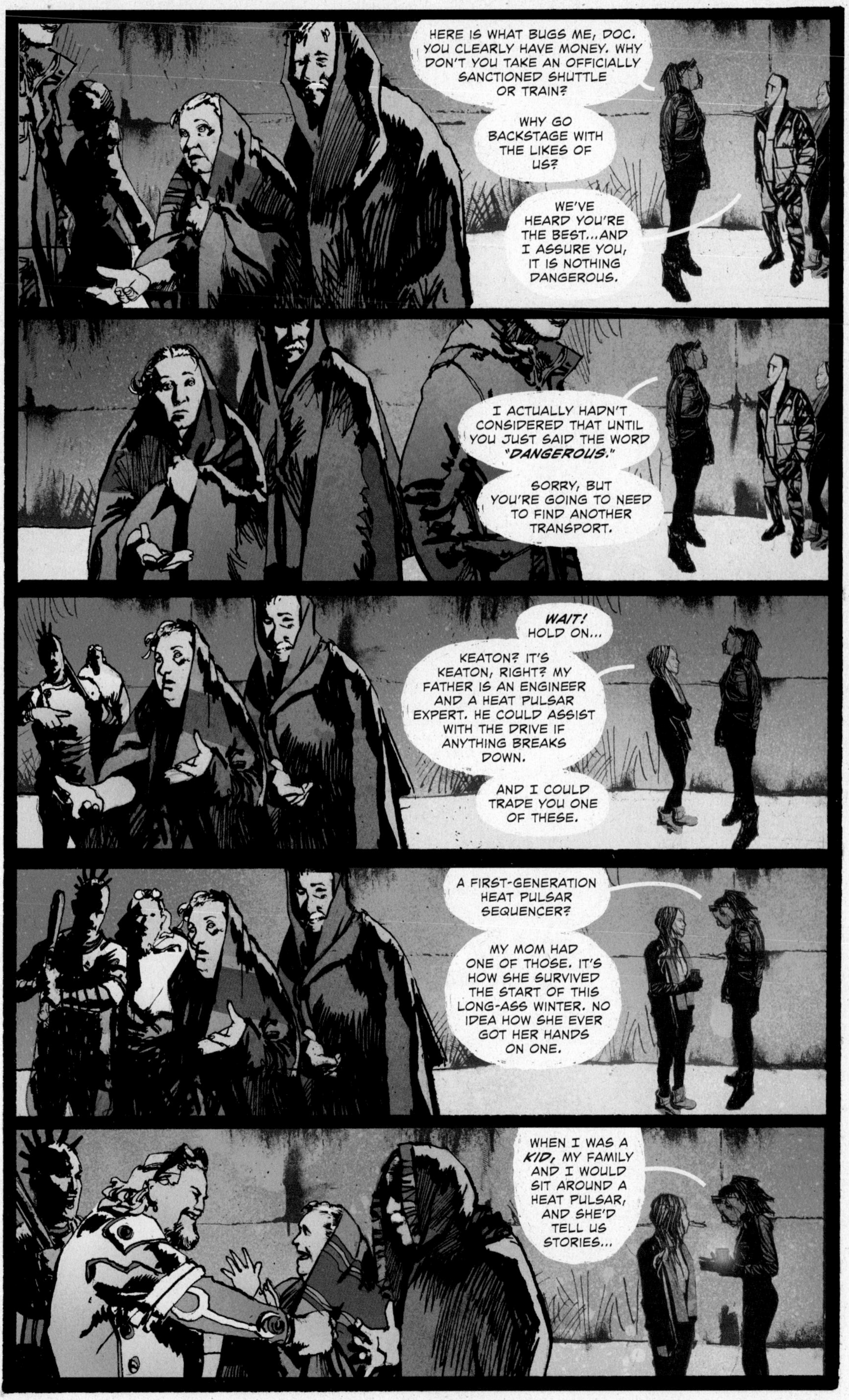

HERE IS WHAT BUGS ME, DOC. YOU CLEARLY HAVE MONEY. WHY DON'T YOU TAKE AN OFFICIALLY SANCTIONED SHUTTLE OR TRAIN?
WHY GO BACKSTAGE WITH THE LIKES OF US?
WE'VE HEARD YOU'RE THE BEST...AND I ASSURE YOU, IT IS NOTHING DANGEROUS.
I ACTUALLY HADN'T CONSIDERED THAT UNTIL YOU JUST SAID THE WORD "DANGEROUS."
SORRY, BUT YOU'RE GOING TO NEED TO FIND ANOTHER TRANSPORT.
WAIT! HOLD ON...
KEATON? IT'S KEATON, RIGHT? MY FATHER IS AN ENGINEER AND A HEAT PULSAR EXPERT. HE COULD ASSIST WITH THE DRIVE IF ANYTHING BREAKS DOWN.
AND I COULD TRADE YOU ONE OF THESE.
A FIRST-GENERATION HEAT PULSAR SEQUENCER?
MY MOM HAD ONE OF THOSE. IT'S HOW SHE SURVIVED THE START OF THIS LONG-ASS WINTER. NO IDEA HOW SHE EVER GOT HER HANDS ON ONE.
WHEN I WAS A KID, MY FAMILY AND I WOULD SIT AROUND A HEAT PULSAR, AND SHE'D TELL US STORIES...

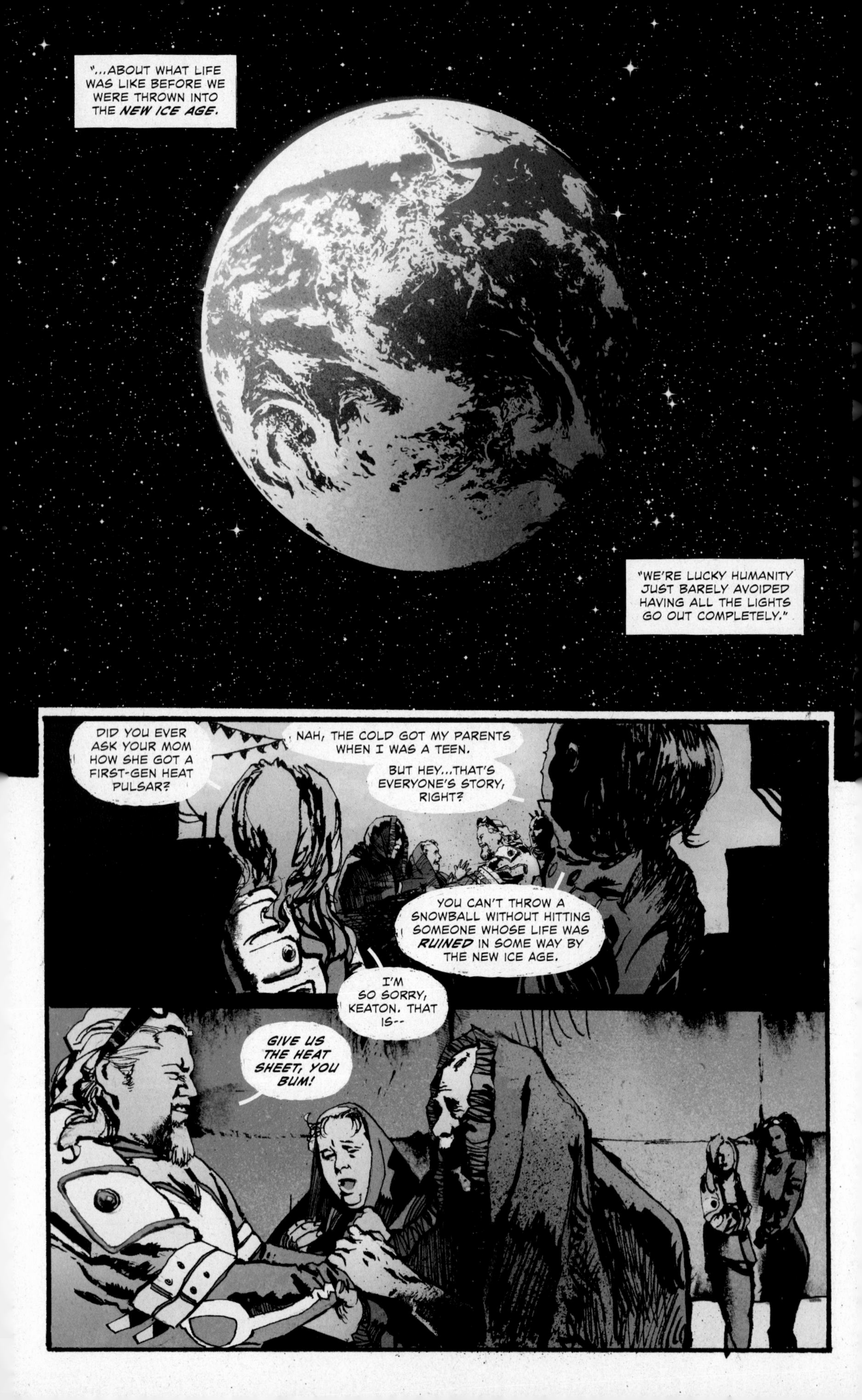
"...ABOUT WHAT LIFE WAS LIKE BEFORE WE WERE THROWN INTO THE *NEW ICE AGE*.
"WE'RE LUCKY HUMANITY JUST BARELY AVOIDED HAVING ALL THE LIGHTS GO OUT COMPLETELY."
DID YOU EVER ASK YOUR MOM HOW SHE GOT A FIRST-GEN HEAT PULSAR?
NAH, THE COLD GOT MY PARENTS WHEN I WAS A TEEN.
BUT HEY...THAT'S EVERYONE'S STORY, RIGHT?
YOU CAN'T THROW A SNOWBALL WITHOUT HITTING SOMEONE WHOSE LIFE WAS *RUINED* IN SOME WAY BY THE NEW ICE AGE.
I'M SO SORRY, KEATON. THAT IS--
*GIVE US THE HEAT SHEET, YOU BUM!*

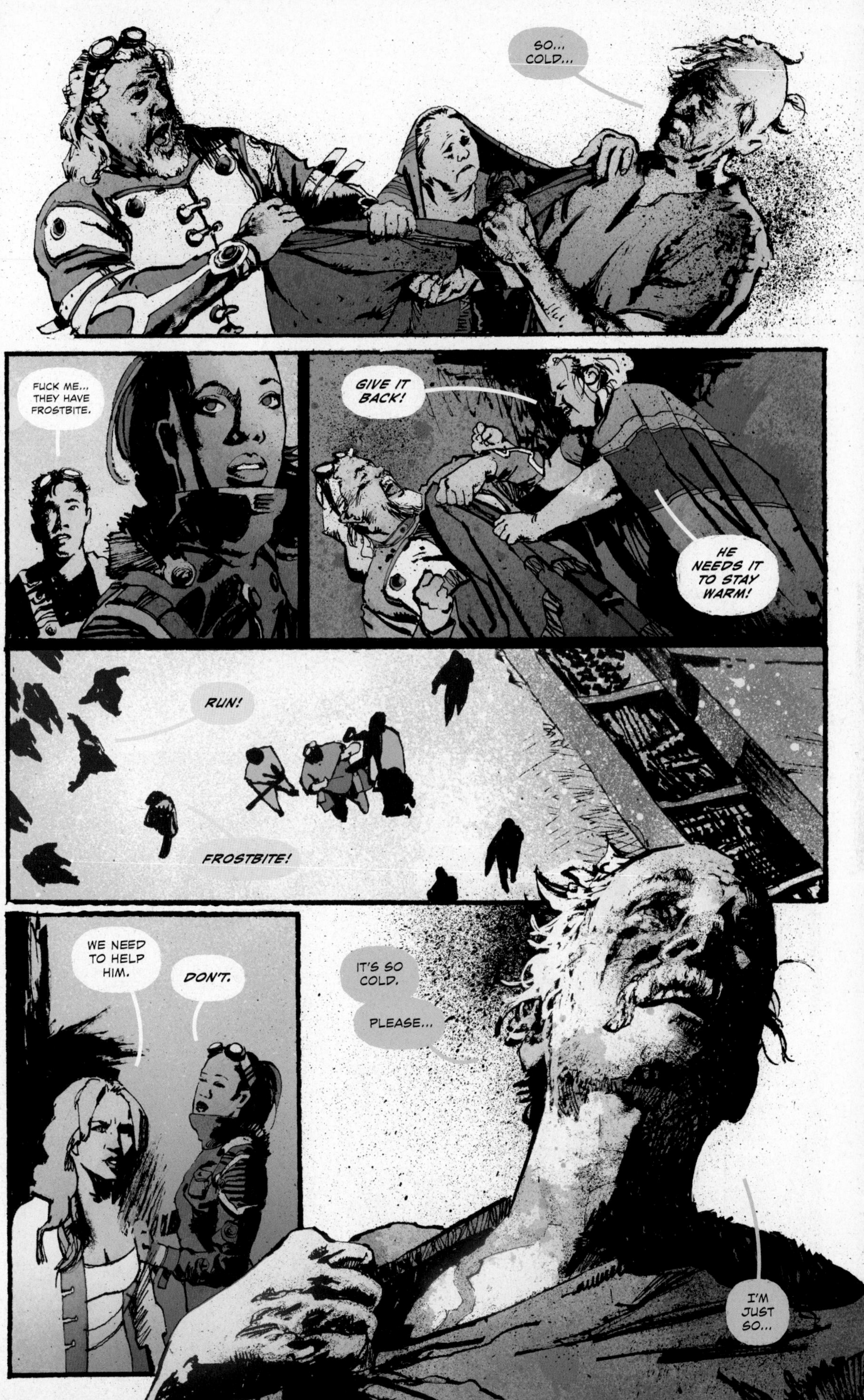
SO... COLD...
FUCK ME... THEY HAVE FROSTBITE.
GIVE IT BACK!
HE NEEDS IT TO STAY WARM!
RUN!
FROSTBITE!
WE NEED TO HELP HIM.
DON'T.
IT'S SO COLD.
PLEASE...
I'M JUST SO...

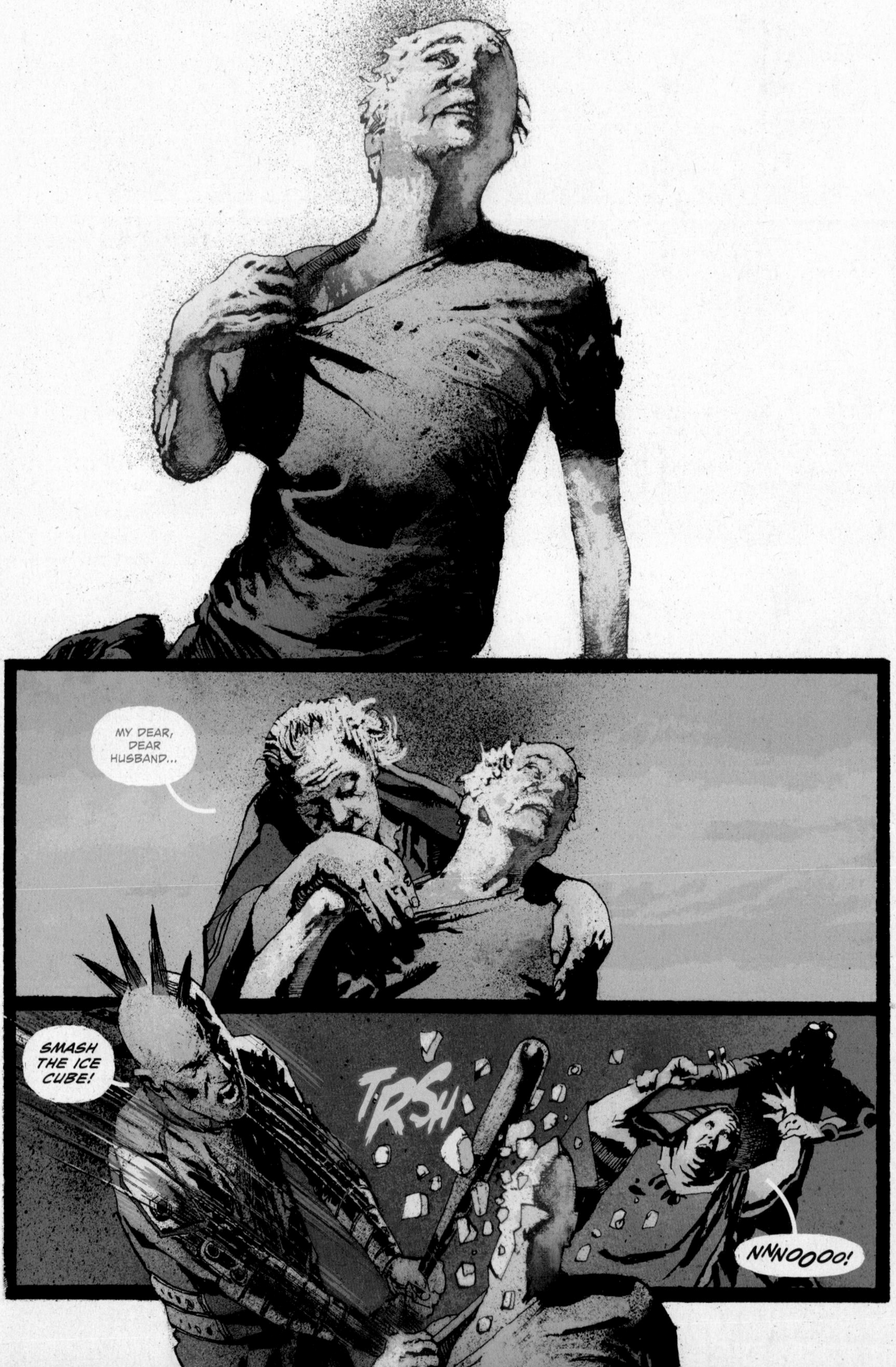
MY DEAR, DEAR HUSBAND...
SMASH THE ICE CUBE!
TRSH
NNNOOOO!

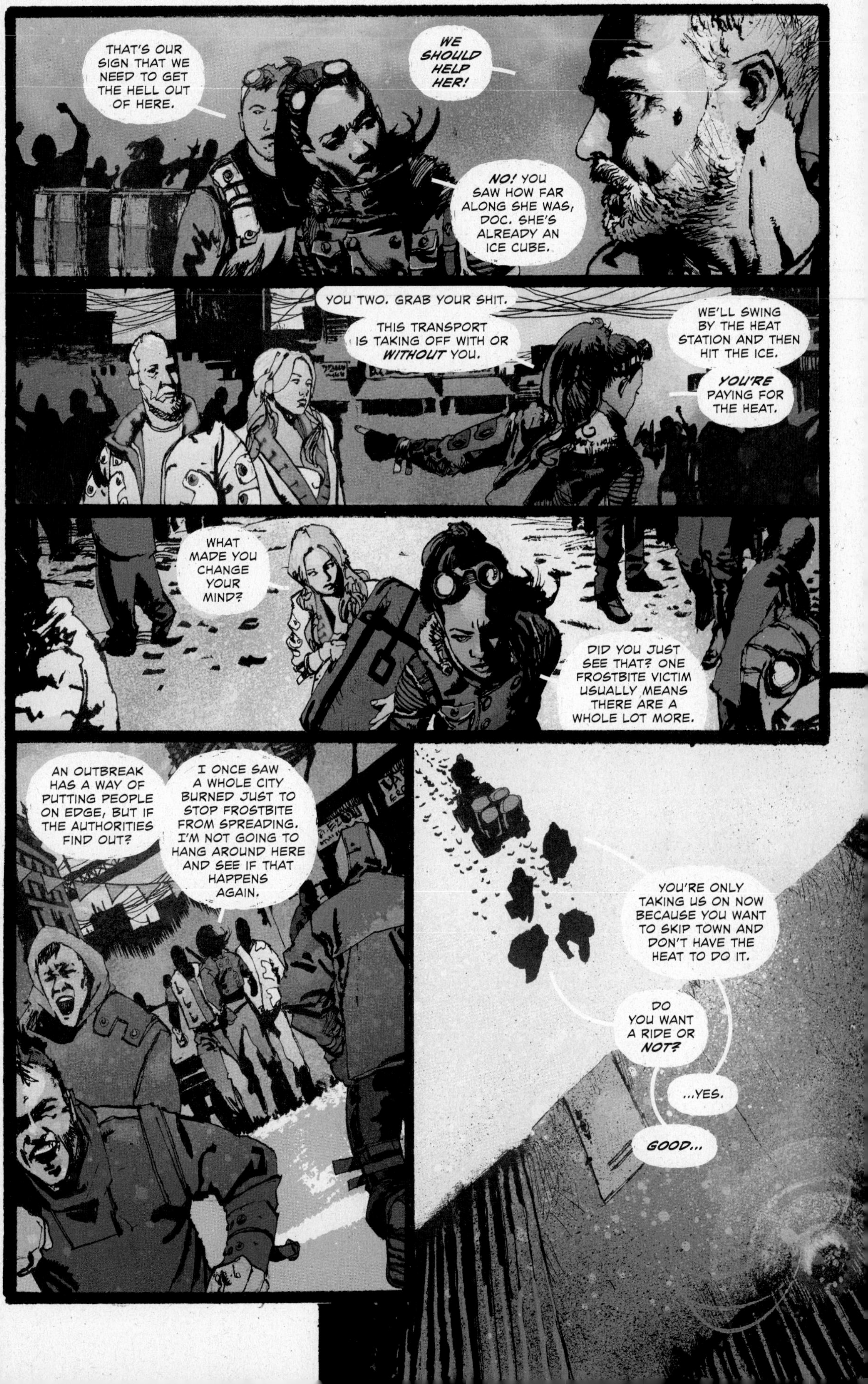
THAT'S OUR SIGN THAT WE NEED TO GET THE HELL OUT OF HERE.
WE SHOULD HELP HER!
NO! YOU SAW HOW FAR ALONG SHE WAS, DOC. SHE'S ALREADY AN ICE CUBE.
YOU TWO. GRAB YOUR SHIT.
THIS TRANSPORT IS TAKING OFF WITH OR WITHOUT YOU.
WE'LL SWING BY THE HEAT STATION AND THEN HIT THE ICE.
YOU'RE PAYING FOR THE HEAT.
WHAT MADE YOU CHANGE YOUR MIND?
DID YOU JUST SEE THAT? ONE FROSTBITE VICTIM USUALLY MEANS THERE ARE A WHOLE LOT MORE.
AN OUTBREAK HAS A WAY OF PUTTING PEOPLE ON EDGE, BUT IF THE AUTHORITIES FIND OUT?
I ONCE SAW A WHOLE CITY BURNED JUST TO STOP FROSTBITE FROM SPREADING. I'M NOT GOING TO HANG AROUND HERE AND SEE IF THAT HAPPENS AGAIN.
YOU'RE ONLY TAKING US ON NOW BECAUSE YOU WANT TO SKIP TOWN AND DON'T HAVE THE HEAT TO DO IT.
DO YOU WANT A RIDE OR NOT?
...YES.
GOOD...

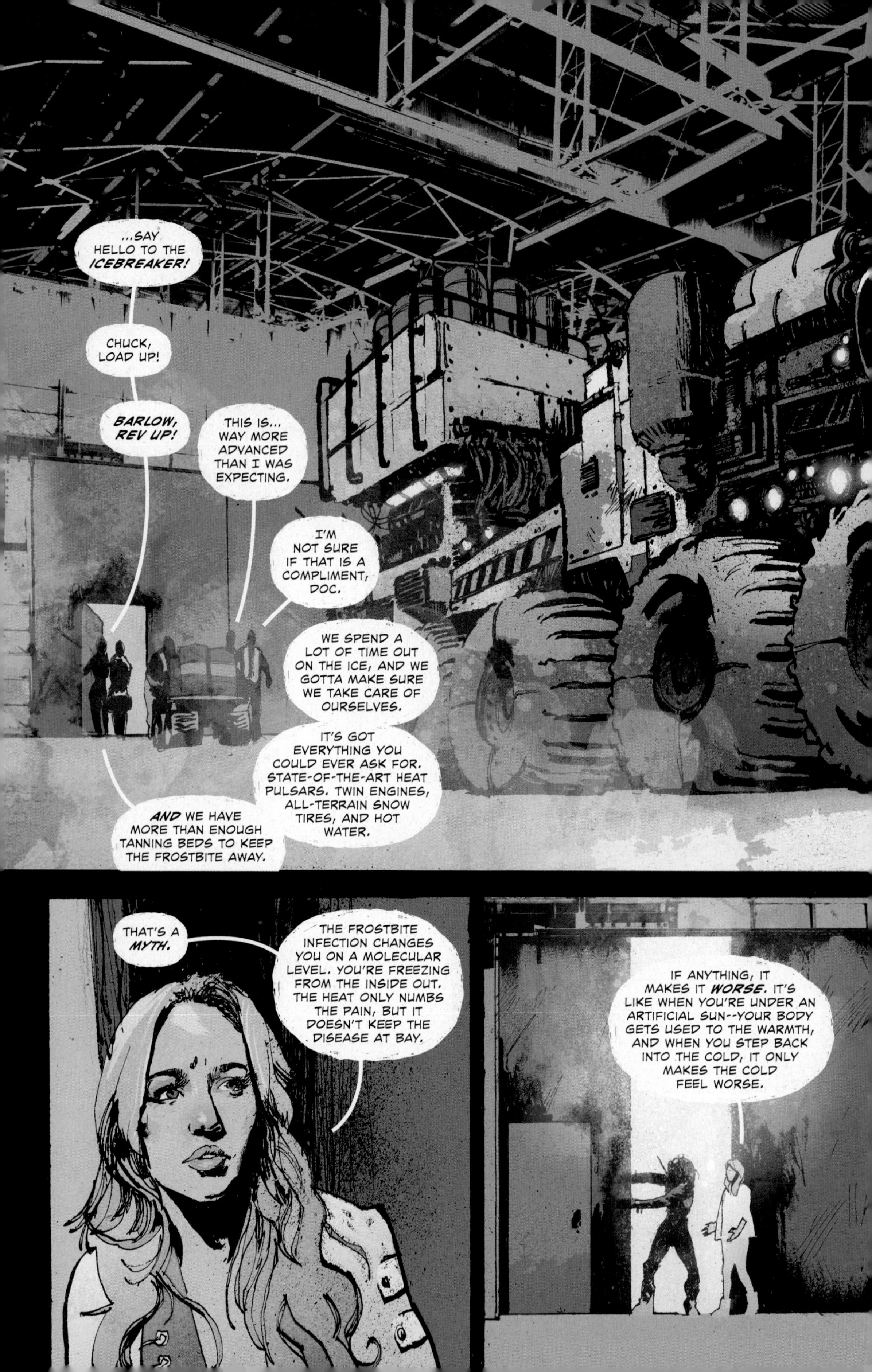
...SAY HELLO TO THE *ICEBREAKER!*
CHUCK, LOAD UP!
*BARLOW, REV UP!*
THIS IS... WAY MORE ADVANCED THAN I WAS EXPECTING.
I'M NOT SURE IF THAT IS A COMPLIMENT, DOC.
WE SPEND A LOT OF TIME OUT ON THE ICE, AND WE GOTTA MAKE SURE WE TAKE CARE OF OURSELVES.
IT'S GOT EVERYTHING YOU COULD EVER ASK FOR. STATE-OF-THE-ART HEAT PULSARS. TWIN ENGINES, ALL-TERRAIN SNOW TIRES, AND HOT WATER.
*AND* WE HAVE MORE THAN ENOUGH TANNING BEDS TO KEEP THE FROSTBITE AWAY.
THAT'S A *MYTH.*
THE FROSTBITE INFECTION CHANGES YOU ON A MOLECULAR LEVEL. YOU'RE FREEZING FROM THE INSIDE OUT. THE HEAT ONLY NUMBS THE PAIN, BUT IT DOESN'T KEEP THE DISEASE AT BAY.
IF ANYTHING, IT MAKES IT *WORSE.* IT'S LIKE WHEN YOU'RE UNDER AN ARTIFICIAL SUN--YOUR BODY GETS USED TO THE WARMTH, AND WHEN YOU STEP BACK INTO THE COLD, IT ONLY MAKES THE COLD FEEL WORSE.

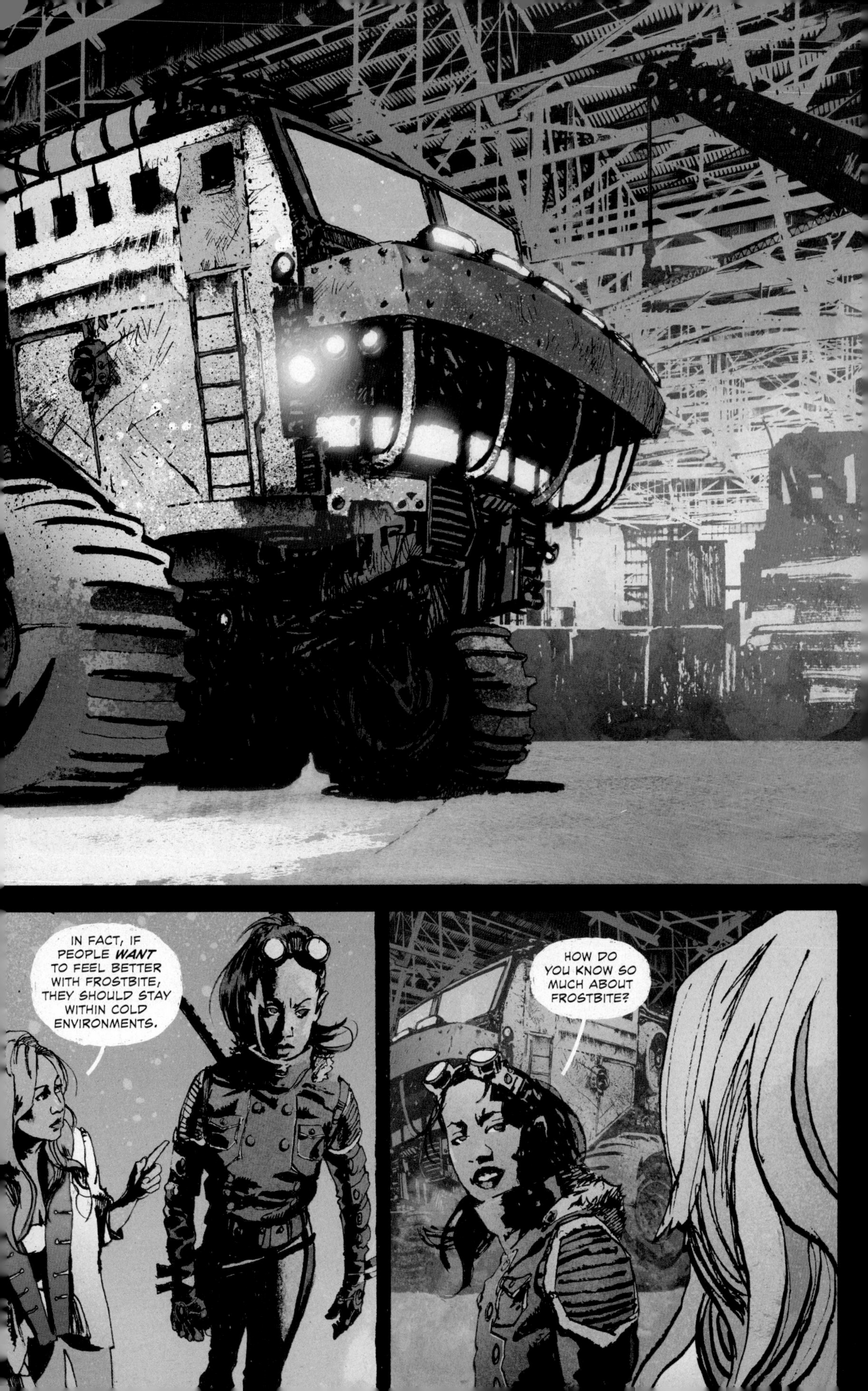
IN FACT, IF PEOPLE *WANT* TO FEEL BETTER WITH FROSTBITE, THEY SHOULD STAY WITHIN COLD ENVIRONMENTS.
HOW DO YOU KNOW SO MUCH ABOUT FROSTBITE?

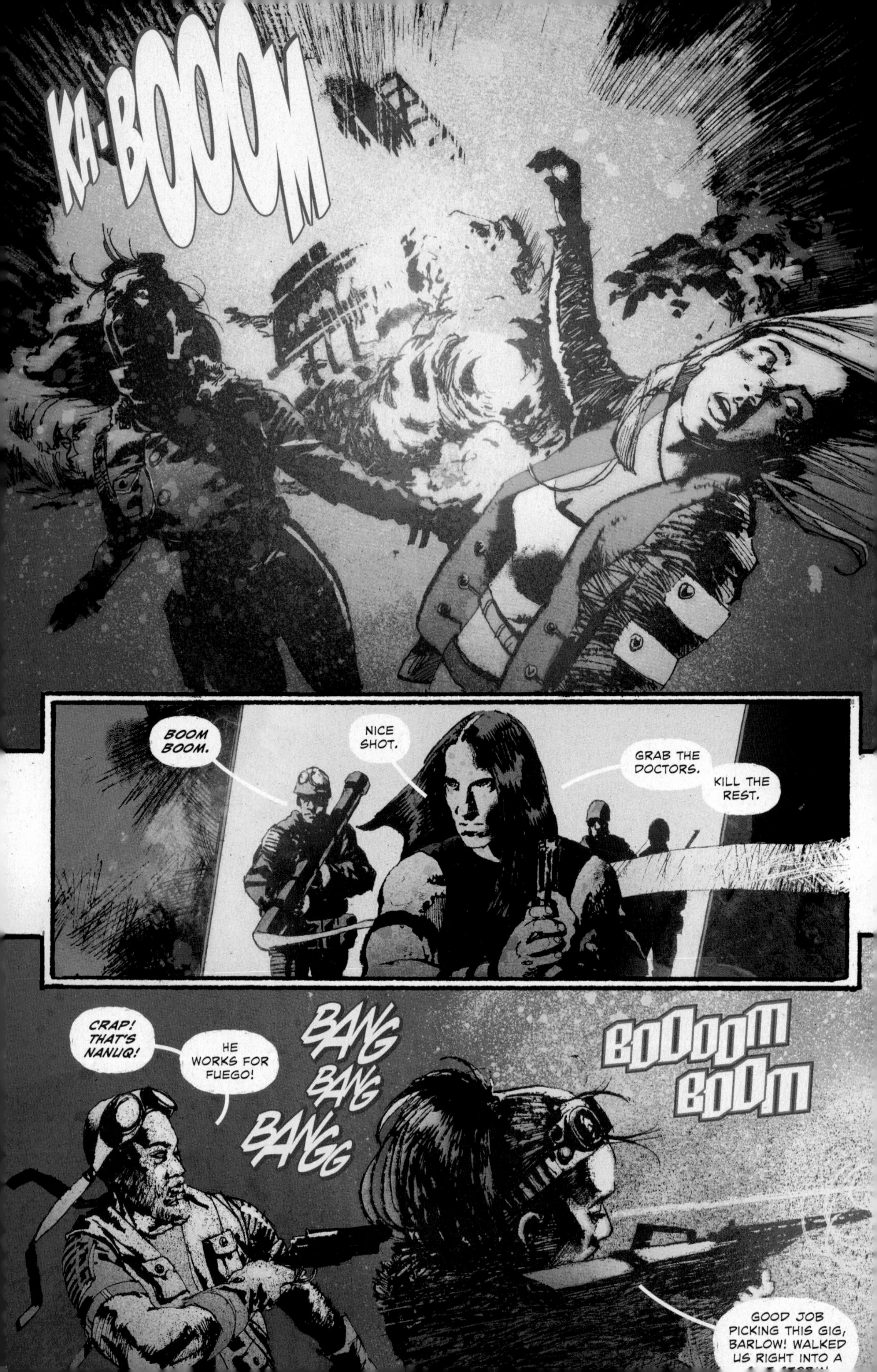
KA-BOOOM
BOOM BOOM.
NICE SHOT.
GRAB THE DOCTORS.
KILL THE REST.
CRAP! THAT'S NANUQ!
HE WORKS FOR FUEGO!
BANG BANG BANGG
BOOOOM BOOM
GOOD JOB PICKING THIS GIG, BARLOW! WALKED US RIGHT INTO A

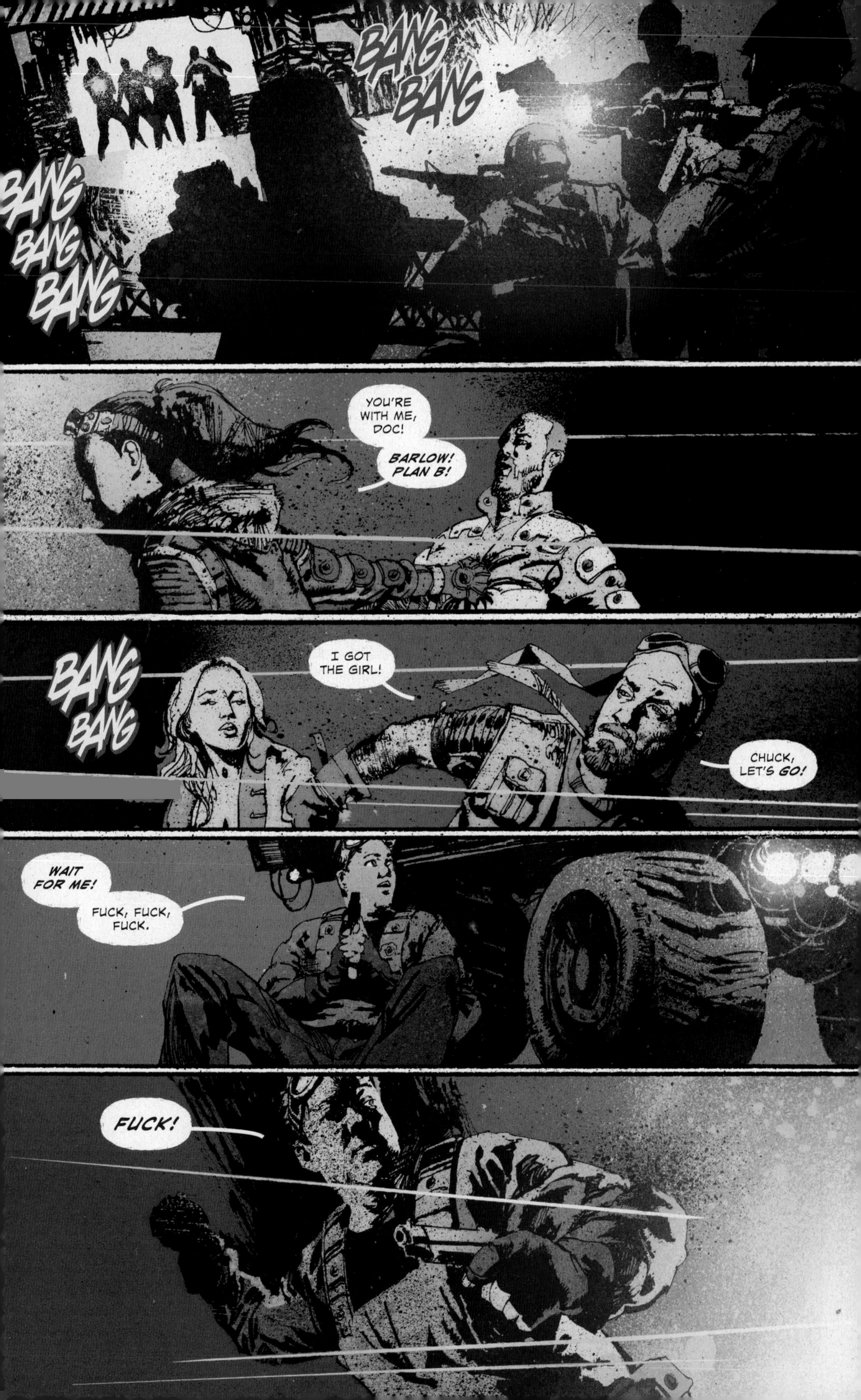
BANG
BANG
BANG
BANG
BANG
YOU'RE WITH ME, DOC!
BARLOW! PLAN B!
BANG
BANG
I GOT THE GIRL!
CHUCK, LET'S GO!
WAIT FOR ME!
FUCK, FUCK, FUCK.
FUCK!

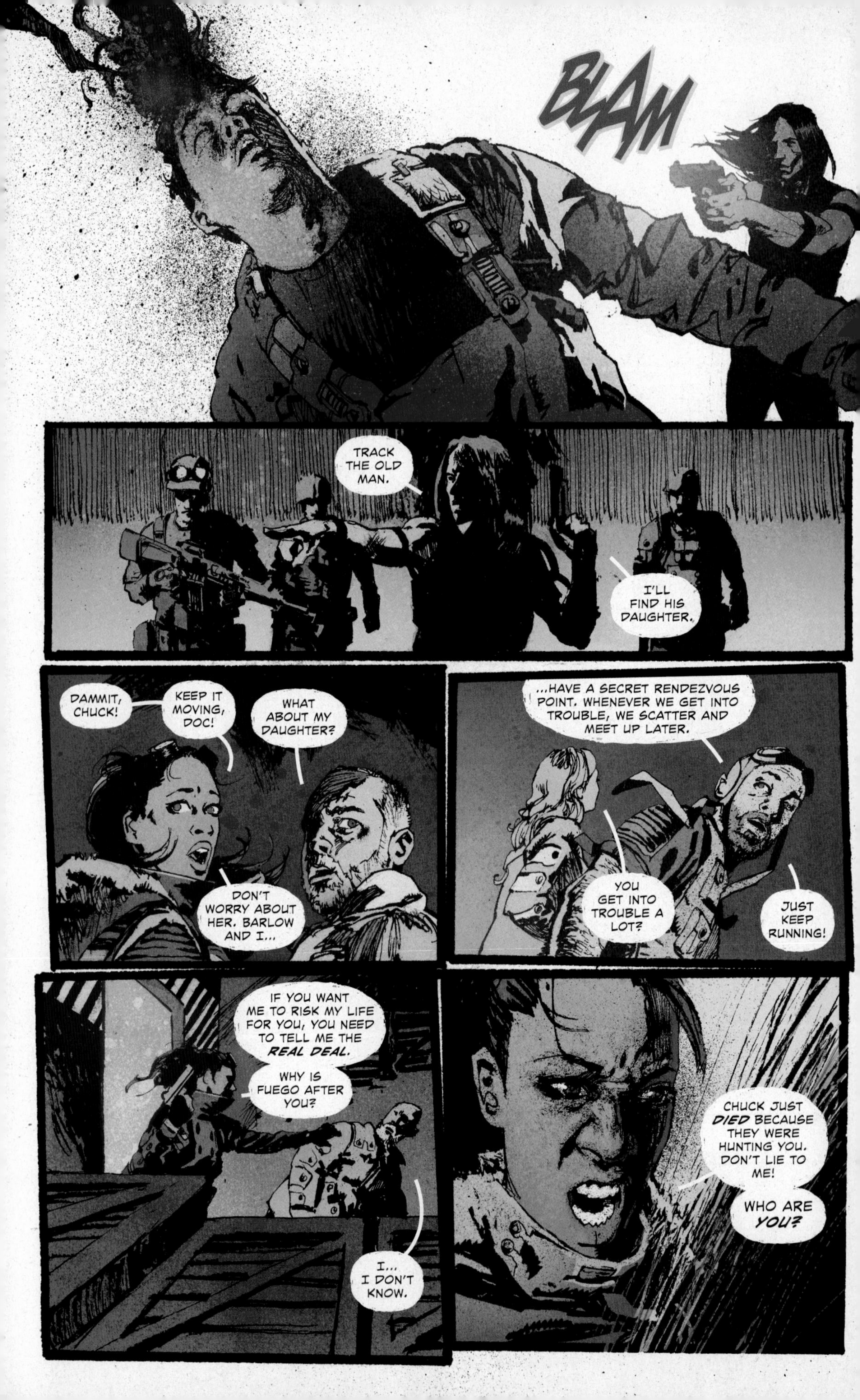
BLAM
TRACK THE OLD MAN.
I'LL FIND HIS DAUGHTER.
DAMMIT, CHUCK!
KEEP IT MOVING, DOC!
WHAT ABOUT MY DAUGHTER?
DON'T WORRY ABOUT HER. BARLOW AND I...
...HAVE A SECRET RENDEZVOUS POINT. WHENEVER WE GET INTO TROUBLE, WE SCATTER AND MEET UP LATER.
YOU GET INTO TROUBLE A LOT?
JUST KEEP RUNNING!
IF YOU WANT ME TO RISK MY LIFE FOR YOU, YOU NEED TO TELL ME THE REAL DEAL.
WHY IS FUEGO AFTER YOU?
I... I DON'T KNOW.
CHUCK JUST DIED BECAUSE THEY WERE HUNTING YOU. DON'T LIE TO ME!
WHO ARE YOU?

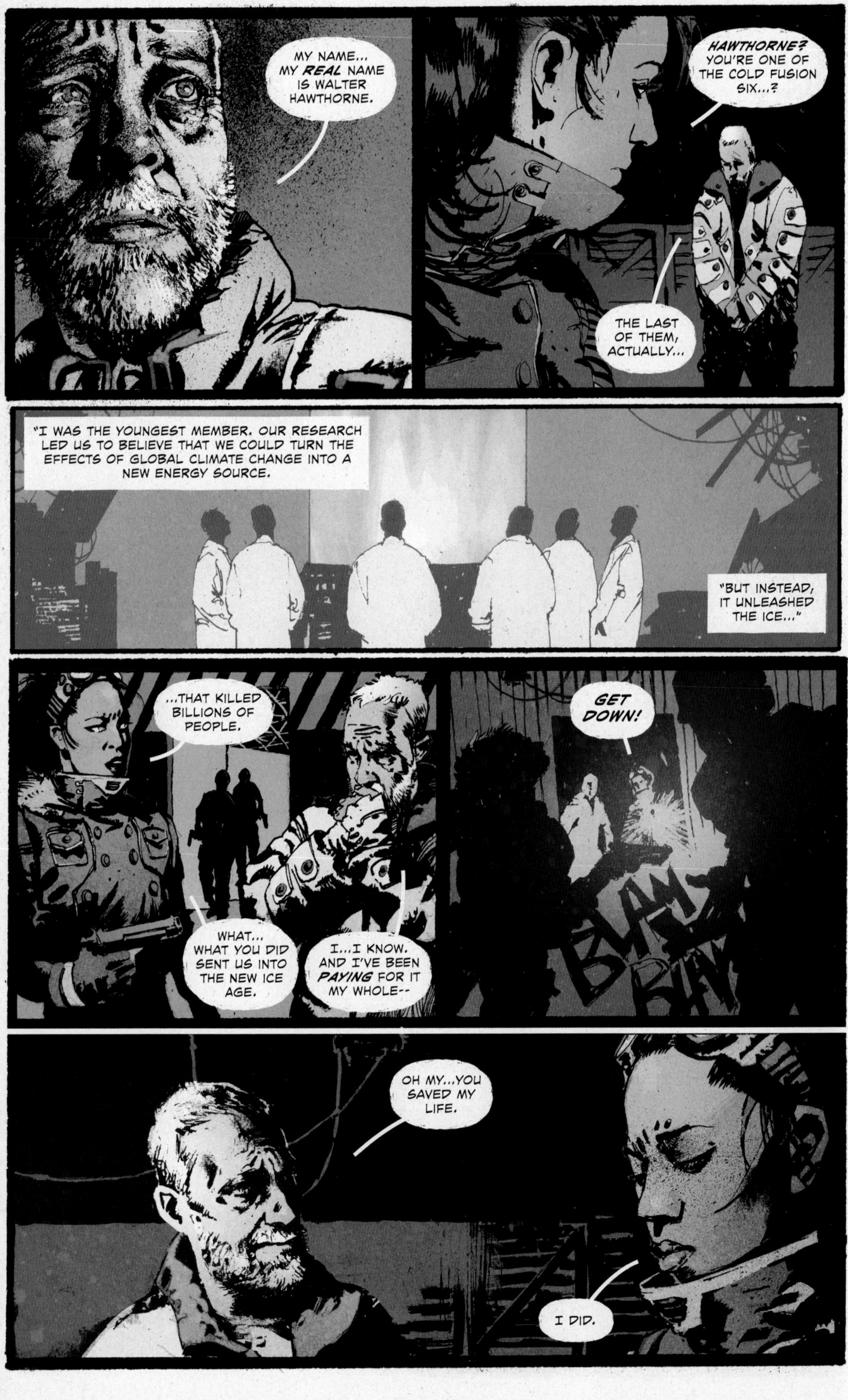
MY NAME... MY *REAL* NAME IS WALTER HAWTHORNE.
*HAWTHORNE?* YOU'RE ONE OF THE COLD FUSION SIX...?
THE LAST OF THEM, ACTUALLY...
"I WAS THE YOUNGEST MEMBER. OUR RESEARCH LED US TO BELIEVE THAT WE COULD TURN THE EFFECTS OF GLOBAL CLIMATE CHANGE INTO A NEW ENERGY SOURCE.
"BUT INSTEAD, IT UNLEASHED THE ICE..."
...THAT KILLED BILLIONS OF PEOPLE.
WHAT... WHAT YOU DID SENT US INTO THE NEW ICE AGE.
I...I KNOW. AND I'VE BEEN *PAYING* FOR IT MY WHOLE--
*GET DOWN!*
OH MY...YOU SAVED MY LIFE.
I DID.

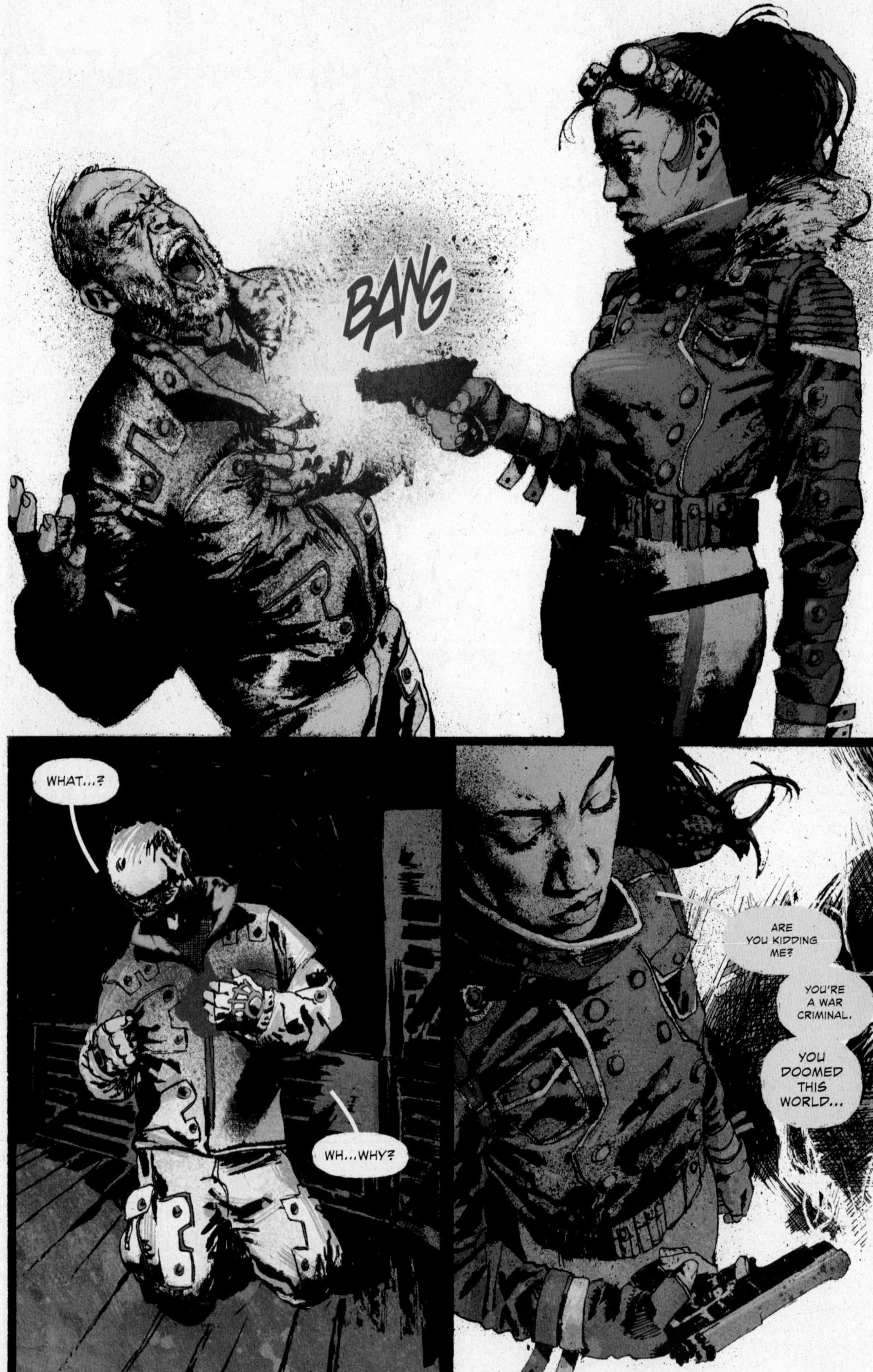
BANG
WHAT...?
WH...WHY?
ARE YOU KIDDING ME?
YOU'RE A WAR CRIMINAL.
YOU DOOMED THIS WORLD...

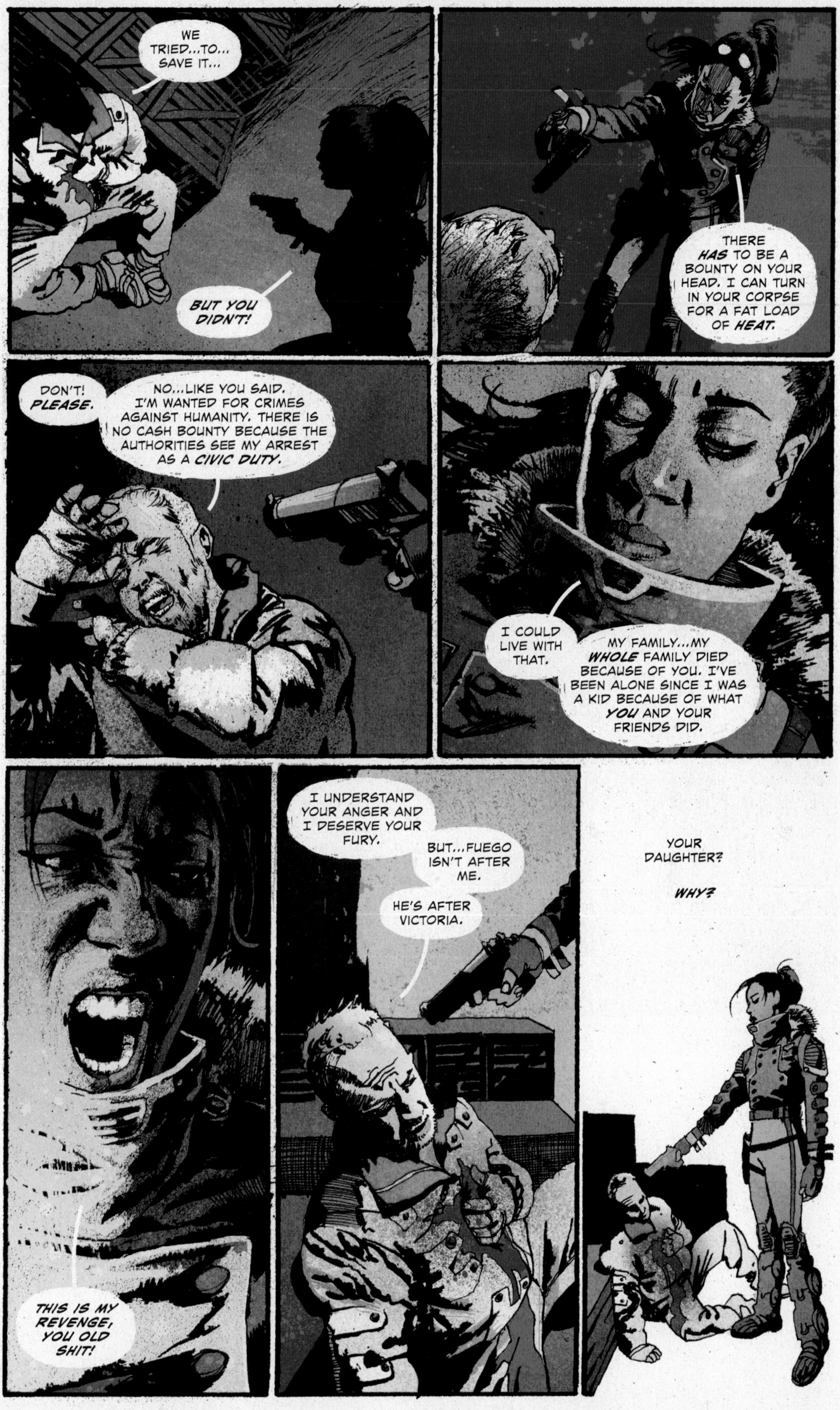
WE TRIED...TO... SAVE IT...
BUT YOU DIDN'T!
THERE HAS TO BE A BOUNTY ON YOUR HEAD. I CAN TURN IN YOUR CORPSE FOR A FAT LOAD OF HEAT.
DON'T! PLEASE.
NO...LIKE YOU SAID. I'M WANTED FOR CRIMES AGAINST HUMANITY. THERE IS NO CASH BOUNTY BECAUSE THE AUTHORITIES SEE MY ARREST AS A CIVIC DUTY.
I COULD LIVE WITH THAT.
MY FAMILY...MY WHOLE FAMILY DIED BECAUSE OF YOU. I'VE BEEN ALONE SINCE I WAS A KID BECAUSE OF WHAT YOU AND YOUR FRIENDS DID.
THIS IS MY REVENGE, YOU OLD SHIT!
I UNDERSTAND YOUR ANGER AND I DESERVE YOUR FURY.
BUT...FUEGO ISN'T AFTER ME.
HE'S AFTER VICTORIA.
YOUR DAUGHTER?
WHY?

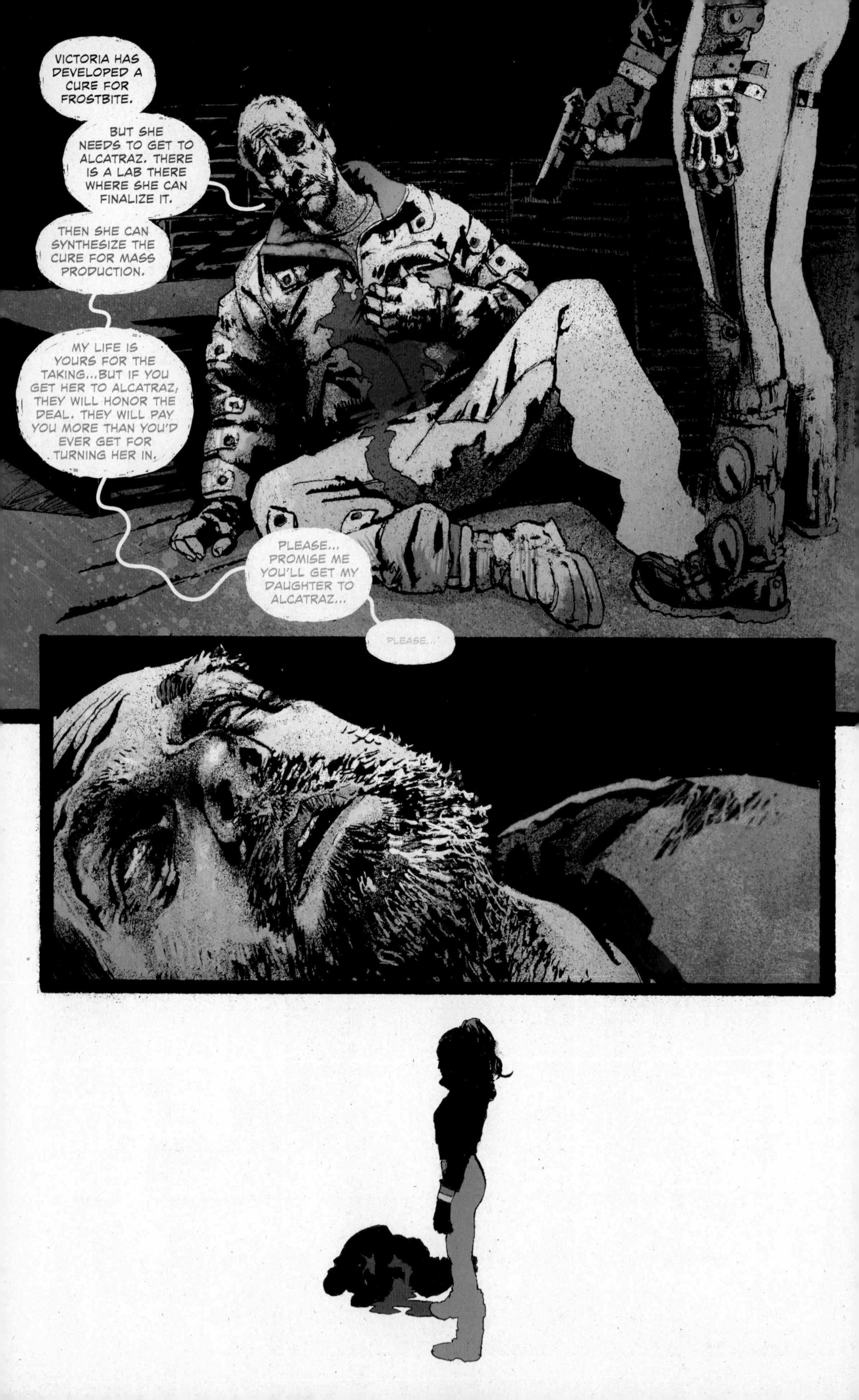
VICTORIA HAS DEVELOPED A CURE FOR FROSTBITE.
BUT SHE NEEDS TO GET TO ALCATRAZ. THERE IS A LAB THERE WHERE SHE CAN FINALIZE IT.
THEN SHE CAN SYNTHESIZE THE CURE FOR MASS PRODUCTION.
MY LIFE IS YOURS FOR THE TAKING...BUT IF YOU GET HER TO ALCATRAZ, THEY WILL HONOR THE DEAL. THEY WILL PAY YOU MORE THAN YOU'D EVER GET FOR TURNING HER IN.
PLEASE... PROMISE ME YOU'LL GET MY DAUGHTER TO ALCATRAZ...
PLEASE...

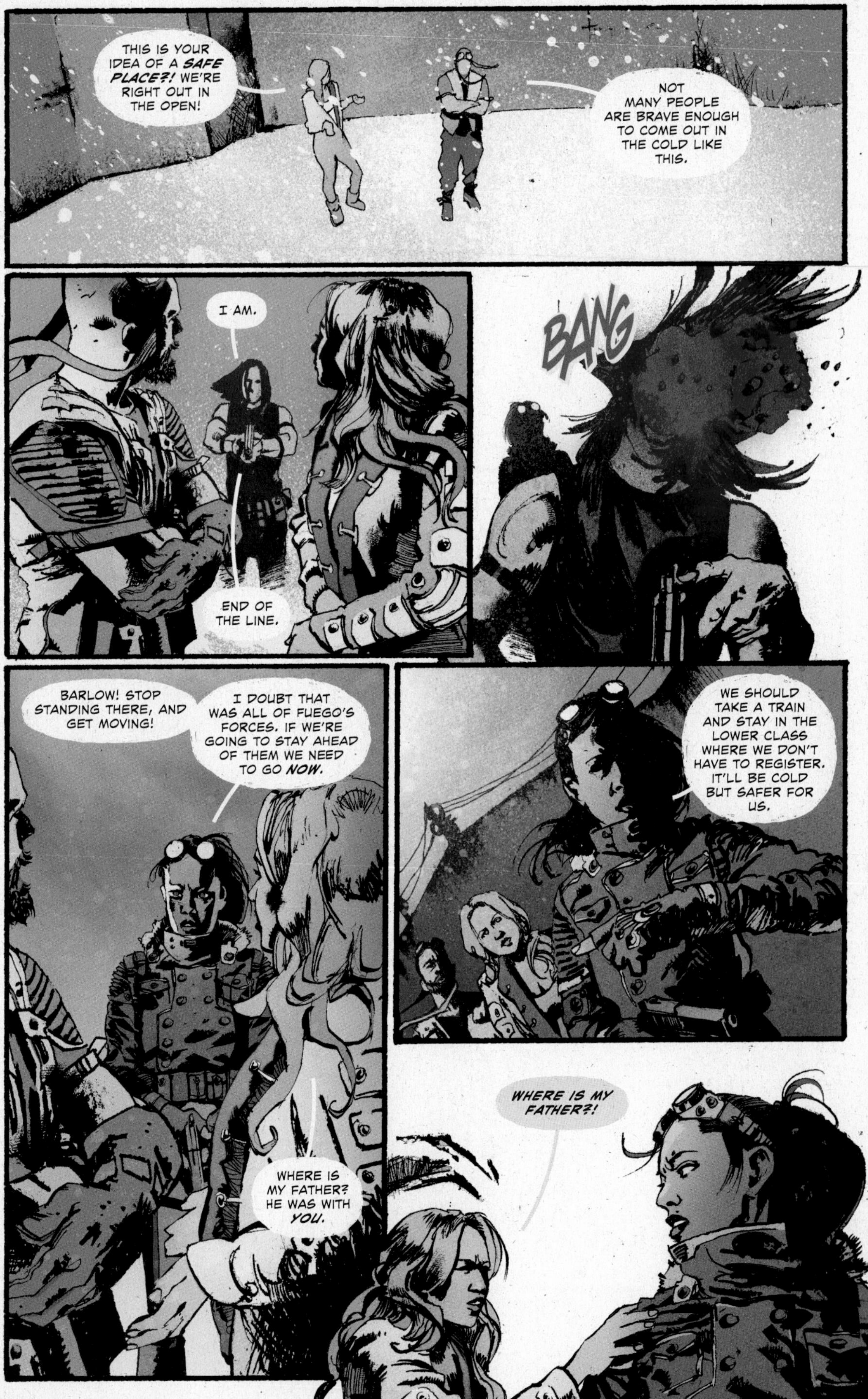
THIS IS YOUR IDEA OF A SAFE PLACE?! WE'RE RIGHT OUT IN THE OPEN!
NOT MANY PEOPLE ARE BRAVE ENOUGH TO COME OUT IN THE COLD LIKE THIS.
I AM.
END OF THE LINE.
BANG
BARLOW! STOP STANDING THERE, AND GET MOVING!
I DOUBT THAT WAS ALL OF FUEGO'S FORCES. IF WE'RE GOING TO STAY AHEAD OF THEM WE NEED TO GO NOW.
WE SHOULD TAKE A TRAIN AND STAY IN THE LOWER CLASS WHERE WE DON'T HAVE TO REGISTER. IT'LL BE COLD BUT SAFER FOR US.
WHERE IS MY FATHER? HE WAS WITH YOU.
WHERE IS MY FATHER?!

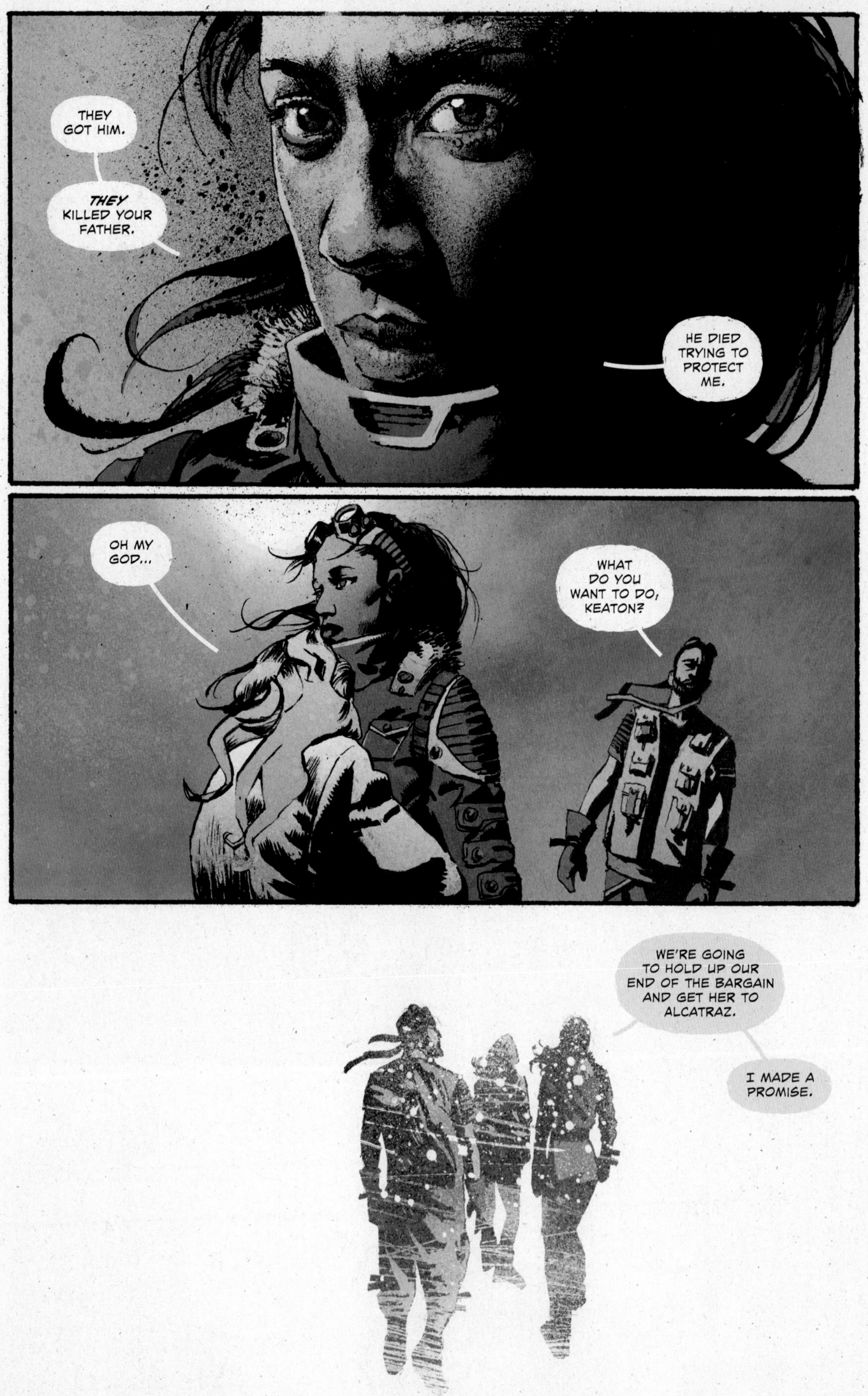
THEY GOT HIM.
THEY KILLED YOUR FATHER.
HE DIED TRYING TO PROTECT ME.
OH MY GOD...
WHAT DO YOU WANT TO DO, KEATON?
WE'RE GOING TO HOLD UP OUR END OF THE BARGAIN AND GET HER TO ALCATRAZ.
I MADE A PROMISE.

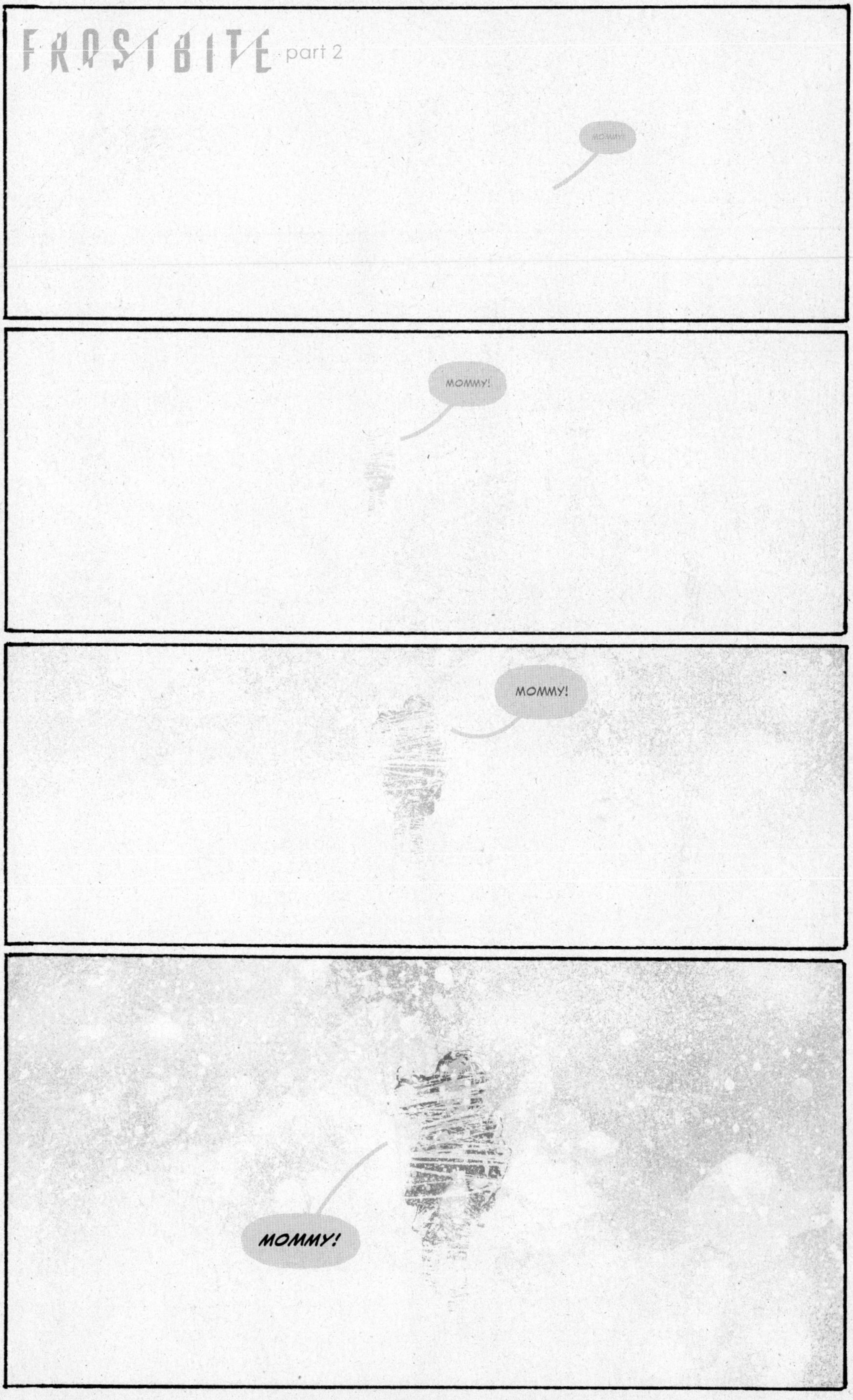
FROSTBITE part 2
MOMMY
MOMMY!
MOMMY!
MOMMY!

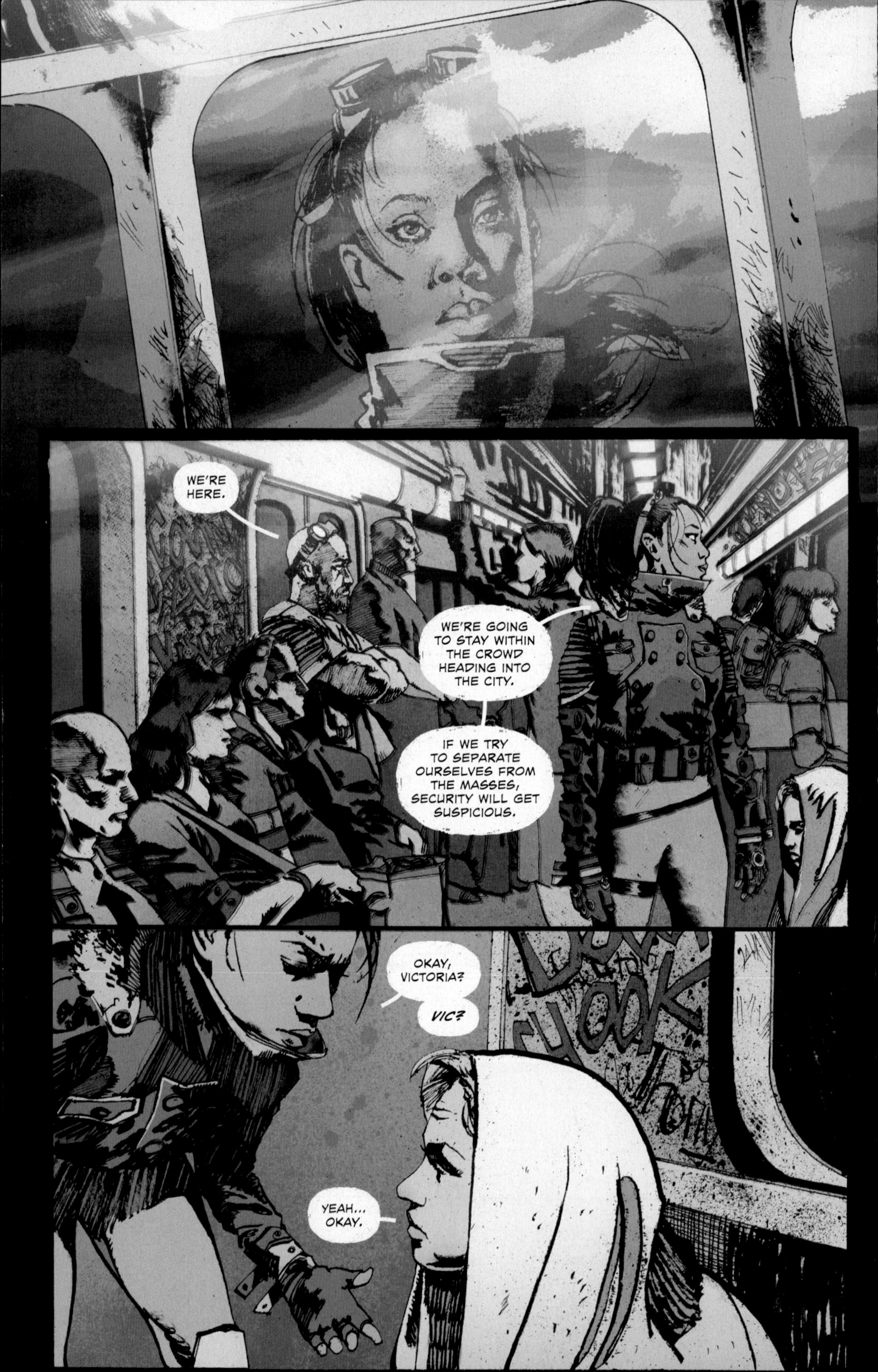
WE'RE HERE.
WE'RE GOING TO STAY WITHIN THE CROWD HEADING INTO THE CITY.
IF WE TRY TO SEPARATE OURSELVES FROM THE MASSES, SECURITY WILL GET SUSPICIOUS.
OKAY, VICTORIA?
VIC?
YEAH... OKAY.

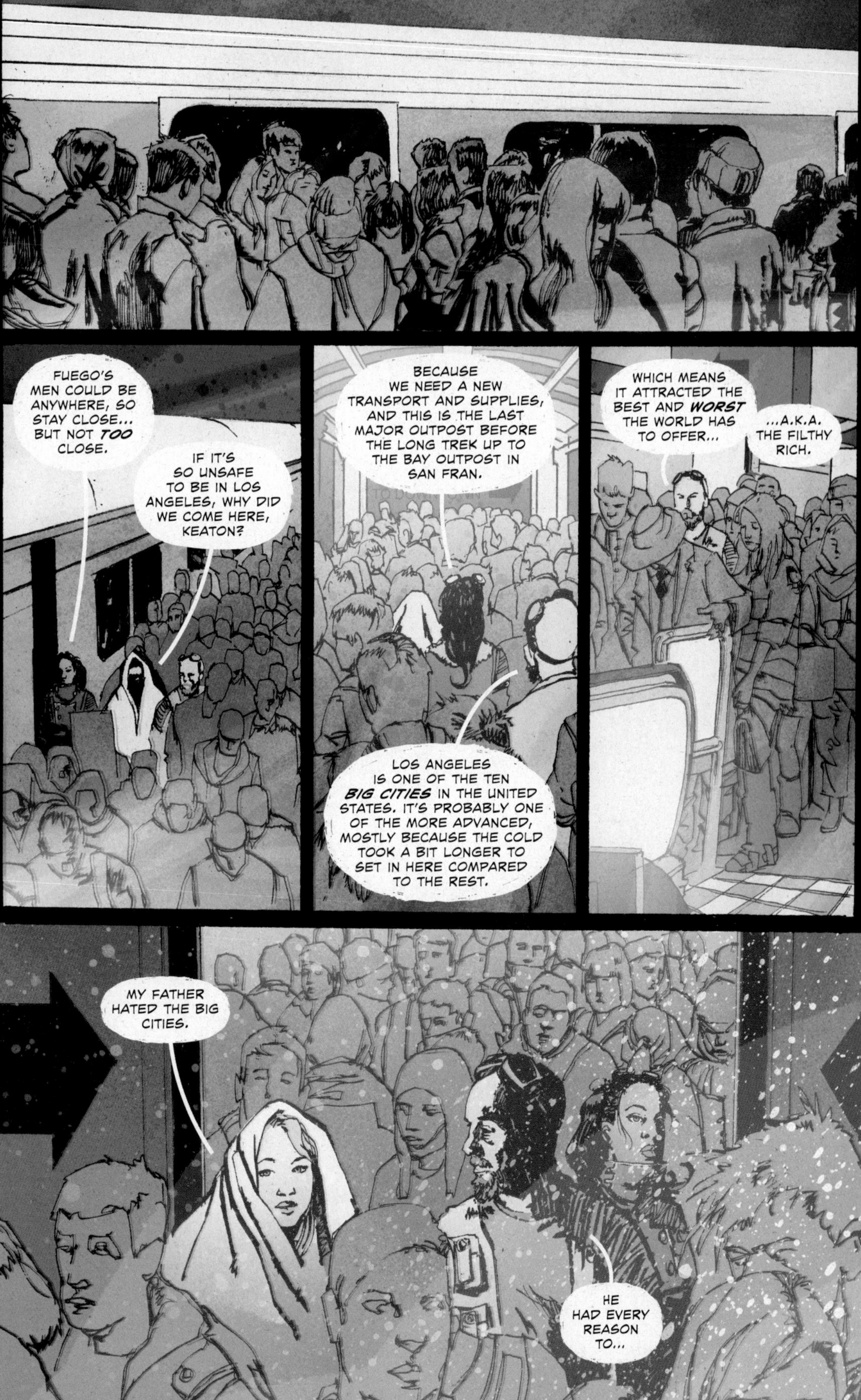
FUEGO'S MEN COULD BE ANYWHERE, SO STAY CLOSE... BUT NOT *TOO* CLOSE.
IF IT'S SO UNSAFE TO BE IN LOS ANGELES, WHY DID WE COME HERE, KEATON?
BECAUSE WE NEED A NEW TRANSPORT AND SUPPLIES, AND THIS IS THE LAST MAJOR OUTPOST BEFORE THE LONG TREK UP TO THE BAY OUTPOST IN SAN FRAN.
LOS ANGELES IS ONE OF THE TEN ***BIG CITIES*** IN THE UNITED STATES. IT'S PROBABLY ONE OF THE MORE ADVANCED, MOSTLY BECAUSE THE COLD TOOK A BIT LONGER TO SET IN HERE COMPARED TO THE REST.
WHICH MEANS IT ATTRACTED THE BEST AND ***WORST*** THE WORLD HAS TO OFFER...
...A.K.A. THE FILTHY RICH.
MY FATHER HATED THE BIG CITIES.
HE HAD EVERY REASON TO...

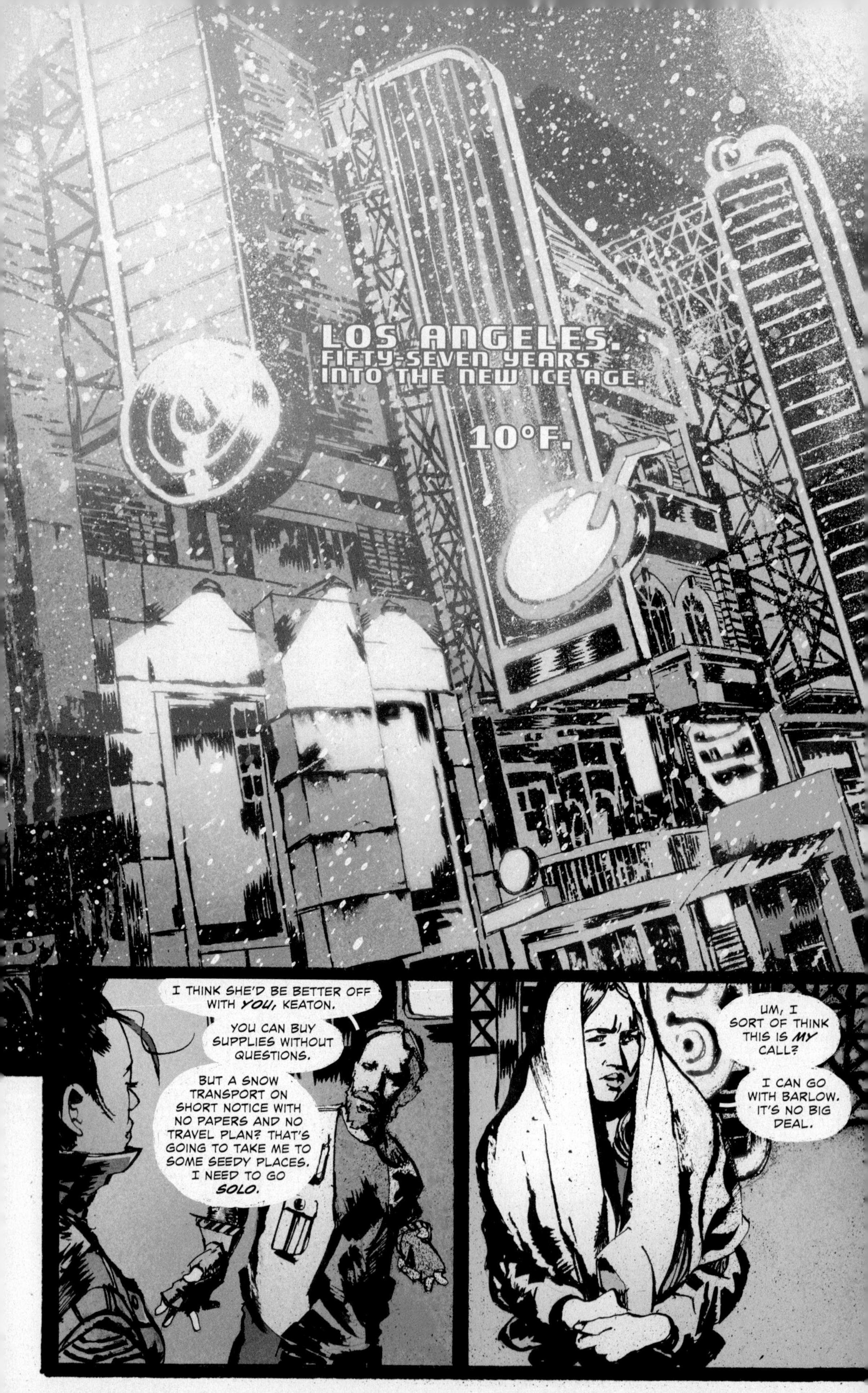
LOS ANGELES.
FIFTY-SEVEN YEARS INTO THE NEW ICE AGE.
10°F.
I THINK SHE'D BE BETTER OFF WITH YOU, KEATON.
YOU CAN BUY SUPPLIES WITHOUT QUESTIONS.
BUT A SNOW TRANSPORT ON SHORT NOTICE WITH NO PAPERS AND NO TRAVEL PLAN? THAT'S GOING TO TAKE ME TO SOME SEEDY PLACES. I NEED TO GO SOLO.
UM, I SORT OF THINK THIS IS MY CALL?
I CAN GO WITH BARLOW. IT'S NO BIG DEAL.

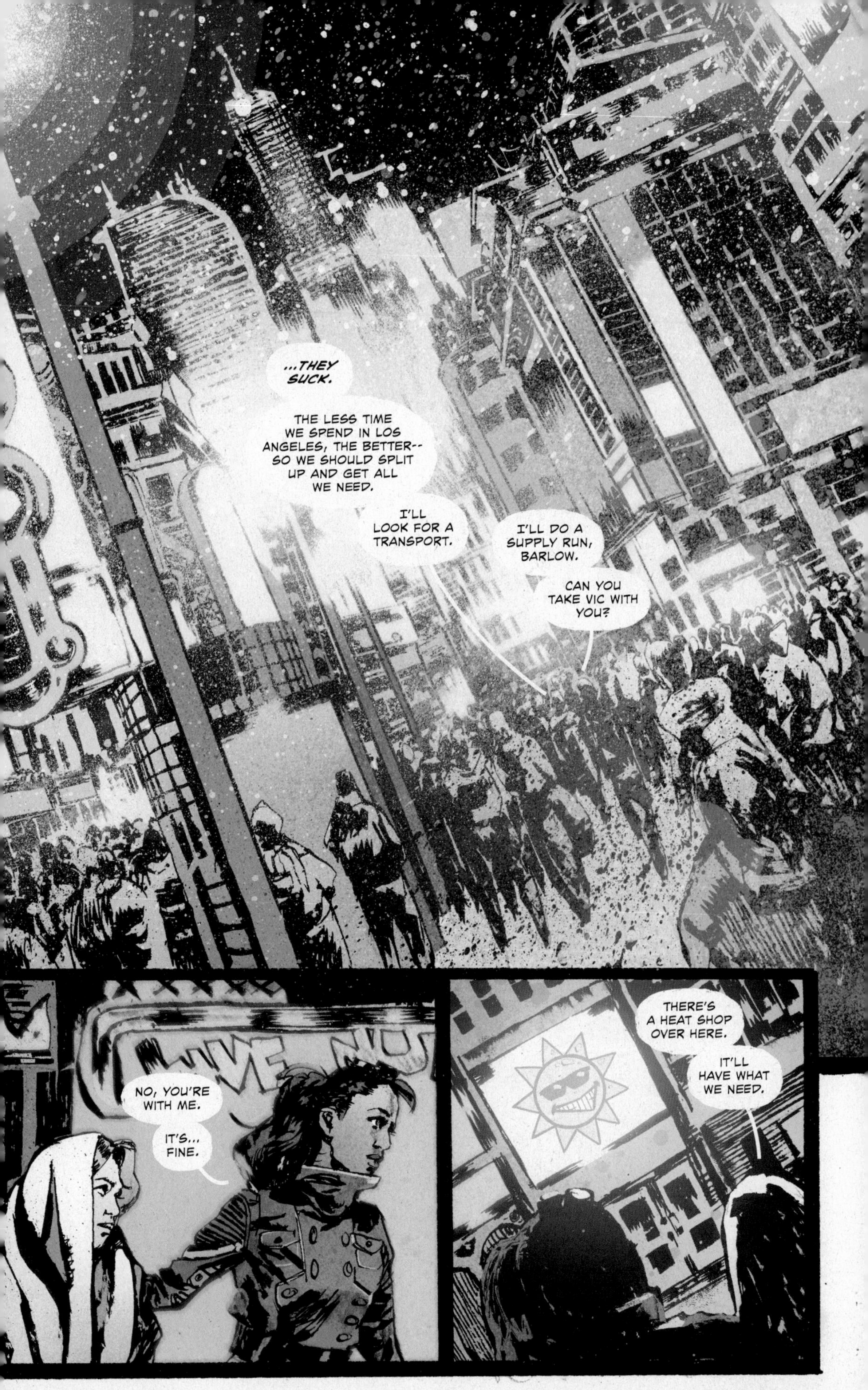
...THEY SUCK.
THE LESS TIME WE SPEND IN LOS ANGELES, THE BETTER-- SO WE SHOULD SPLIT UP AND GET ALL WE NEED.
I'LL LOOK FOR A TRANSPORT.
I'LL DO A SUPPLY RUN, BARLOW.
CAN YOU TAKE VIC WITH YOU?
NO, YOU'RE WITH ME.
IT'S... FINE.
THERE'S A HEAT SHOP OVER HERE.
IT'LL HAVE WHAT WE NEED.

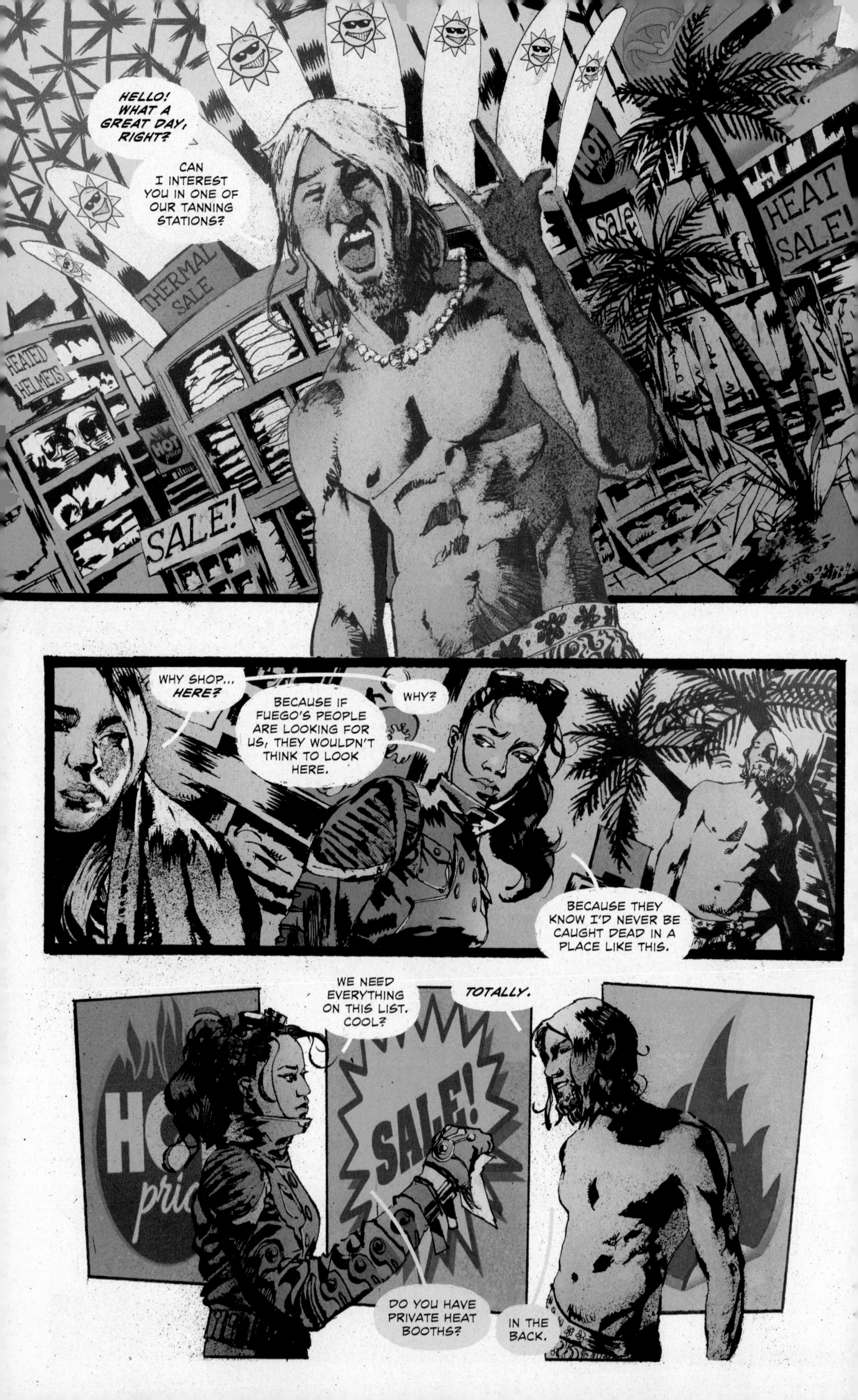
HELLO! WHAT A GREAT DAY, RIGHT?
CAN I INTEREST YOU IN ONE OF OUR TANNING STATIONS?
THERMAL SALE
HEATED HELMETS
HOT price
SALE!
HOT price
Sale
HEAT SALE!
WHY SHOP... HERE?
WHY?
BECAUSE IF FUEGO'S PEOPLE ARE LOOKING FOR US, THEY WOULDN'T THINK TO LOOK HERE.
BECAUSE THEY KNOW I'D NEVER BE CAUGHT DEAD IN A PLACE LIKE THIS.
WE NEED EVERYTHING ON THIS LIST. COOL?
TOTALLY.
SALE!
DO YOU HAVE PRIVATE HEAT BOOTHS?
IN THE BACK.

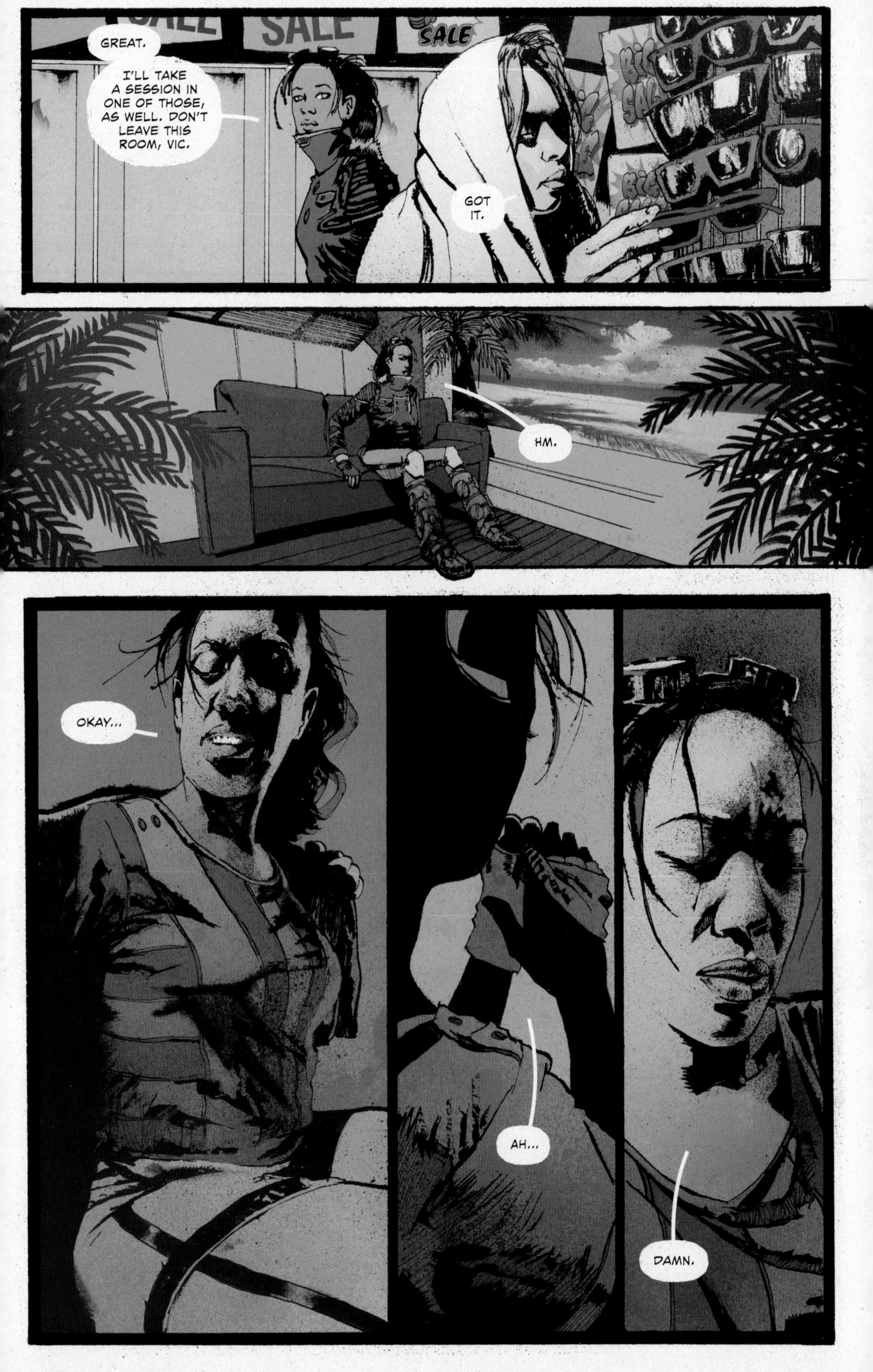
SALE
SALE
SALE
GREAT.
I'LL TAKE A SESSION IN ONE OF THOSE, AS WELL. DON'T LEAVE THIS ROOM, VIC.
GOT IT.
HM.
OKAY...
AH...
DAMN.

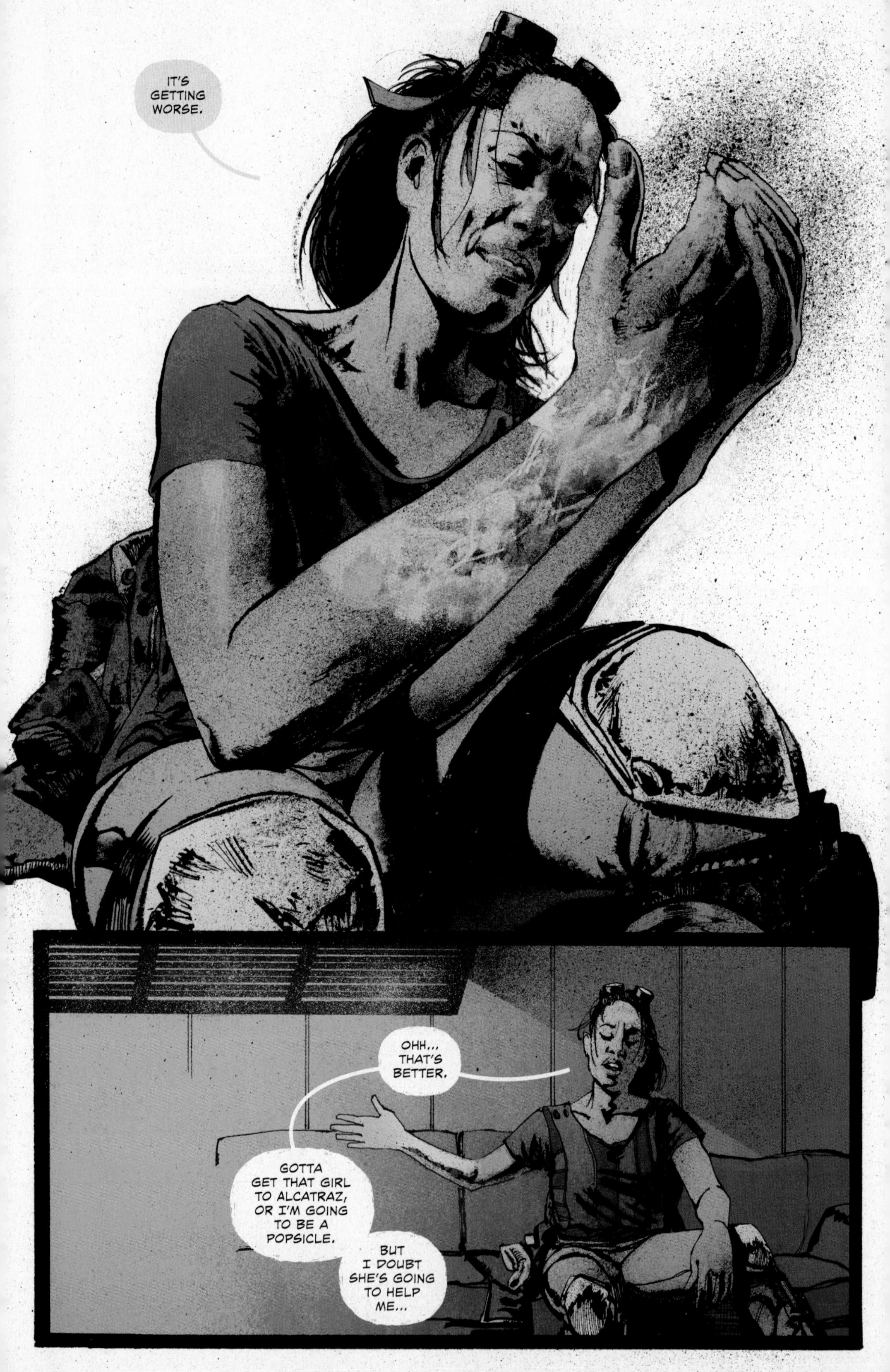
IT'S GETTING WORSE.
OHH... THAT'S BETTER.
GOTTA GET THAT GIRL TO ALCATRAZ, OR I'M GOING TO BE A POPSICLE.
BUT I DOUBT SHE'S GOING TO HELP ME...

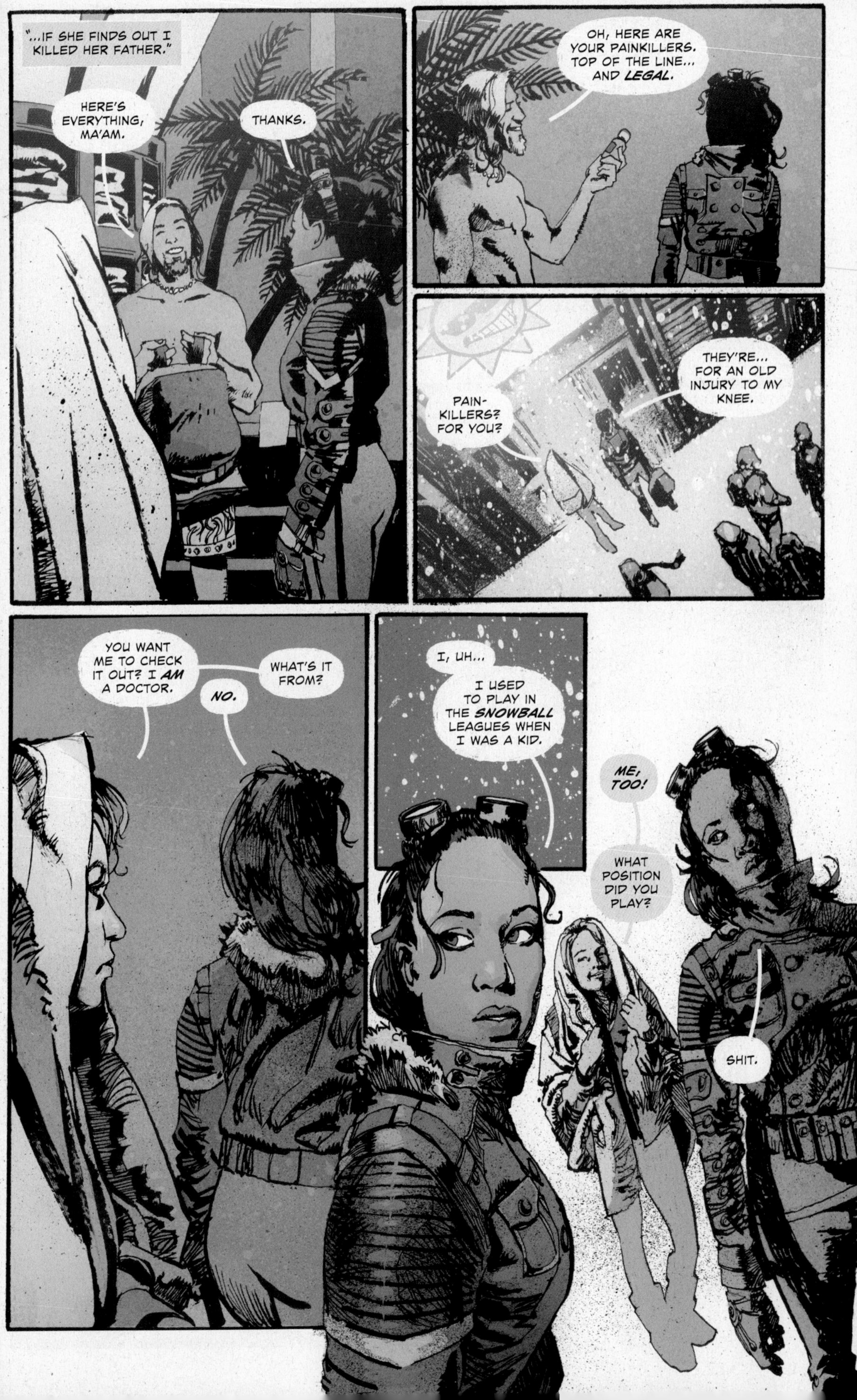
"...IF SHE FINDS OUT I KILLED HER FATHER."
HERE'S EVERYTHING, MA'AM.
THANKS.
OH, HERE ARE YOUR PAINKILLERS. TOP OF THE LINE... AND *LEGAL.*
PAIN-KILLERS? FOR YOU?
THEY'RE... FOR AN OLD INJURY TO MY KNEE.
YOU WANT ME TO CHECK IT OUT? I *AM* A DOCTOR.
*NO.*
WHAT'S IT FROM?
I, UH...
I USED TO PLAY IN THE *SNOWBALL* LEAGUES WHEN I WAS A KID.
*ME, TOO!*
WHAT POSITION DID YOU PLAY?
SHIT.

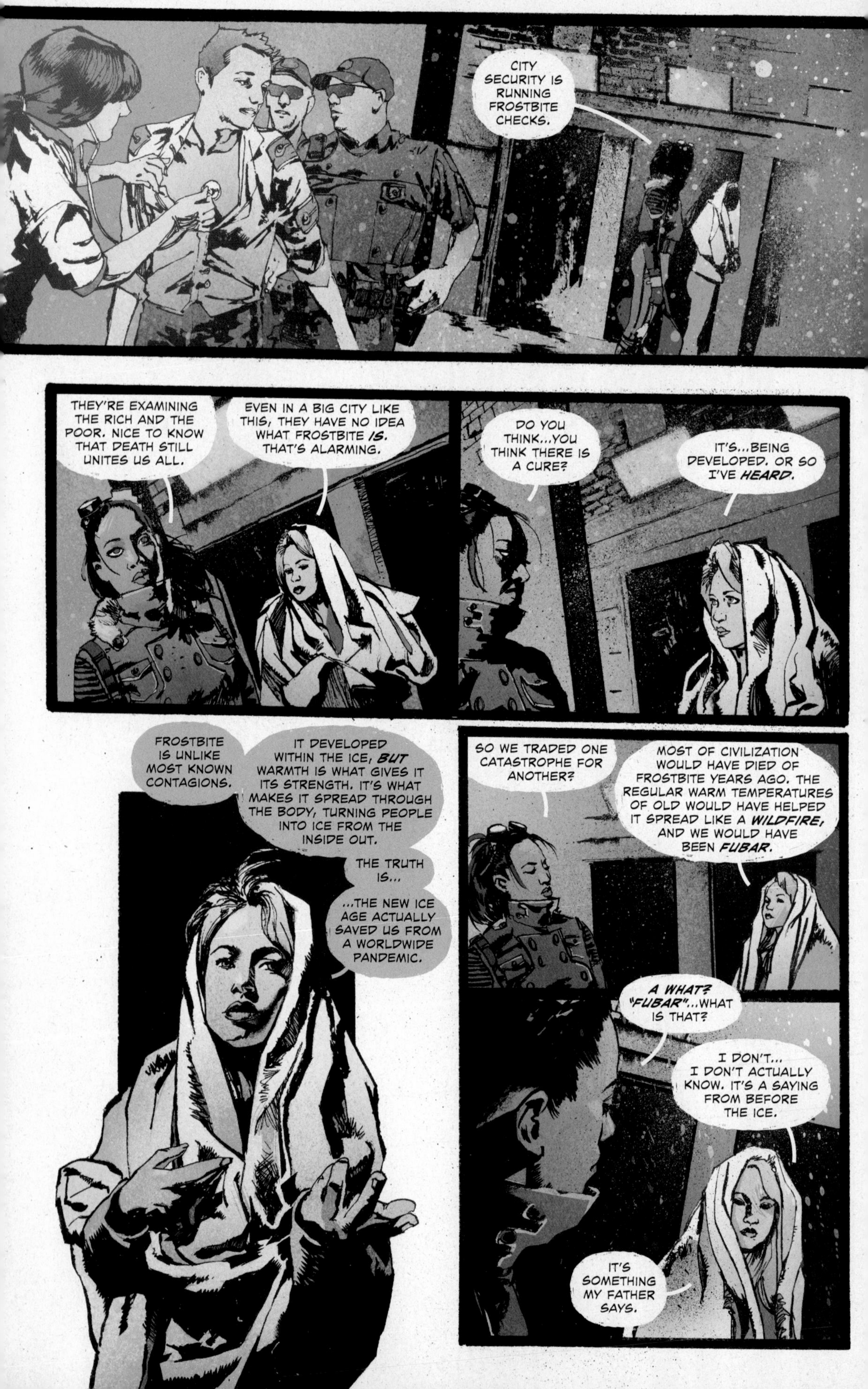
CITY SECURITY IS RUNNING FROSTBITE CHECKS.
THEY'RE EXAMINING THE RICH AND THE POOR. NICE TO KNOW THAT DEATH STILL UNITES US ALL.
EVEN IN A BIG CITY LIKE THIS, THEY HAVE NO IDEA WHAT FROSTBITE *IS.* THAT'S ALARMING.
DO YOU THINK...YOU THINK THERE IS A CURE?
IT'S...BEING DEVELOPED. OR SO I'VE *HEARD.*
FROSTBITE IS UNLIKE MOST KNOWN CONTAGIONS.
IT DEVELOPED WITHIN THE ICE, *BUT* WARMTH IS WHAT GIVES IT ITS STRENGTH. IT'S WHAT MAKES IT SPREAD THROUGH THE BODY, TURNING PEOPLE INTO ICE FROM THE INSIDE OUT.
THE TRUTH IS...
...THE NEW ICE AGE ACTUALLY SAVED US FROM A WORLDWIDE PANDEMIC.
SO WE TRADED ONE CATASTROPHE FOR ANOTHER?
MOST OF CIVILIZATION WOULD HAVE DIED OF FROSTBITE YEARS AGO. THE REGULAR WARM TEMPERATURES OF OLD WOULD HAVE HELPED IT SPREAD LIKE A *WILDFIRE,* AND WE WOULD HAVE BEEN *FUBAR.*
*A WHAT? "FUBAR"*...WHAT IS THAT?
I DON'T... I DON'T ACTUALLY KNOW. IT'S A SAYING FROM BEFORE THE ICE.
IT'S SOMETHING MY FATHER SAYS.

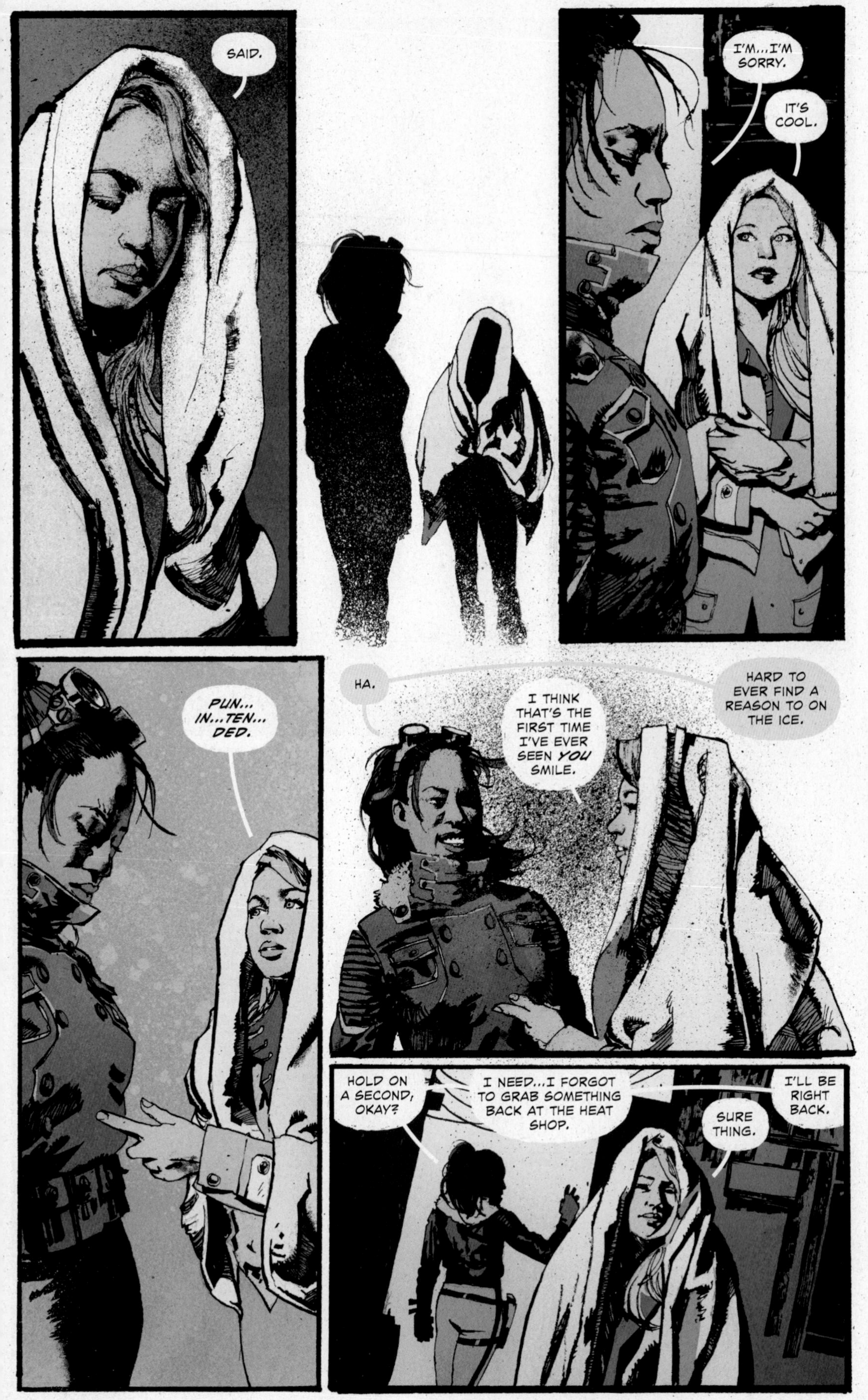
SAID.
I'M...I'M SORRY.
IT'S COOL.
PUN... IN...TEN... DED.
HA.
I THINK THAT'S THE FIRST TIME I'VE EVER SEEN YOU SMILE.
HARD TO EVER FIND A REASON TO ON THE ICE.
HOLD ON A SECOND, OKAY?
I NEED...I FORGOT TO GRAB SOMETHING BACK AT THE HEAT SHOP.
I'LL BE RIGHT BACK.
SURE THING.

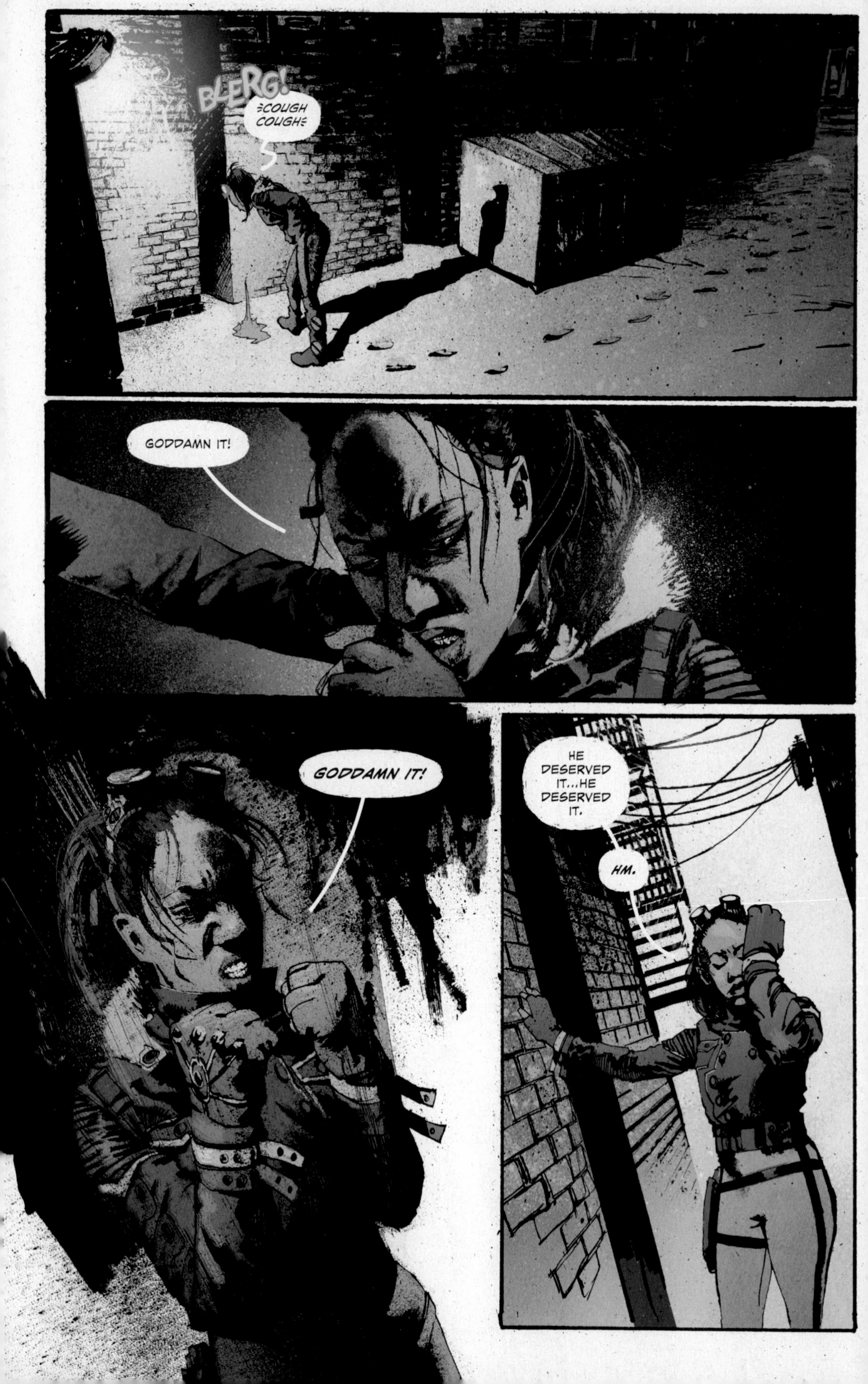
BLERG!
COUGH COUGH
GODDAMN IT!
GODDAMN IT!
HE DESERVED IT...HE DESERVED IT.
HM.

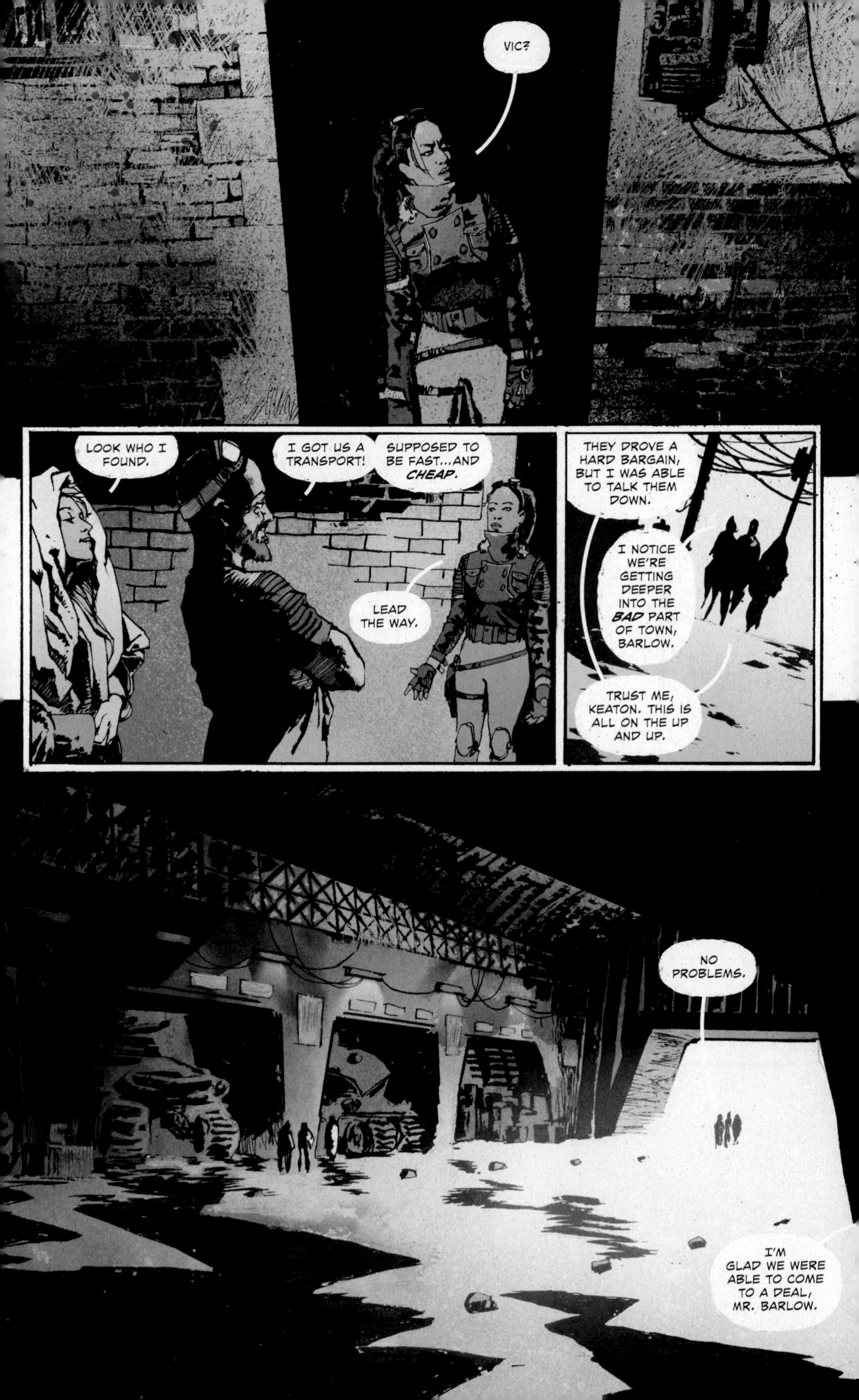
VIC?
LOOK WHO I FOUND.
I GOT US A TRANSPORT!
SUPPOSED TO BE FAST...AND *CHEAP.*
LEAD THE WAY.
THEY DROVE A HARD BARGAIN, BUT I WAS ABLE TO TALK THEM DOWN.
I NOTICE WE'RE GETTING DEEPER INTO THE *BAD* PART OF TOWN, BARLOW.
TRUST ME, KEATON. THIS IS ALL ON THE UP AND UP.
NO PROBLEMS.
I'M GLAD WE WERE ABLE TO COME TO A DEAL, MR. BARLOW.

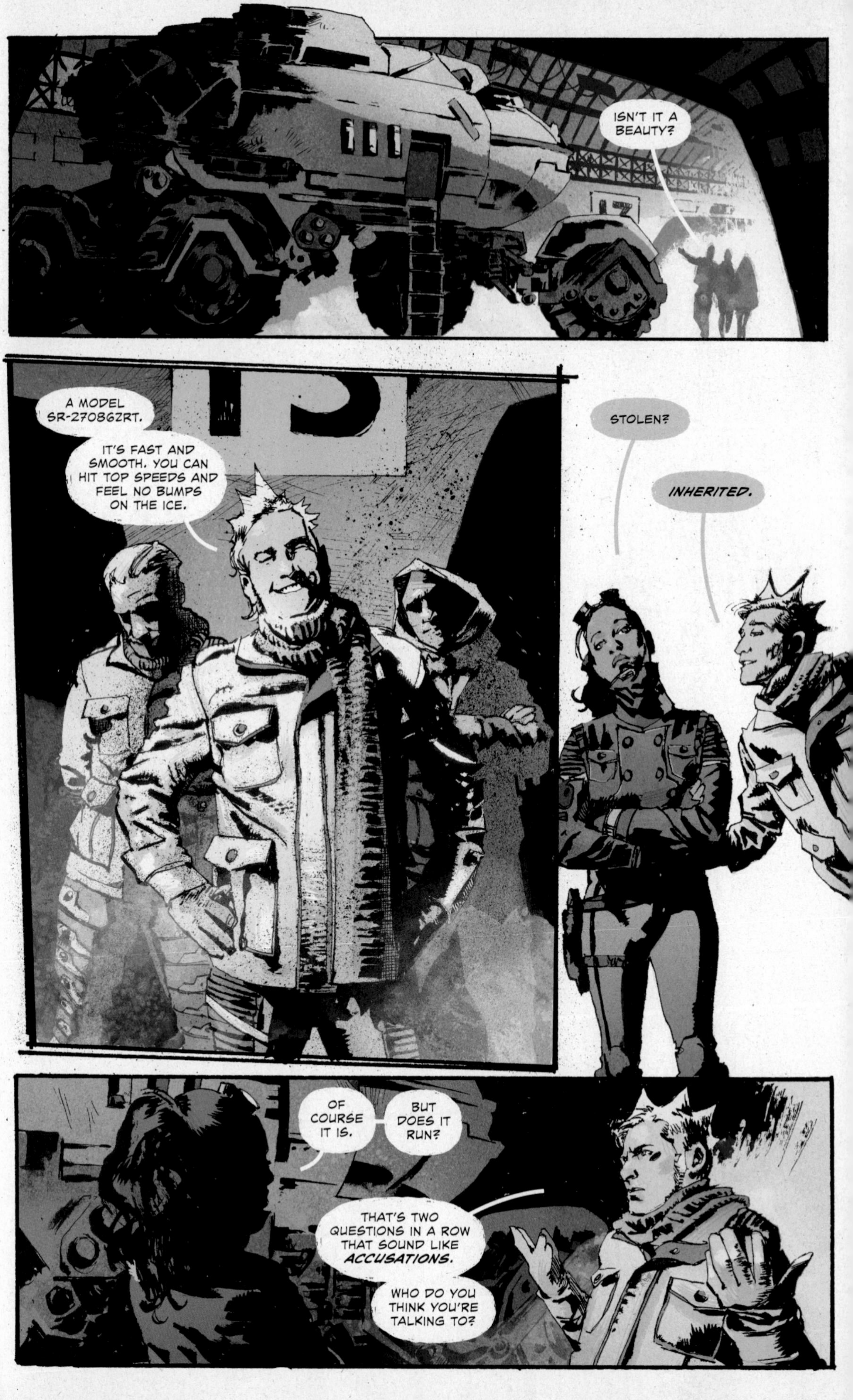
ISN'T IT A BEAUTY?
A MODEL SR-27086ZRT.
IT'S FAST AND SMOOTH. YOU CAN HIT TOP SPEEDS AND FEEL NO BUMPS ON THE ICE.
STOLEN?
INHERITED.
OF COURSE IT IS.
BUT DOES IT RUN?
THAT'S TWO QUESTIONS IN A ROW THAT SOUND LIKE ACCUSATIONS.
WHO DO YOU THINK YOU'RE TALKING TO?

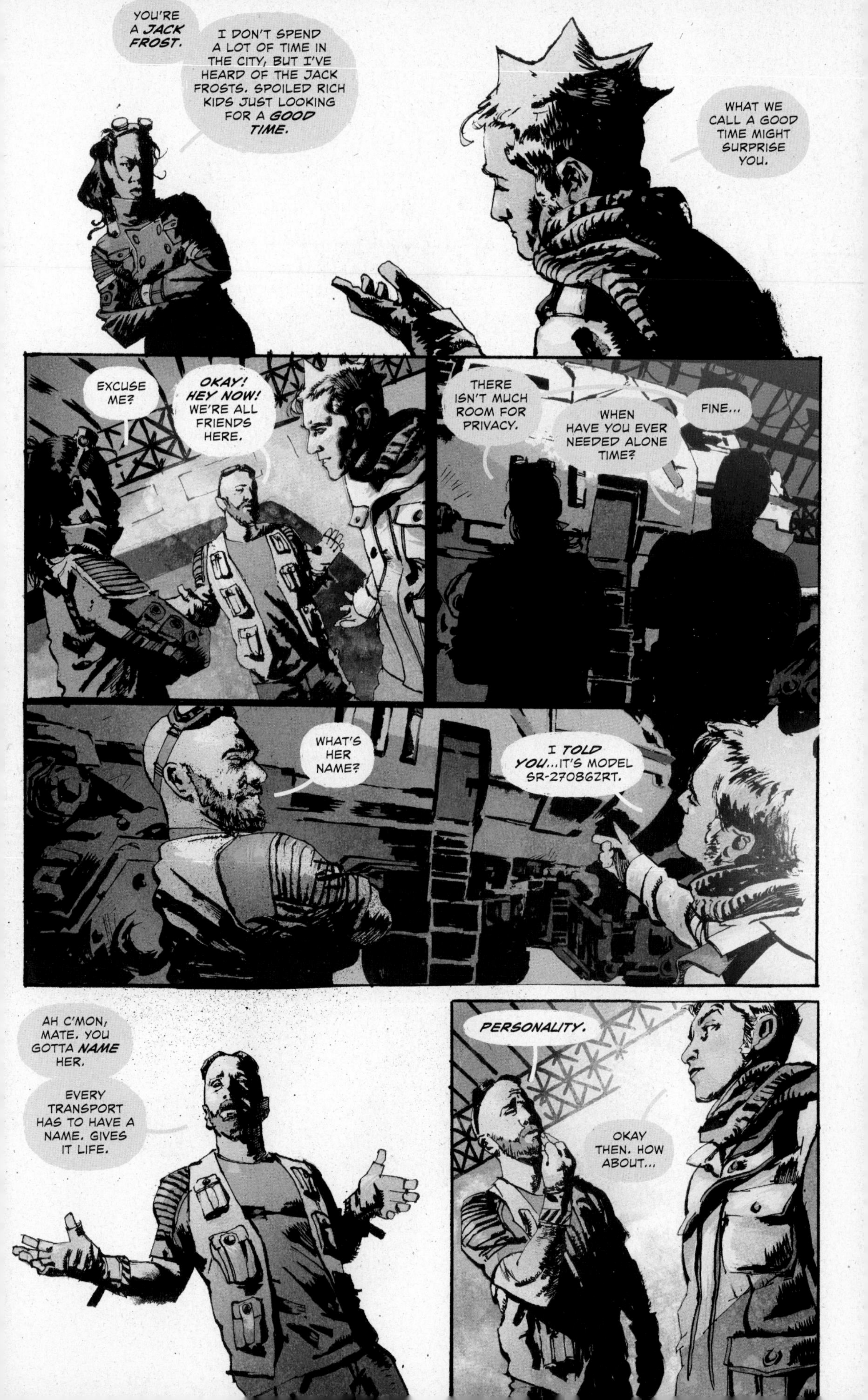
YOU'RE A JACK FROST.
I DON'T SPEND A LOT OF TIME IN THE CITY, BUT I'VE HEARD OF THE JACK FROSTS. SPOILED RICH KIDS JUST LOOKING FOR A GOOD TIME.
WHAT WE CALL A GOOD TIME MIGHT SURPRISE YOU.
EXCUSE ME?
OKAY! HEY NOW! WE'RE ALL FRIENDS HERE.
THERE ISN'T MUCH ROOM FOR PRIVACY.
WHEN HAVE YOU EVER NEEDED ALONE TIME?
FINE...
WHAT'S HER NAME?
I TOLD YOU...IT'S MODEL SR-27086ZRT.
AH C'MON, MATE. YOU GOTTA NAME HER.
EVERY TRANSPORT HAS TO HAVE A NAME. GIVES IT LIFE.
PERSONALITY.
OKAY THEN. HOW ABOUT...

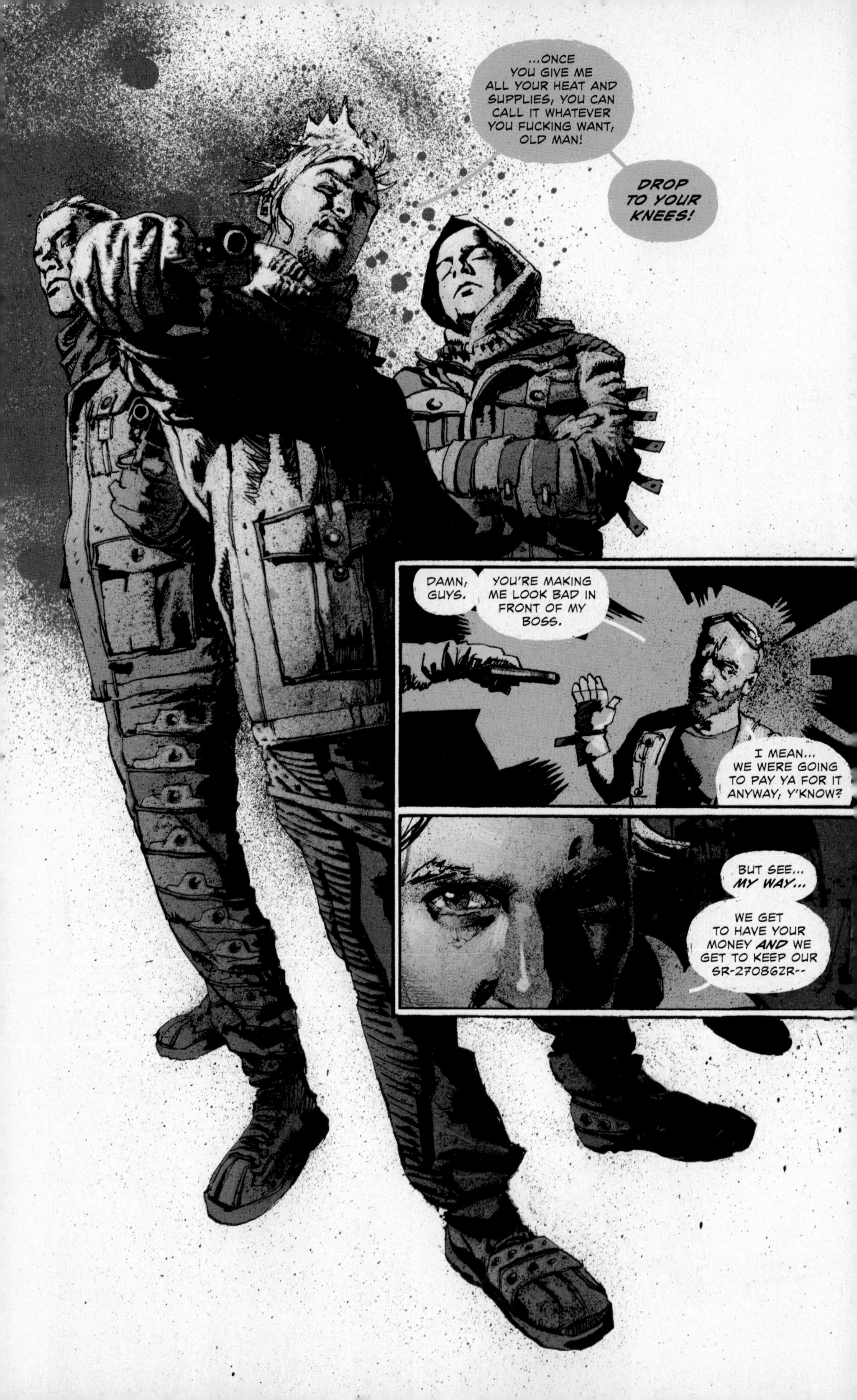
...ONCE YOU GIVE ME ALL YOUR HEAT AND SUPPLIES, YOU CAN CALL IT WHATEVER YOU FUCKING WANT, OLD MAN!
DROP TO YOUR KNEES!
DAMN, GUYS.
YOU'RE MAKING ME LOOK BAD IN FRONT OF MY BOSS.
I MEAN... WE WERE GOING TO PAY YA FOR IT ANYWAY, Y'KNOW?
BUT SEE... MY WAY...
WE GET TO HAVE YOUR MONEY AND WE GET TO KEEP OUR SR-27086ZR--

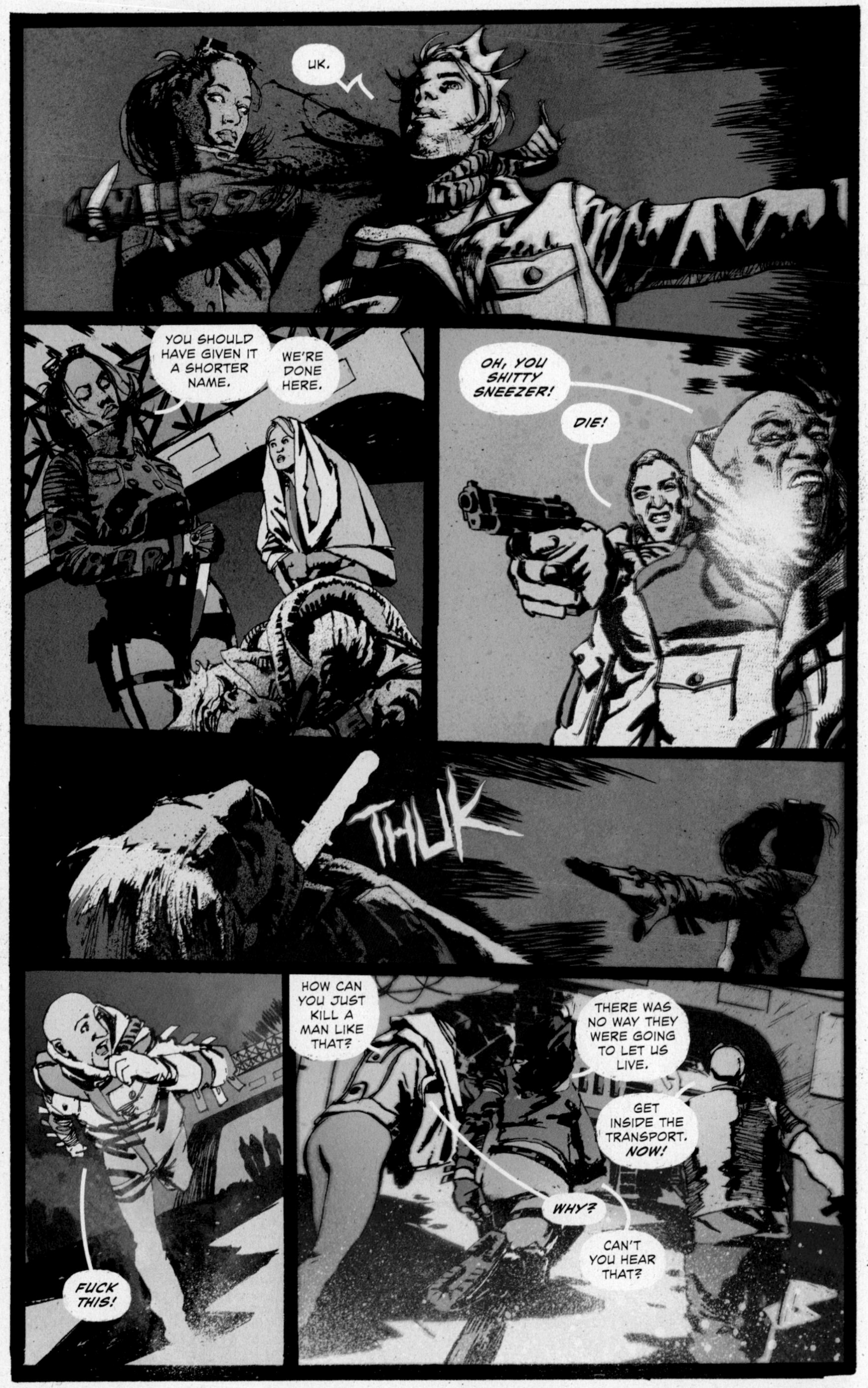
UK.
YOU SHOULD HAVE GIVEN IT A SHORTER NAME.
WE'RE DONE HERE.
OH, YOU SHITTY SNEEZER!
DIE!
THUK
FUCK THIS!
HOW CAN YOU JUST KILL A MAN LIKE THAT?
THERE WAS NO WAY THEY WERE GOING TO LET US LIVE.
GET INSIDE THE TRANSPORT. NOW!
WHY?
CAN'T YOU HEAR THAT?

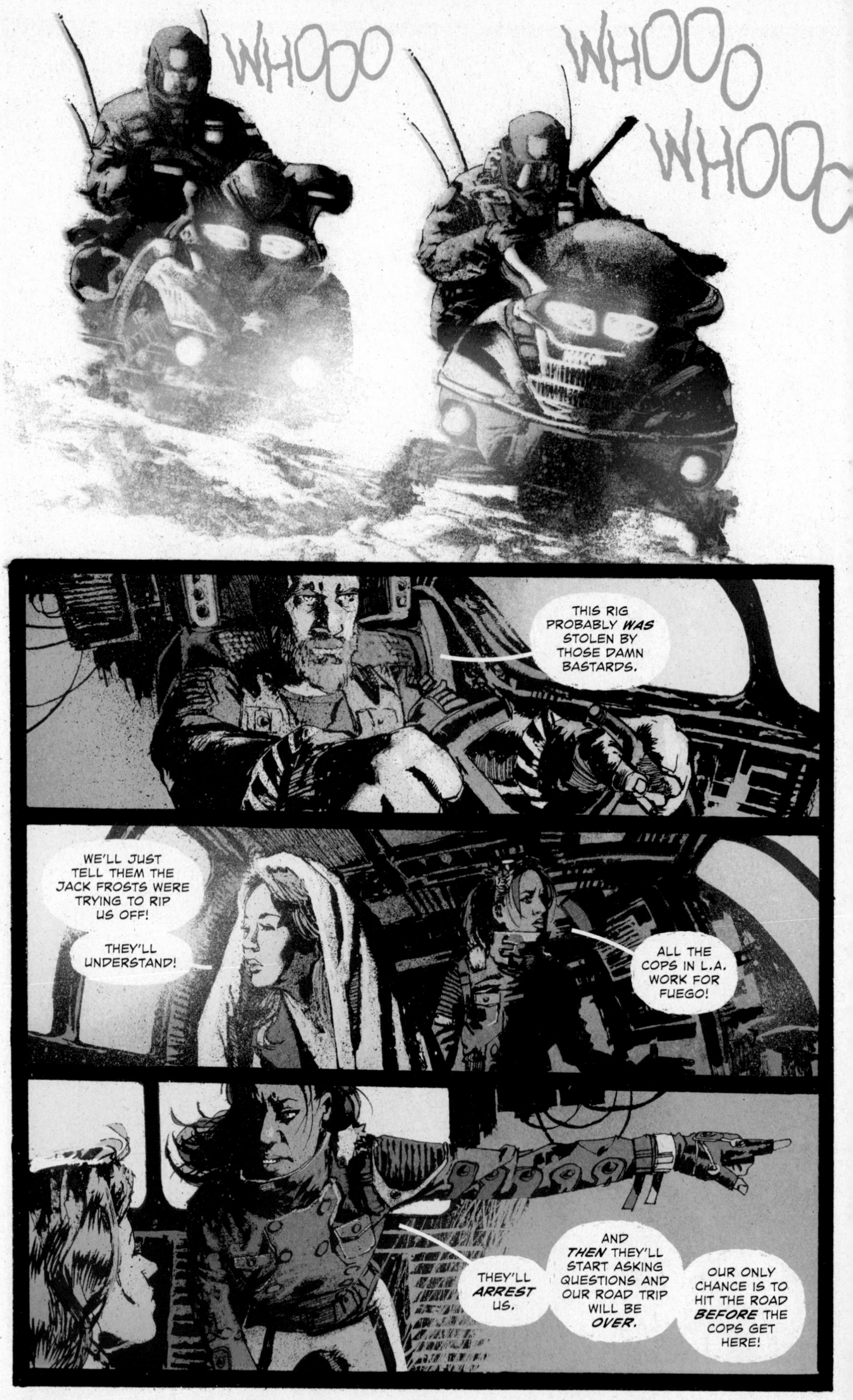
WHOOO
WHOOO
WHOOO
THIS RIG PROBABLY WAS STOLEN BY THOSE DAMN BASTARDS.
WE'LL JUST TELL THEM THE JACK FROSTS WERE TRYING TO RIP US OFF!
THEY'LL UNDERSTAND!
ALL THE COPS IN L.A. WORK FOR FUEGO!
THEY'LL ARREST US.
AND THEN THEY'LL START ASKING QUESTIONS AND OUR ROAD TRIP WILL BE OVER.
OUR ONLY CHANCE IS TO HIT THE ROAD BEFORE THE COPS GET HERE!

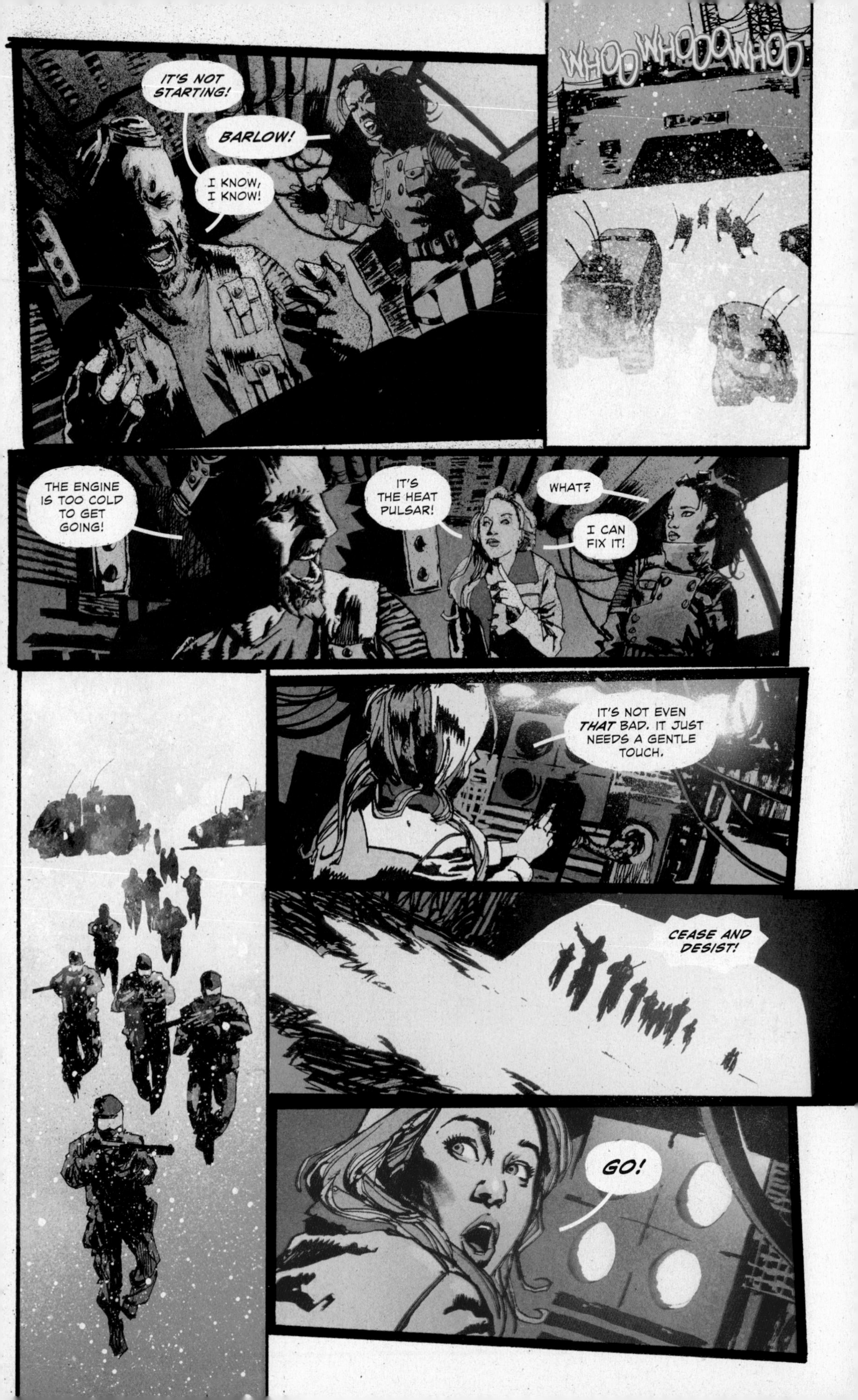
IT'S NOT STARTING!
BARLOW!
I KNOW, I KNOW!
WHOOWHOOOWHOO
THE ENGINE IS TOO COLD TO GET GOING!
IT'S THE HEAT PULSAR!
WHAT?
I CAN FIX IT!
IT'S NOT EVEN THAT BAD. IT JUST NEEDS A GENTLE TOUCH.
CEASE AND DESIST!
GO!

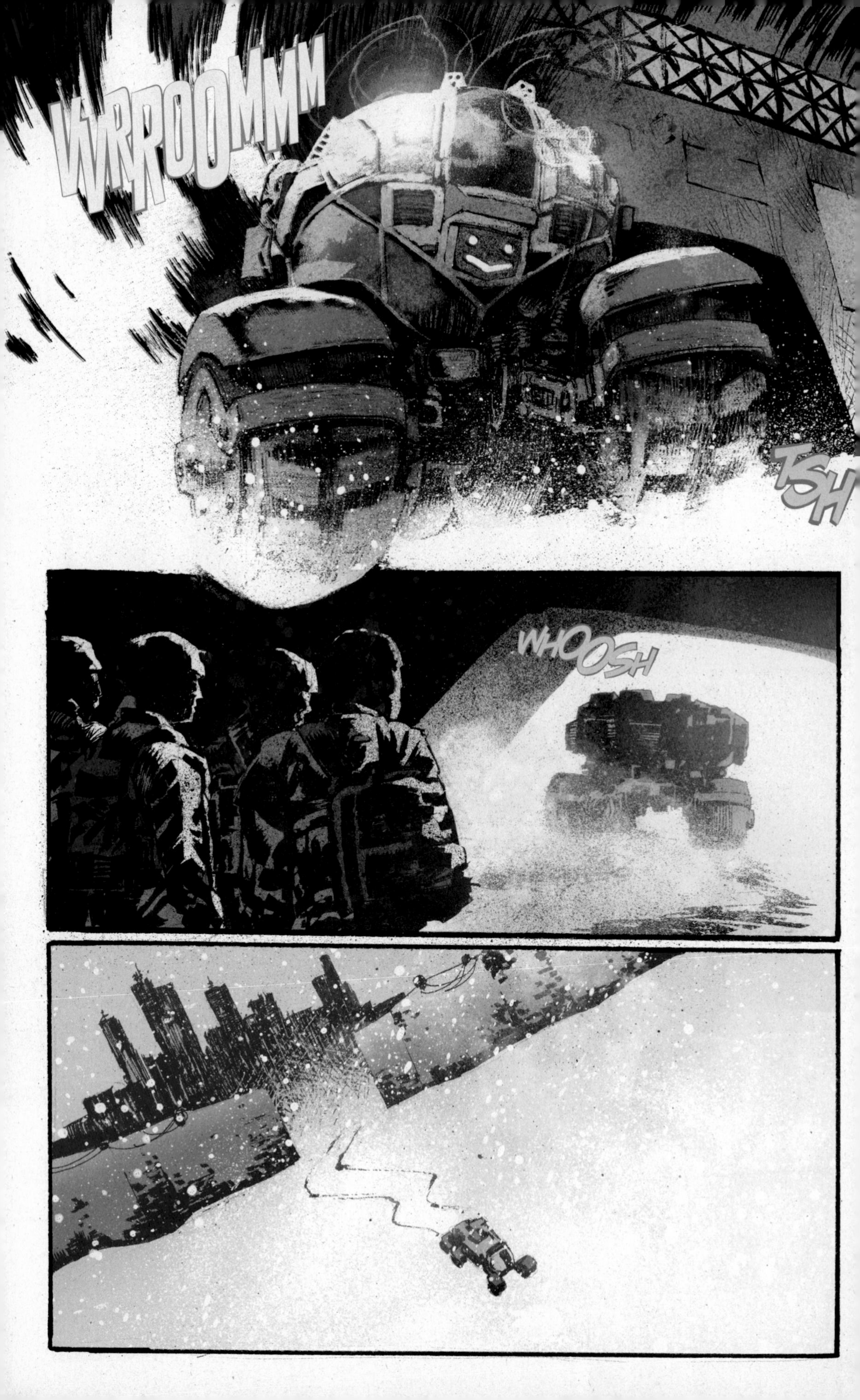
WRROOMMM
TSH
WHOOSH

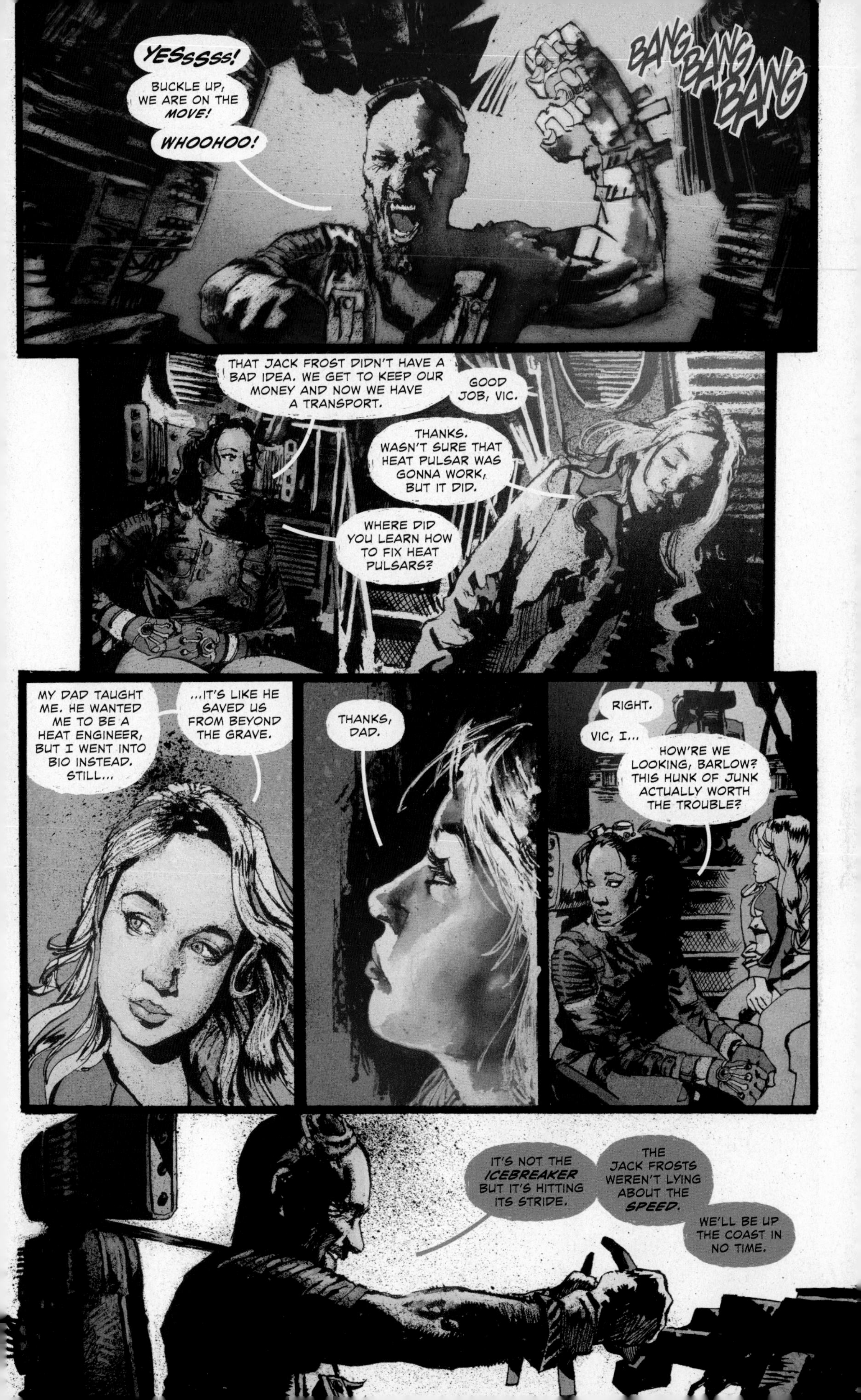
YESssss!
BUCKLE UP, WE ARE ON THE *MOVE!*
WHOOHOO!
BANG BANG BANG
THAT JACK FROST DIDN'T HAVE A BAD IDEA. WE GET TO KEEP OUR MONEY AND NOW WE HAVE A TRANSPORT.
GOOD JOB, VIC.
THANKS. WASN'T SURE THAT HEAT PULSAR WAS GONNA WORK, BUT IT DID.
WHERE DID YOU LEARN HOW TO FIX HEAT PULSARS?
MY DAD TAUGHT ME. HE WANTED ME TO BE A HEAT ENGINEER, BUT I WENT INTO BIO INSTEAD. STILL...
...IT'S LIKE HE SAVED US FROM BEYOND THE GRAVE.
THANKS, DAD.
RIGHT.
VIC, I...
HOW'RE WE LOOKING, BARLOW? THIS HUNK OF JUNK ACTUALLY WORTH THE TROUBLE?
IT'S NOT THE *ICEBREAKER* BUT IT'S HITTING ITS STRIDE.
THE JACK FROSTS WEREN'T LYING ABOUT THE *SPEED.*
WE'LL BE UP THE COAST IN NO TIME.

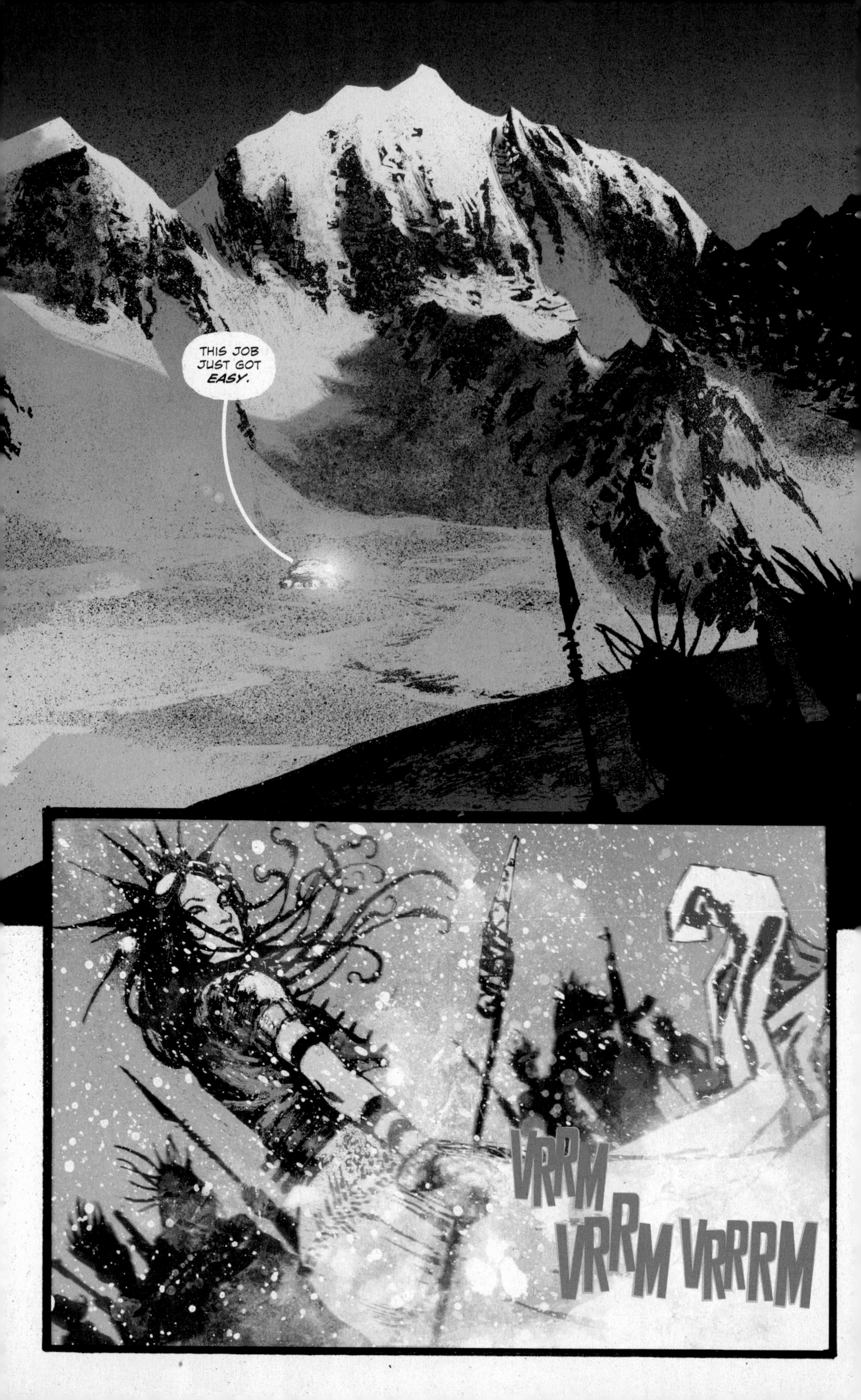
THIS JOB JUST GOT EASY.
VRRM VRRM VRRRM

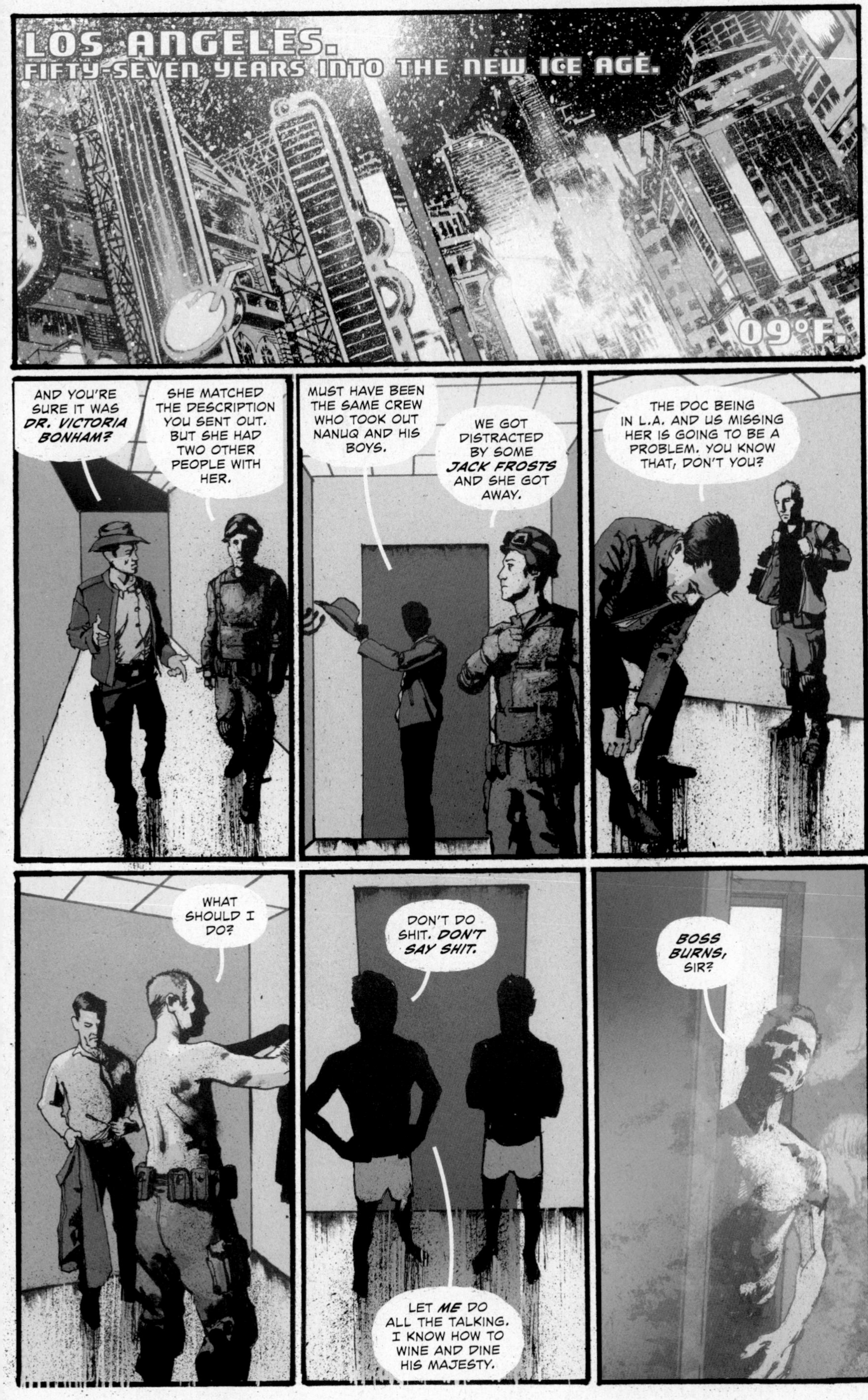
LOS ANGELES.
FIFTY-SEVEN YEARS INTO THE NEW ICE AGE.
09°F.
AND YOU'RE SURE IT WAS DR. VICTORIA BONHAM?
SHE MATCHED THE DESCRIPTION YOU SENT OUT. BUT SHE HAD TWO OTHER PEOPLE WITH HER.
MUST HAVE BEEN THE SAME CREW WHO TOOK OUT NANUQ AND HIS BOYS.
WE GOT DISTRACTED BY SOME JACK FROSTS AND SHE GOT AWAY.
THE DOC BEING IN L.A. AND US MISSING HER IS GOING TO BE A PROBLEM. YOU KNOW THAT, DON'T YOU?
WHAT SHOULD I DO?
DON'T DO SHIT. DON'T SAY SHIT.
LET ME DO ALL THE TALKING. I KNOW HOW TO WINE AND DINE HIS MAJESTY.
BOSS BURNS, SIR?

I'VE ALREADY HEARD ABOUT YOUR COLOSSAL FUCKUPS AS OF LATE, FUEGO.
SO SKIP YOUR SONG AND DANCE AND TELL ME HOW YOU PLAN TO **SOLVE** THIS.
FROSTBITE part 3

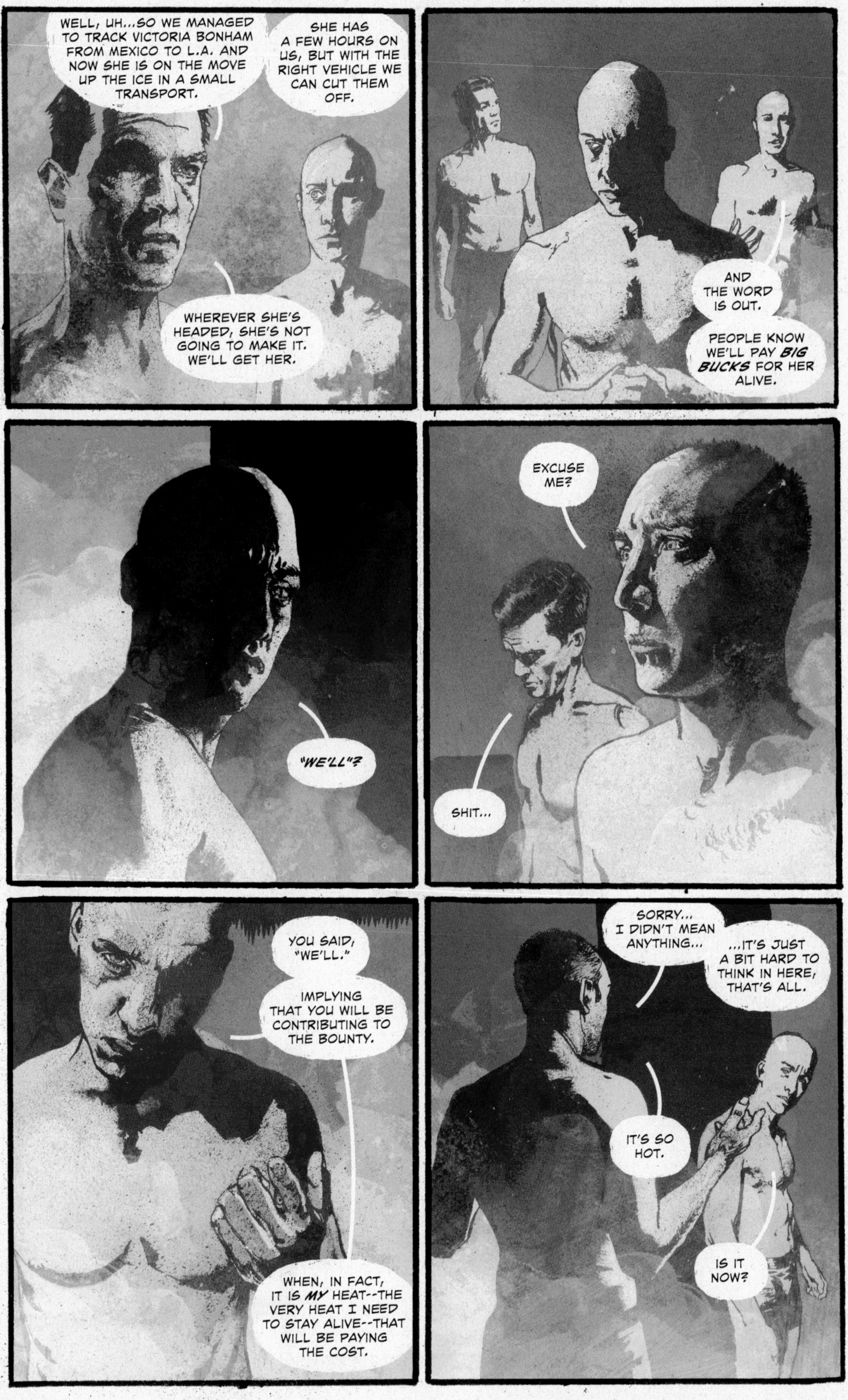
WELL, UH...SO WE MANAGED TO TRACK VICTORIA BONHAM FROM MEXICO TO L.A. AND NOW SHE IS ON THE MOVE UP THE ICE IN A SMALL TRANSPORT.
SHE HAS A FEW HOURS ON US, BUT WITH THE RIGHT VEHICLE WE CAN CUT THEM OFF.
WHEREVER SHE'S HEADED, SHE'S NOT GOING TO MAKE IT. WE'LL GET HER.
AND THE WORD IS OUT.
PEOPLE KNOW WE'LL PAY BIG BUCKS FOR HER ALIVE.
"WE'LL"?
EXCUSE ME?
SHIT...
YOU SAID, "WE'LL."
IMPLYING THAT YOU WILL BE CONTRIBUTING TO THE BOUNTY.
WHEN, IN FACT, IT IS MY HEAT--THE VERY HEAT I NEED TO STAY ALIVE--THAT WILL BE PAYING THE COST.
SORRY... I DIDN'T MEAN ANYTHING...
...IT'S JUST A BIT HARD TO THINK IN HERE, THAT'S ALL.
IT'S SO HOT.
IS IT NOW?

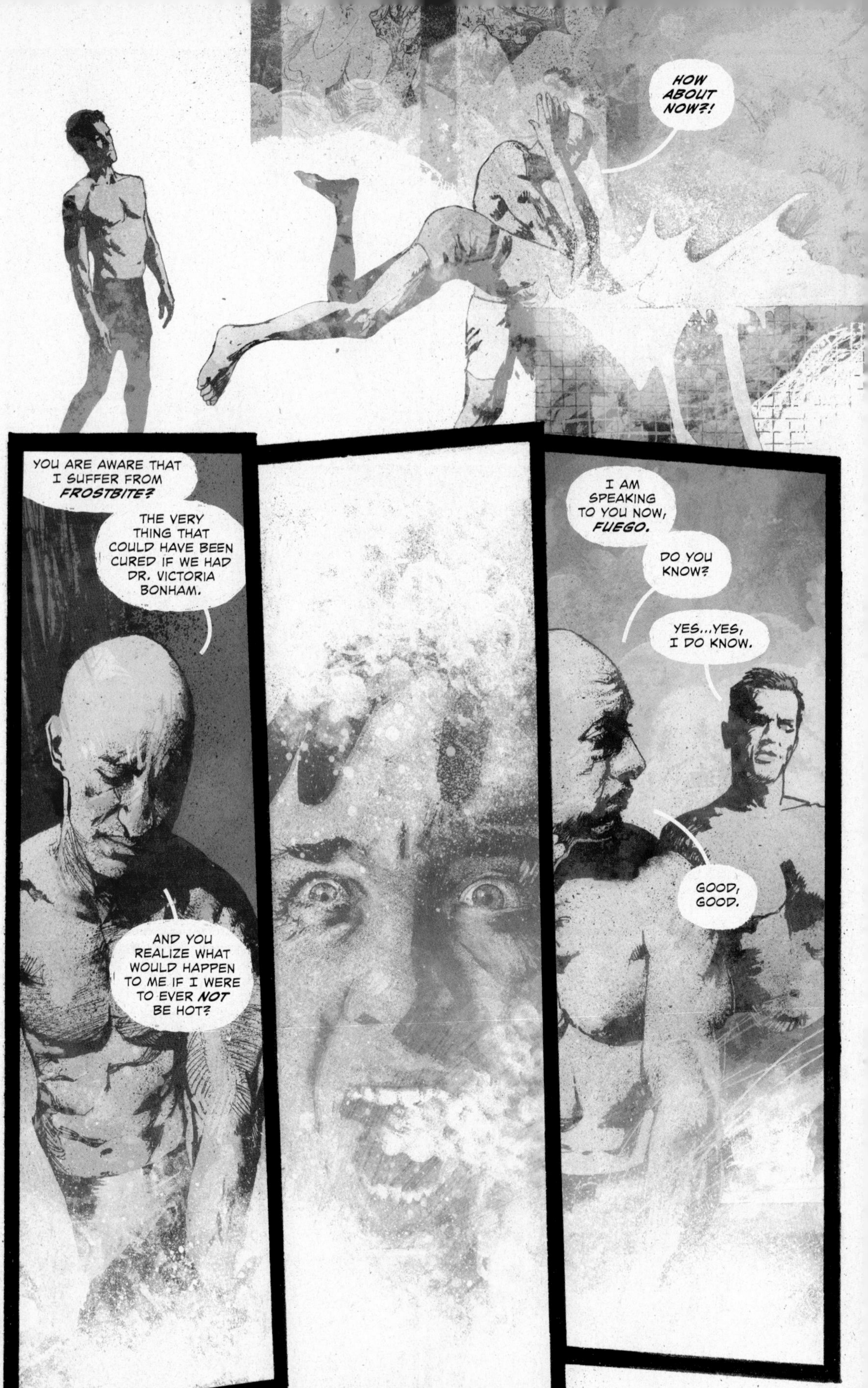
HOW ABOUT NOW?!
YOU ARE AWARE THAT I SUFFER FROM *FROSTBITE?*
THE VERY THING THAT COULD HAVE BEEN CURED IF WE HAD DR. VICTORIA BONHAM.
AND YOU REALIZE WHAT WOULD HAPPEN TO ME IF I WERE TO EVER *NOT* BE HOT?
I AM SPEAKING TO YOU NOW, *FUEGO.*
DO YOU KNOW?
YES...YES, I DO KNOW.
GOOD, GOOD.

YOU CAN TAKE THE *TITANIC*.

REALLY?

VICTORIA AND WHOEVER IS HELPING HER ARE DEAD IN THE ICE, THEN. NO WAY ARE THEY GOING TO OUTRUN THE TITANIC.

ONE LAST THING...

...DID VICTORIA HAVE HER *FATHER* WITH HER WHILE SHE WAS HERE IN LOS ANGELES?

NO. HE KICKED THE BUCKET IN MEXICO.

DR. HENRY BONHAM HAS LEFT US?

IT LOOKS LIKE HE TOOK A HIT DURING THE SHOOTOUT WHEN NANUQ DIED.

LOOKS LIKE?

SOMETHING ABOUT IT DIDN'T SIT RIGHT WITH ME.

THE CRIME SCENE PHOTOS.

IS THE BODY STILL COLD?

UHHH, MORE THAN LIKELY, YEAH.

TAKE A TEAM. *INVESTIGATE.*

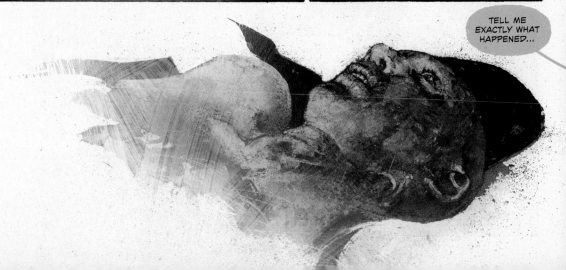

TELL ME EXACTLY WHAT HAPPENED...

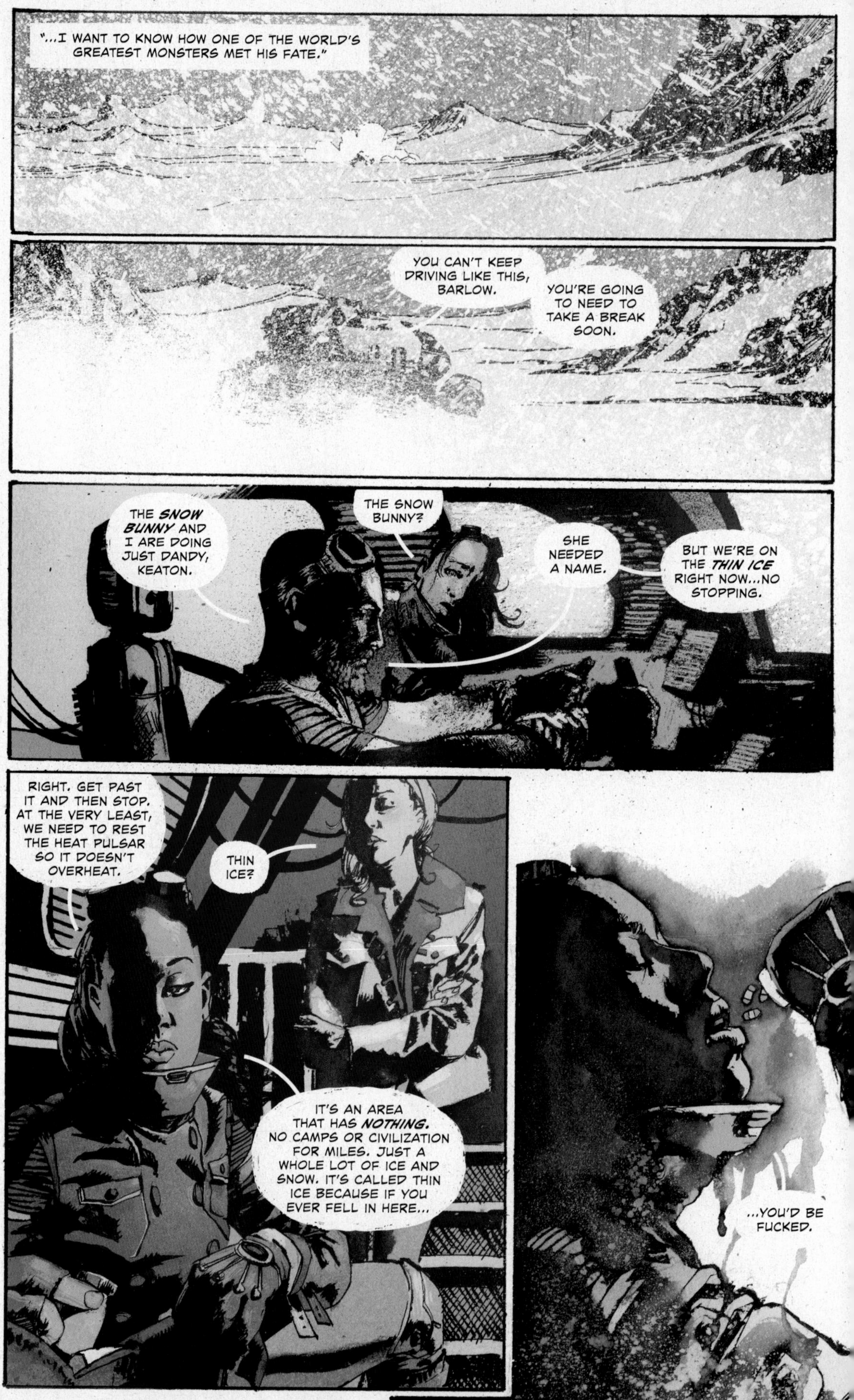
"...I WANT TO KNOW HOW ONE OF THE WORLD'S GREATEST MONSTERS MET HIS FATE."
YOU CAN'T KEEP DRIVING LIKE THIS, BARLOW.
YOU'RE GOING TO NEED TO TAKE A BREAK SOON.
THE *SNOW BUNNY* AND I ARE DOING JUST DANDY, KEATON.
THE SNOW BUNNY?
SHE NEEDED A NAME.
BUT WE'RE ON THE *THIN ICE* RIGHT NOW...NO STOPPING.
RIGHT. GET PAST IT AND THEN STOP. AT THE VERY LEAST, WE NEED TO REST THE HEAT PULSAR SO IT DOESN'T OVERHEAT.
THIN ICE?
IT'S AN AREA THAT HAS *NOTHING.* NO CAMPS OR CIVILIZATION FOR MILES. JUST A WHOLE LOT OF ICE AND SNOW. IT'S CALLED THIN ICE BECAUSE IF YOU EVER FELL IN HERE...
...YOU'D BE FUCKED.

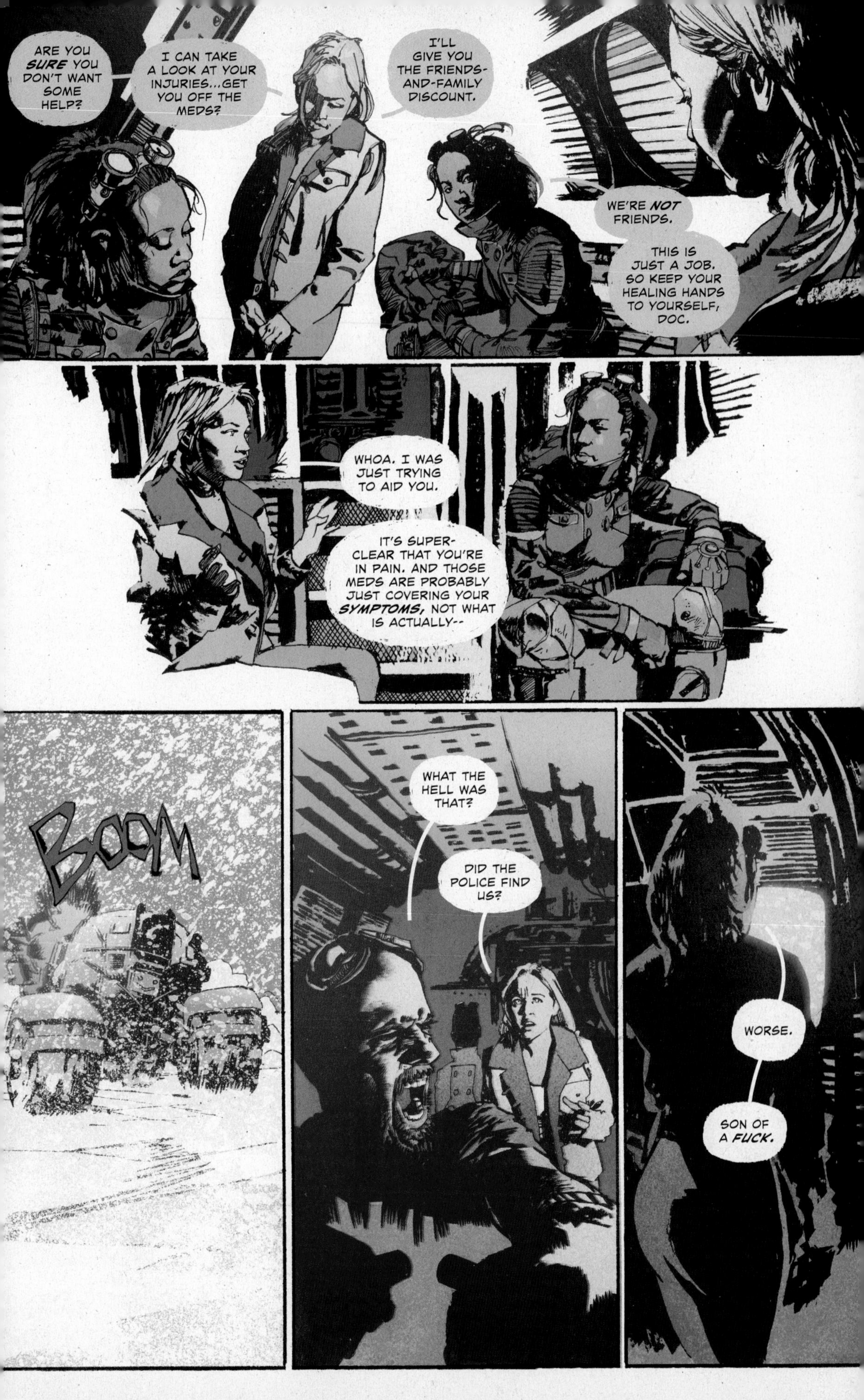
ARE YOU *SURE* YOU DON'T WANT SOME HELP?
I CAN TAKE A LOOK AT YOUR INJURIES...GET YOU OFF THE MEDS?
I'LL GIVE YOU THE FRIENDS-AND-FAMILY DISCOUNT.
WE'RE *NOT* FRIENDS.
THIS IS JUST A JOB. SO KEEP YOUR HEALING HANDS TO YOURSELF, DOC.
WHOA. I WAS JUST TRYING TO AID YOU.
IT'S SUPER-CLEAR THAT YOU'RE IN PAIN. AND THOSE MEDS ARE PROBABLY JUST COVERING YOUR *SYMPTOMS,* NOT WHAT IS ACTUALLY--
BOOM
WHAT THE HELL WAS THAT?
DID THE POLICE FIND US?
WORSE.
SON OF A *FUCK.*

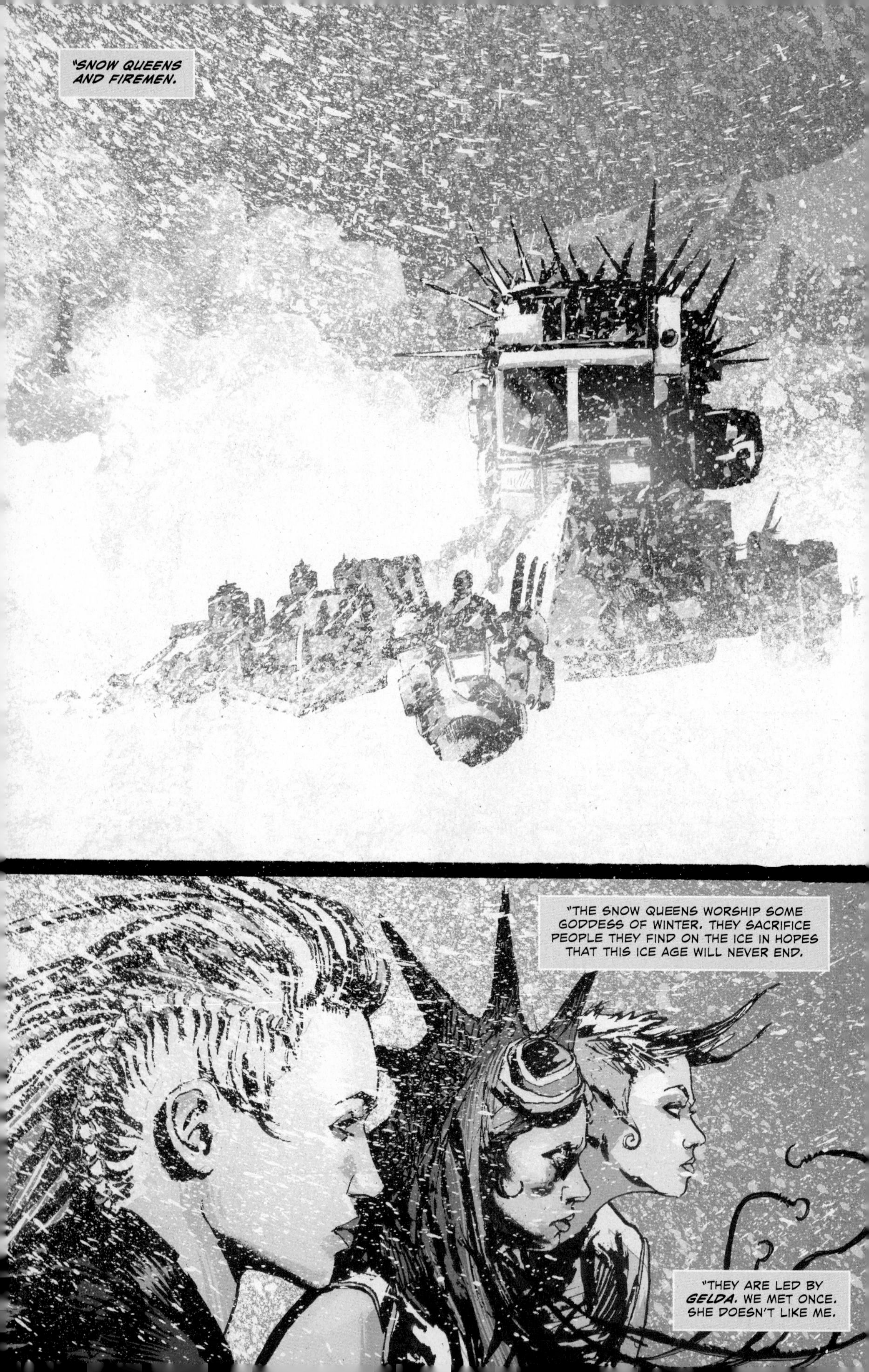
"SNOW QUEENS AND FIREMEN.
"THE SNOW QUEENS WORSHIP SOME GODDESS OF WINTER. THEY SACRIFICE PEOPLE THEY FIND ON THE ICE IN HOPES THAT THIS ICE AGE WILL NEVER END.
"THEY ARE LED BY GELDA. WE MET ONCE. SHE DOESN'T LIKE ME.

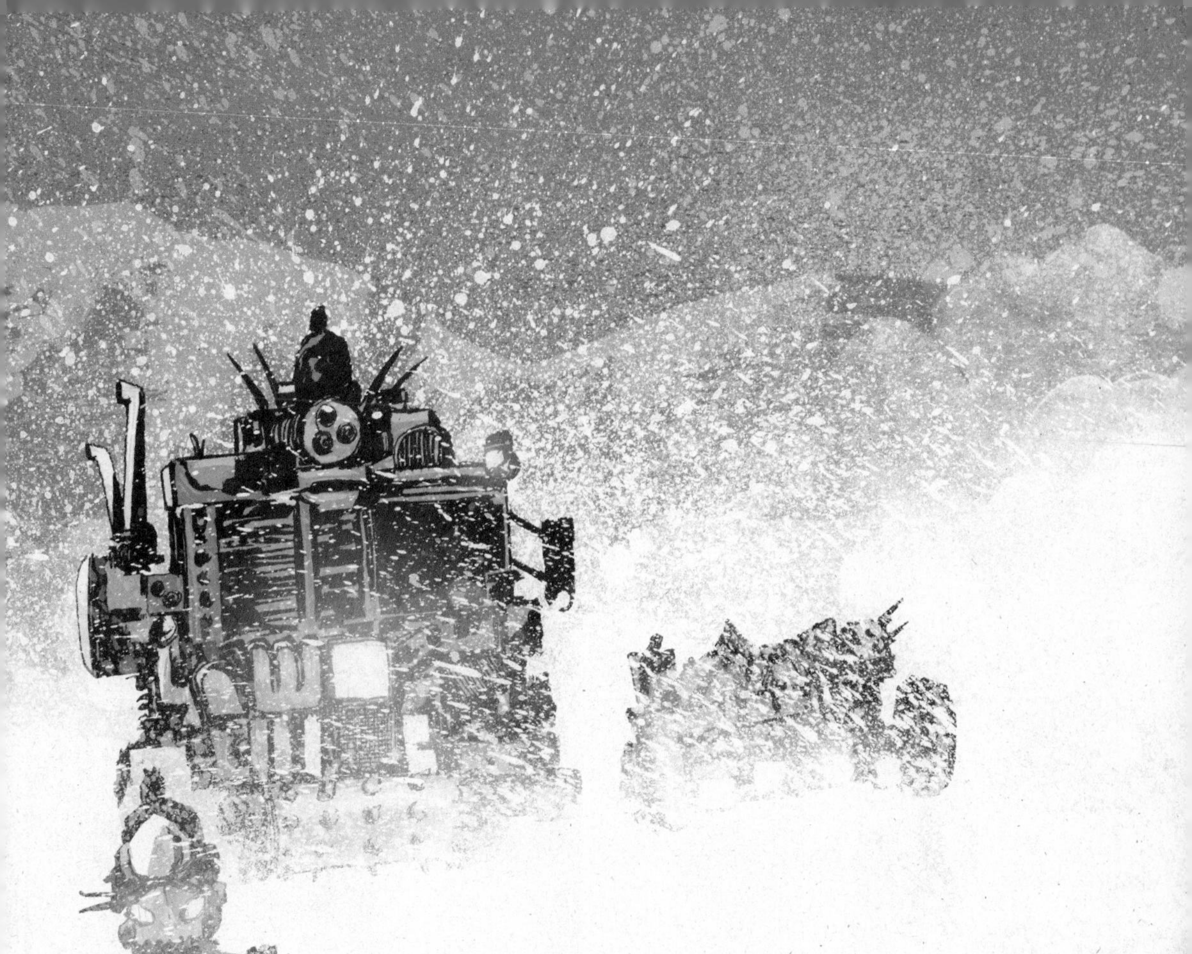

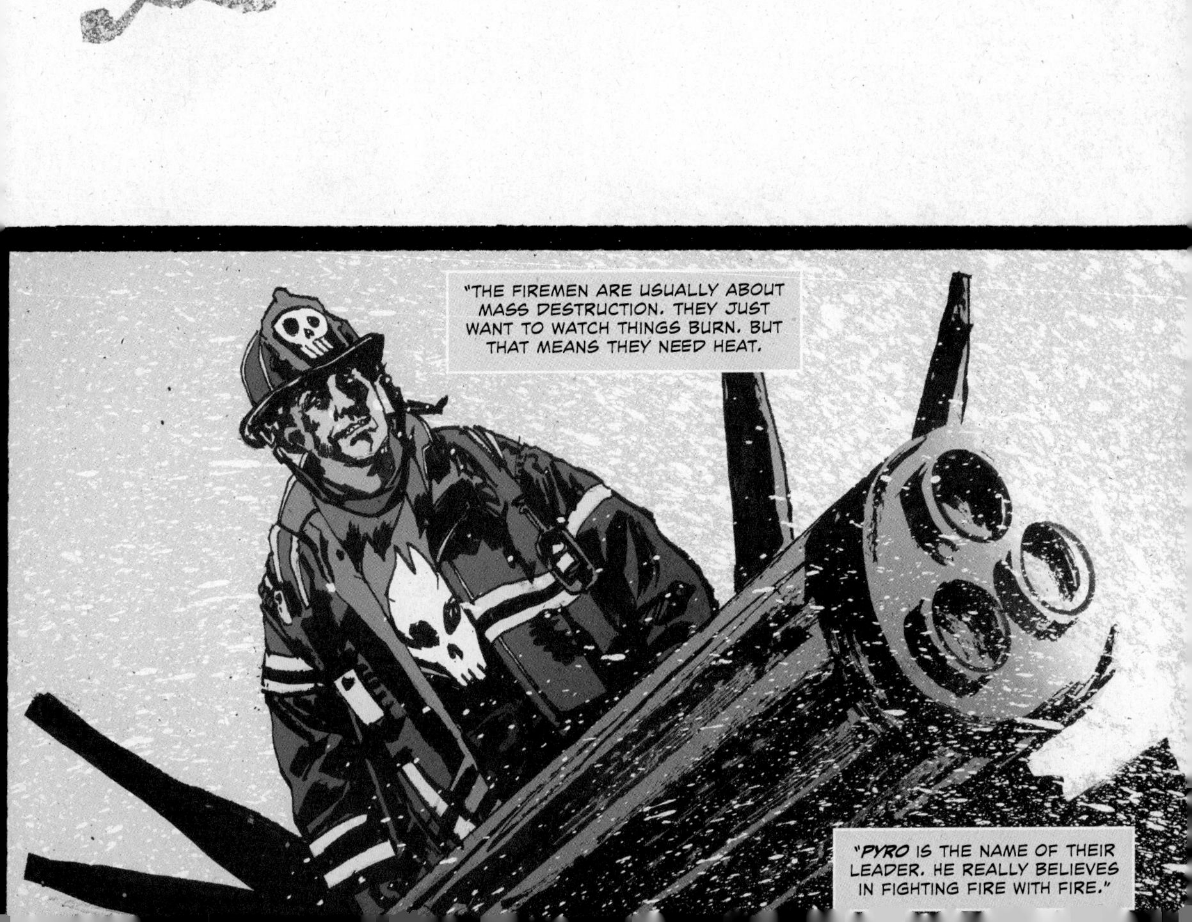
"THE FIREMEN ARE USUALLY ABOUT MASS DESTRUCTION. THEY JUST WANT TO WATCH THINGS BURN. BUT THAT MEANS THEY NEED HEAT.
"PYRO IS THE NAME OF THEIR LEADER. HE REALLY BELIEVES IN FIGHTING FIRE WITH FIRE."

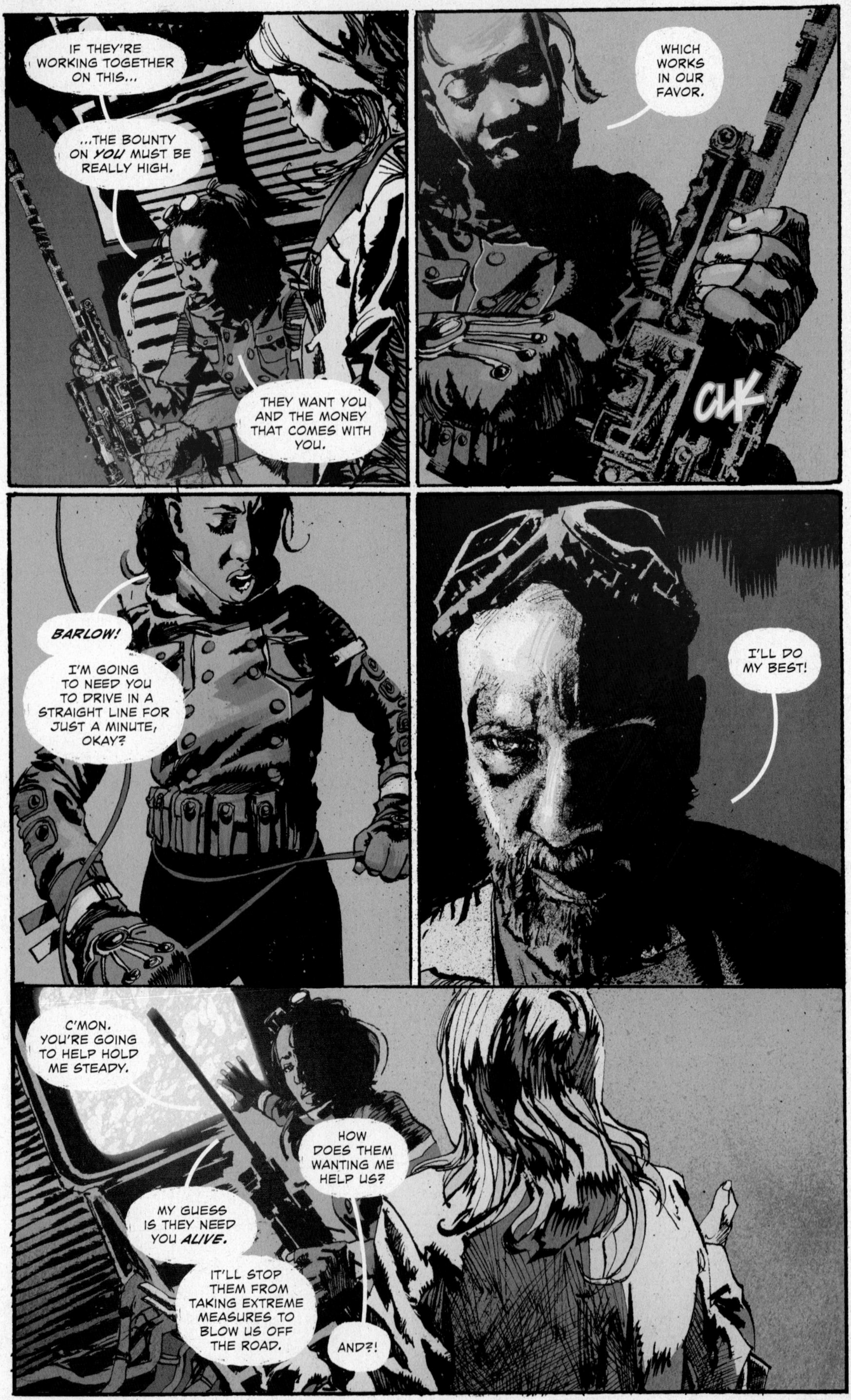
IF THEY'RE WORKING TOGETHER ON THIS...
...THE BOUNTY ON *YOU* MUST BE REALLY HIGH.
THEY WANT YOU AND THE MONEY THAT COMES WITH YOU.
WHICH WORKS IN OUR FAVOR.
CLIK
**BARLOW!**
I'M GOING TO NEED YOU TO DRIVE IN A STRAIGHT LINE FOR JUST A MINUTE, OKAY?
I'LL DO MY BEST!
C'MON. YOU'RE GOING TO HELP HOLD ME STEADY.
HOW DOES THEM WANTING ME HELP US?
MY GUESS IS THEY NEED YOU ***ALIVE.***
IT'LL STOP THEM FROM TAKING EXTREME MEASURES TO BLOW US OFF THE ROAD.
AND?!

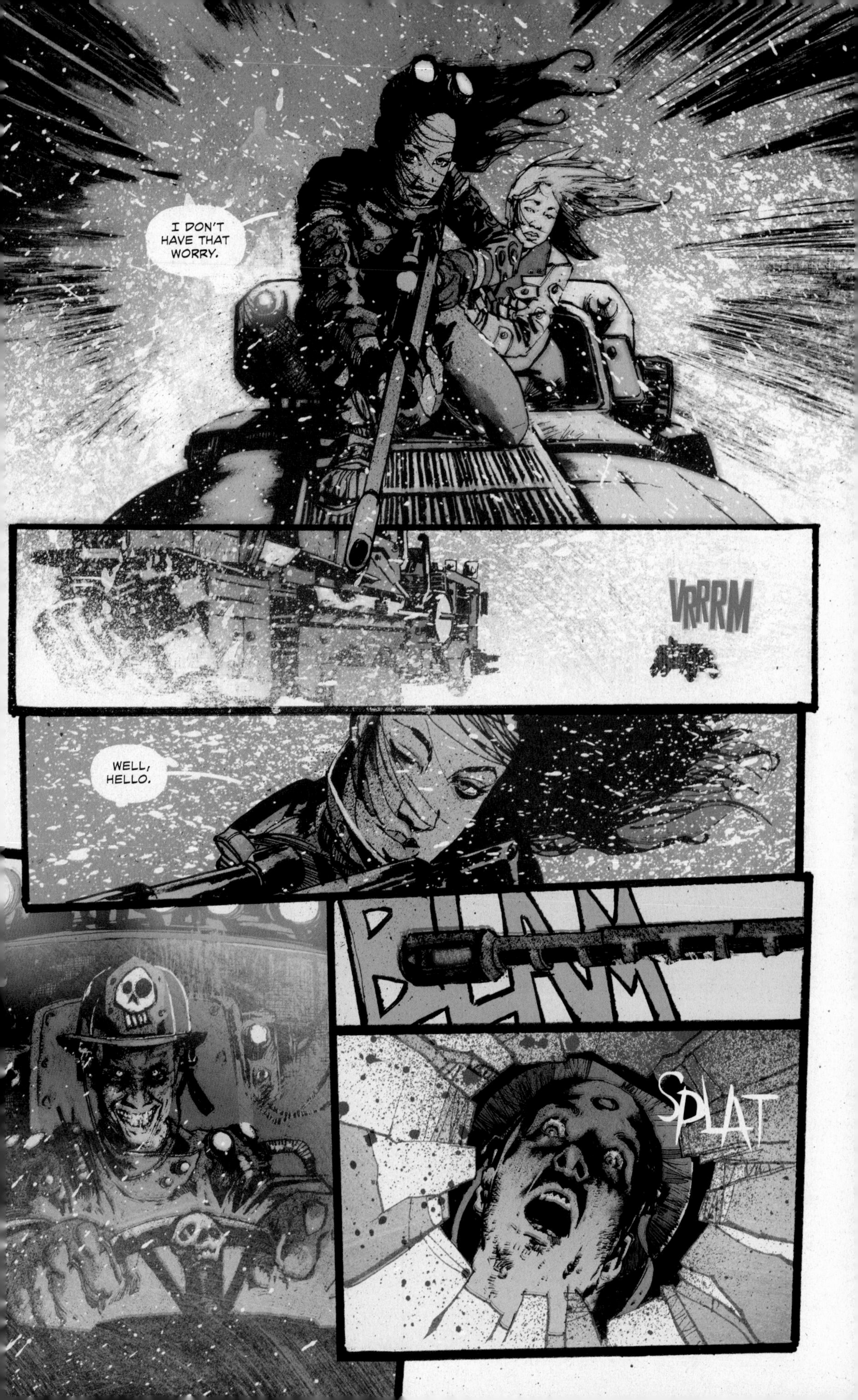
I DON'T HAVE THAT WORRY.
VRRRM
WELL, HELLO.
SPLAT

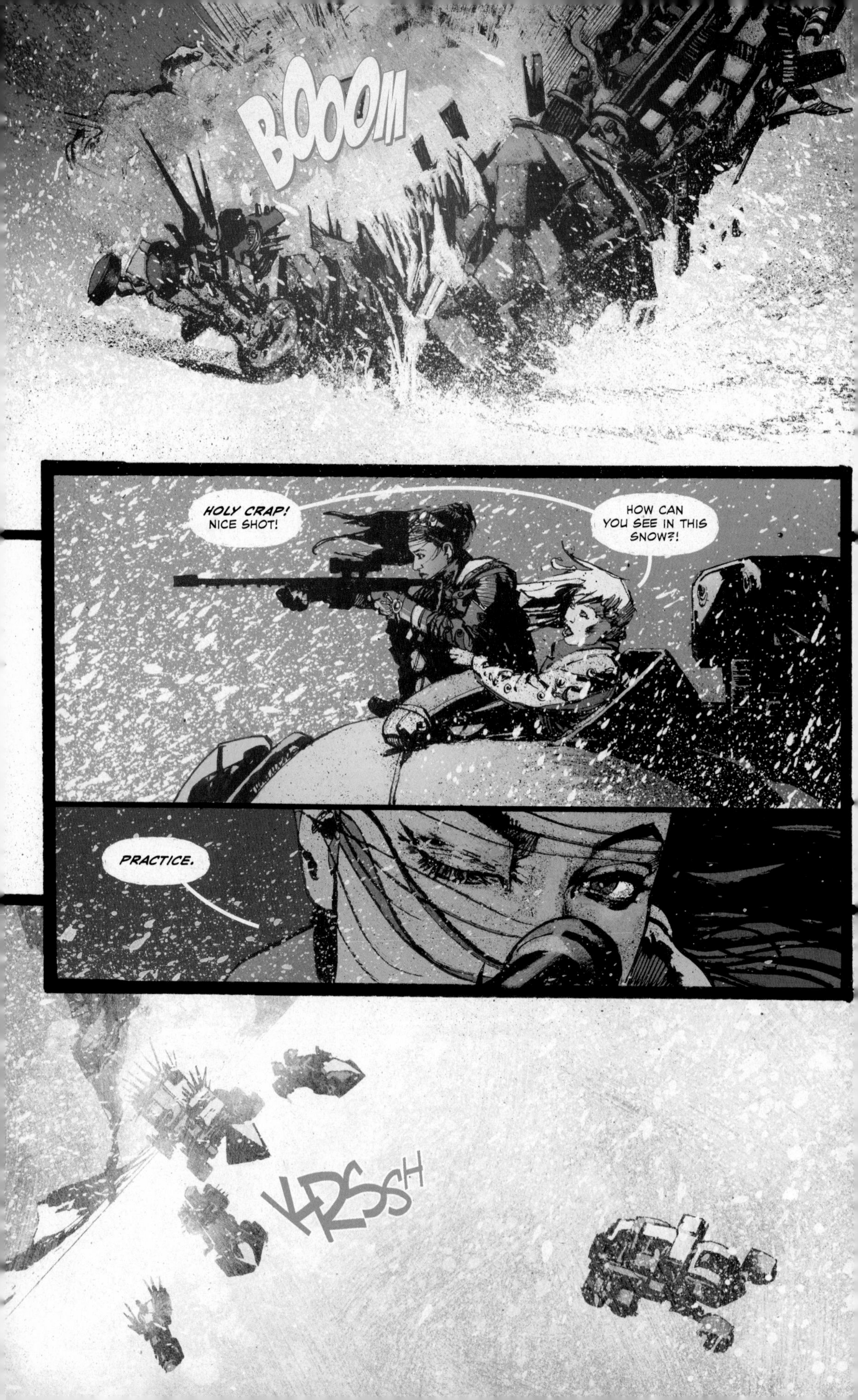
BOOOM
HOLY CRAP! NICE SHOT!
HOW CAN YOU SEE IN THIS SNOW?!
PRACTICE.
KRSSSH

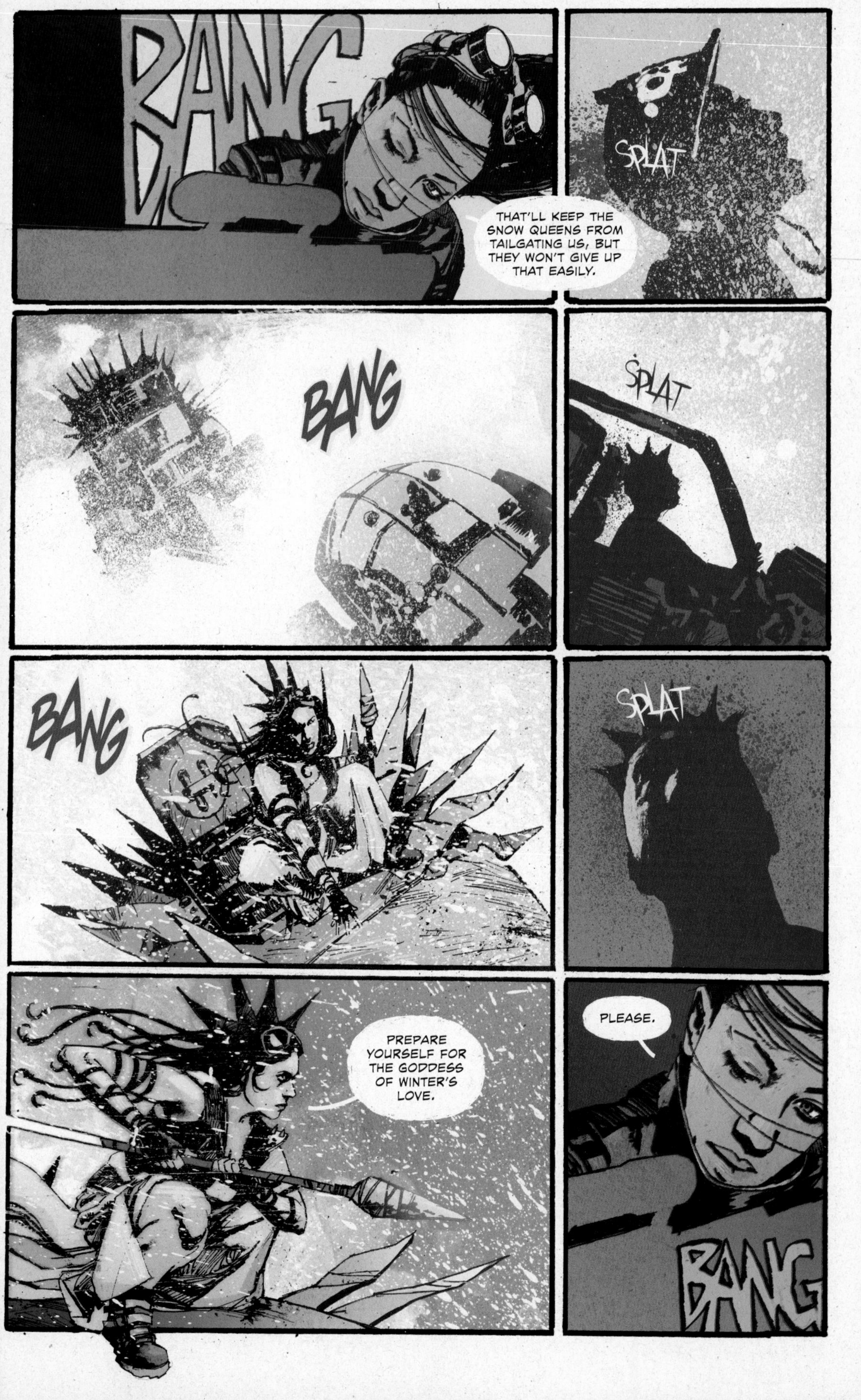
BANG
SPLAT
THAT'LL KEEP THE SNOW QUEENS FROM TAILGATING US, BUT THEY WON'T GIVE UP THAT EASILY.
BANG
SPLAT
BANG
SPLAT
PREPARE YOURSELF FOR THE GODDESS OF WINTER'S LOVE.
PLEASE.
BANG

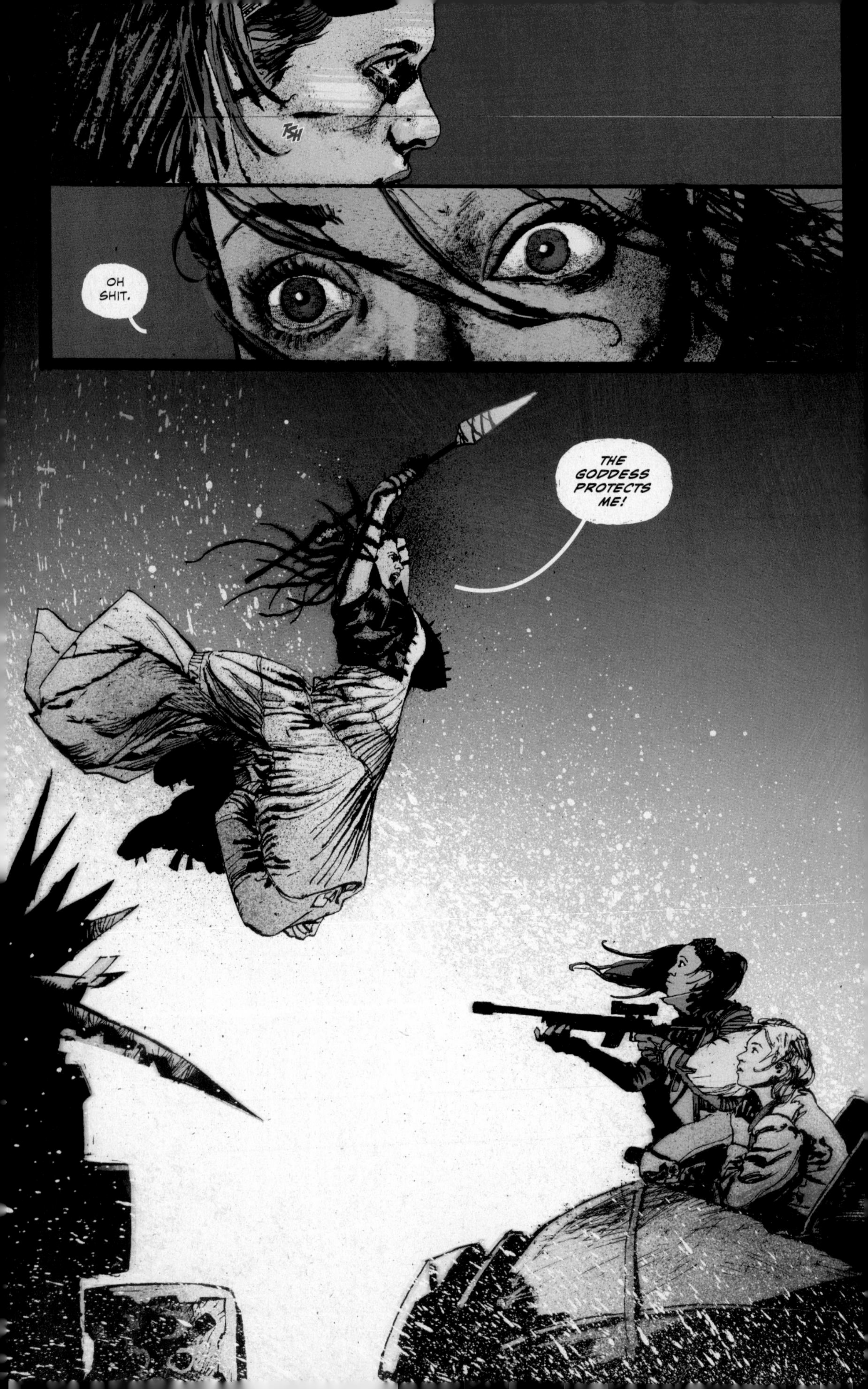
TSH
OH SHIT.
THE GODDESS PROTECTS ME!

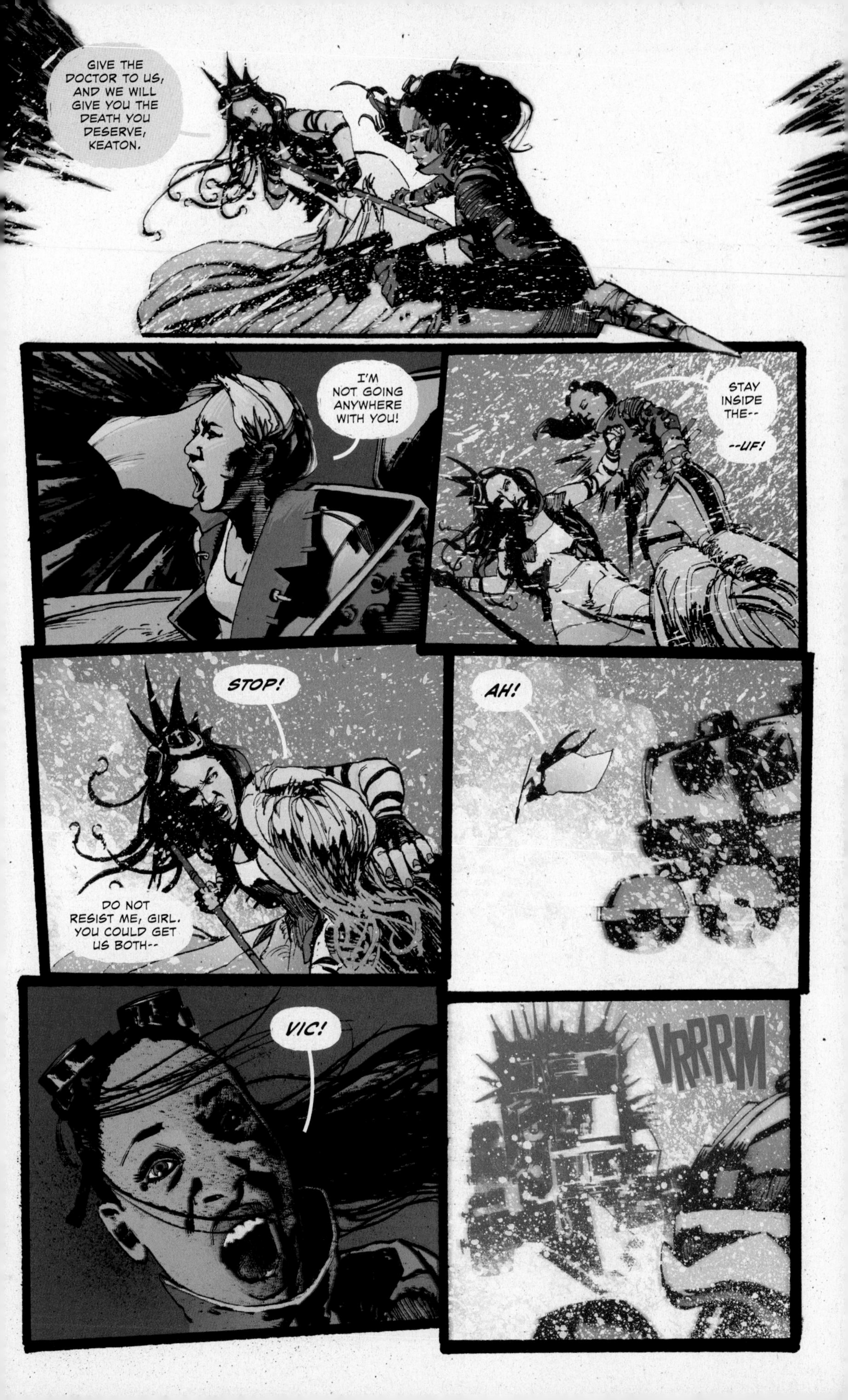
GIVE THE DOCTOR TO US, AND WE WILL GIVE YOU THE DEATH YOU DESERVE, KEATON.
I'M NOT GOING ANYWHERE WITH YOU!
STAY INSIDE THE--
--UF!
STOP!
DO NOT RESIST ME, GIRL. YOU COULD GET US BOTH--
AH!
VIC!
VRRRM

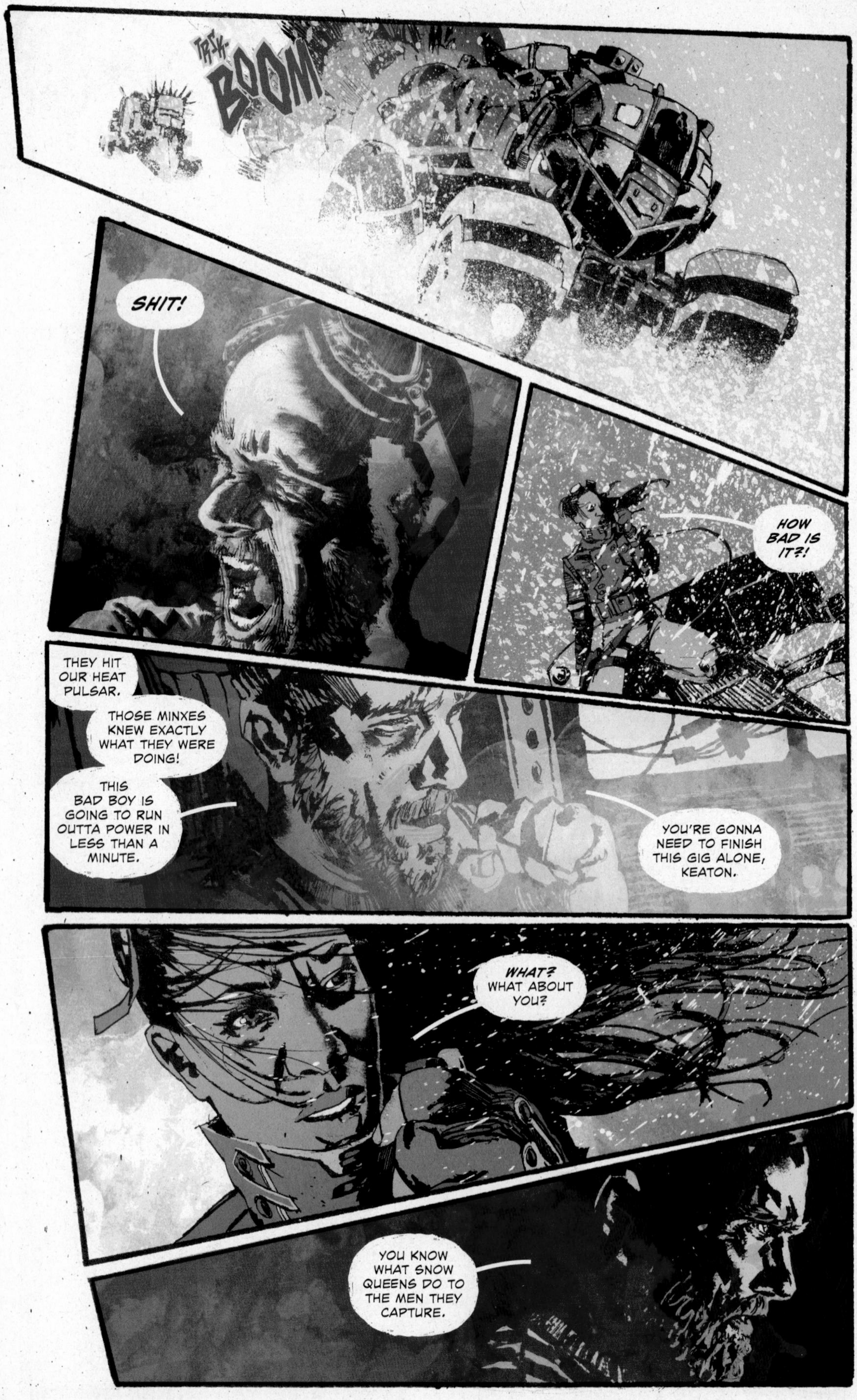
TRSK-BOOM
SHIT!
HOW BAD IS IT?!
THEY HIT OUR HEAT PULSAR.
THOSE MINXES KNEW EXACTLY WHAT THEY WERE DOING!
THIS BAD BOY IS GOING TO RUN OUTTA POWER IN LESS THAN A MINUTE.
YOU'RE GONNA NEED TO FINISH THIS GIG ALONE, KEATON.
WHAT? WHAT ABOUT YOU?
YOU KNOW WHAT SNOW QUEENS DO TO THE MEN THEY CAPTURE.

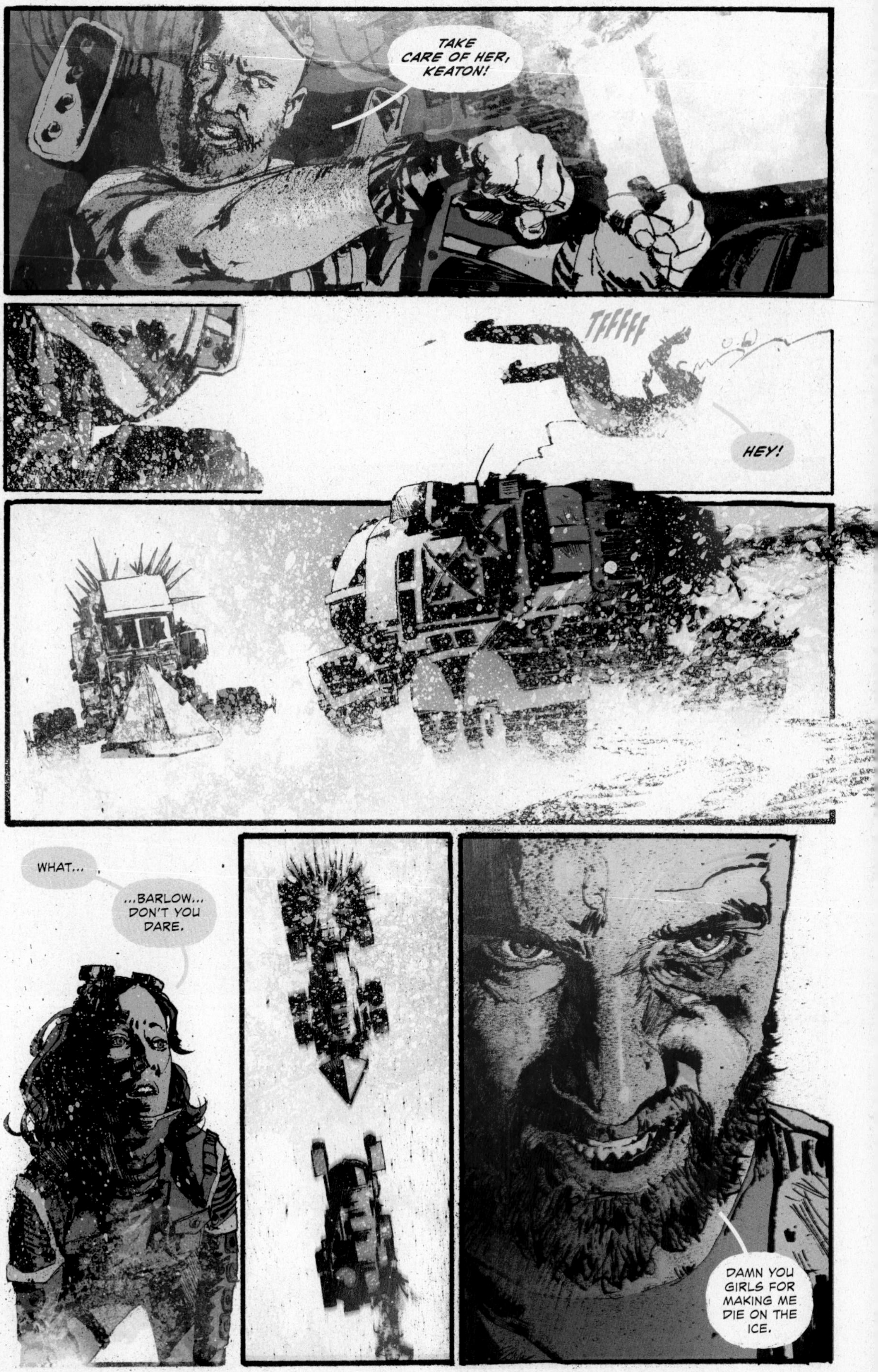
TAKE CARE OF HER, KEATON!
TFFFFF
HEY!
WHAT...
...BARLOW... DON'T YOU DARE.
DAMN YOU GIRLS FOR MAKING ME DIE ON THE ICE.

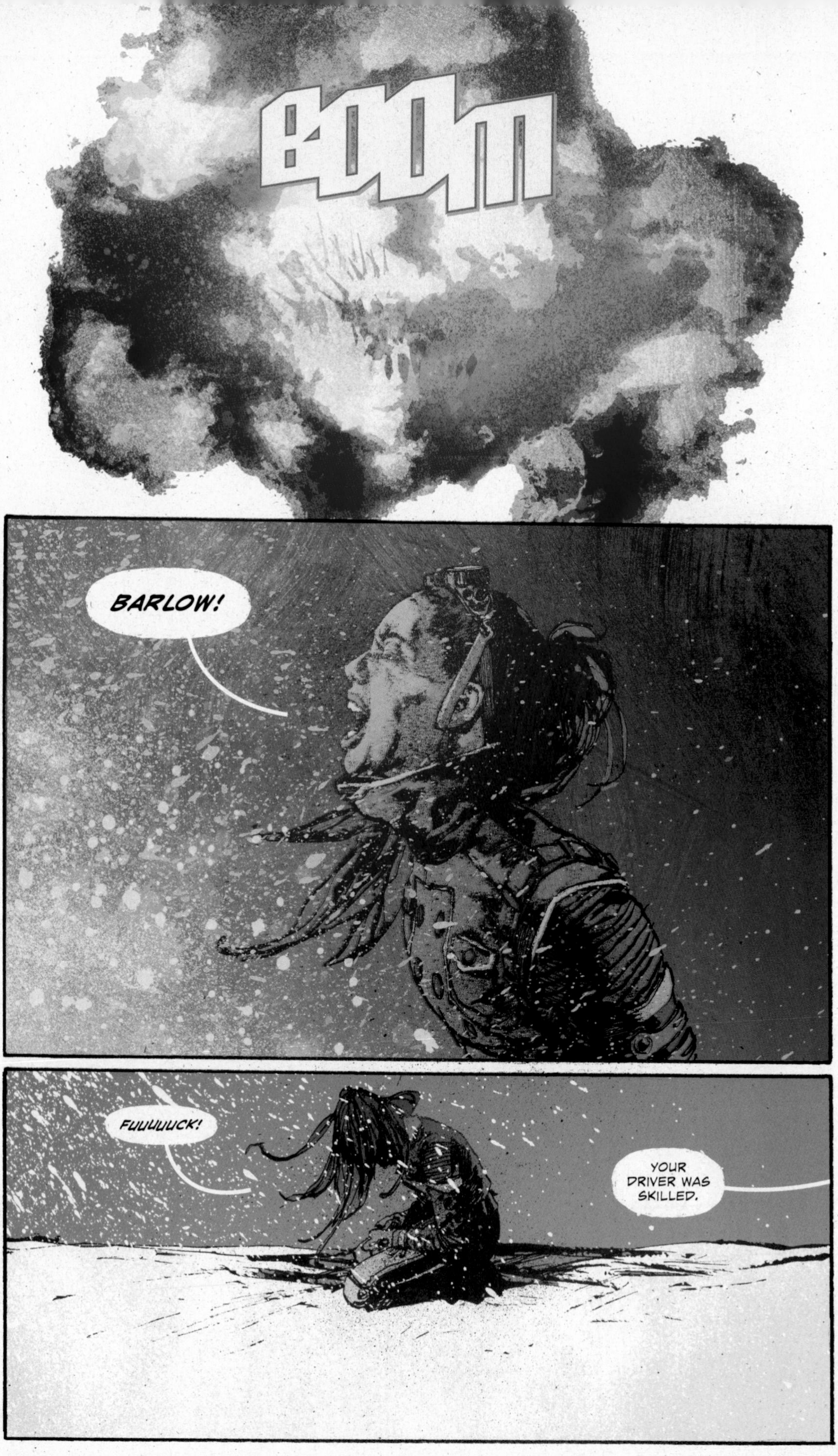
BOOM
BARLOW!
FUUUUUCK!
YOUR DRIVER WAS SKILLED.

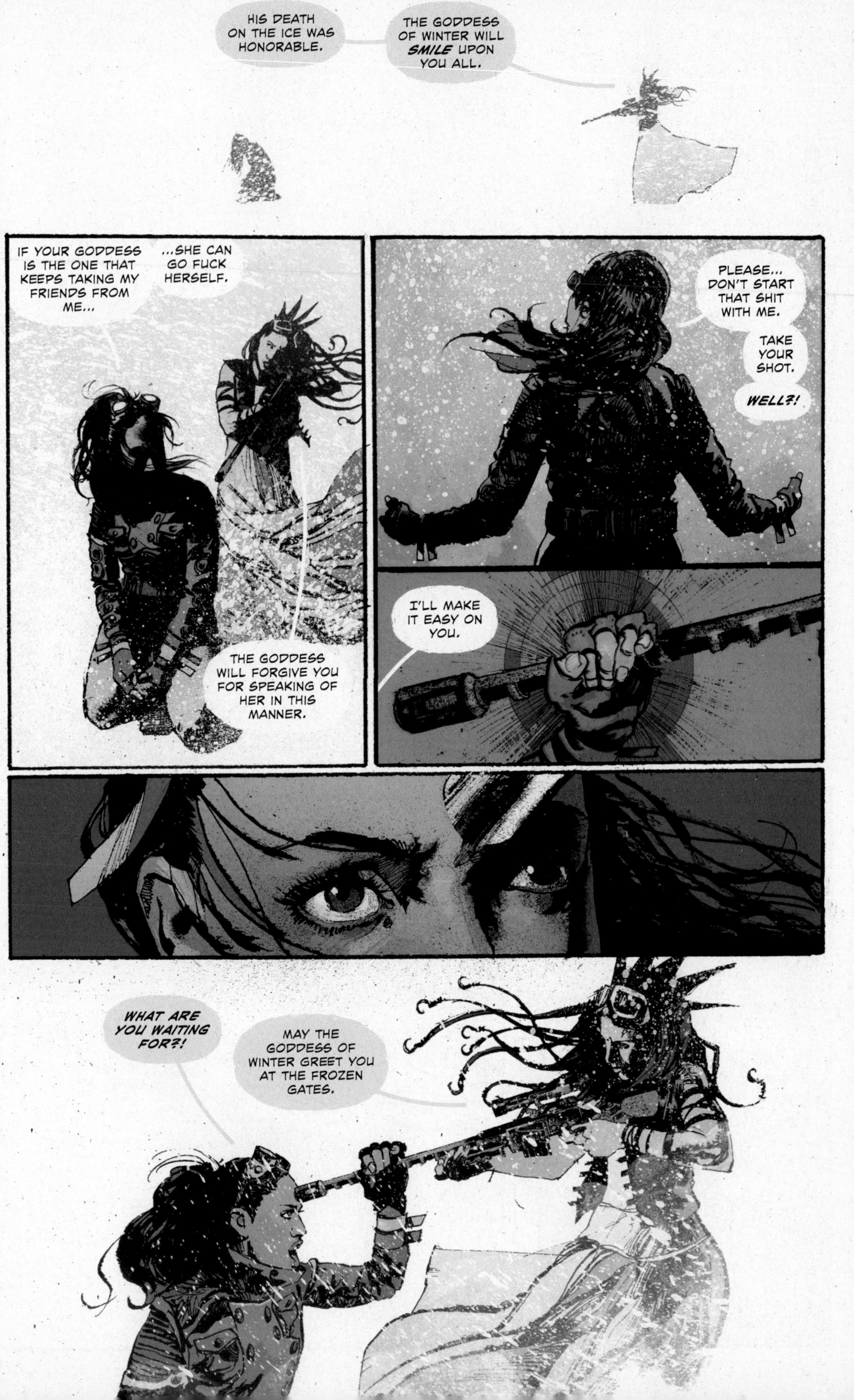
HIS DEATH ON THE ICE WAS HONORABLE.
THE GODDESS OF WINTER WILL SMILE UPON YOU ALL.
IF YOUR GODDESS IS THE ONE THAT KEEPS TAKING MY FRIENDS FROM ME...
...SHE CAN GO FUCK HERSELF.
THE GODDESS WILL FORGIVE YOU FOR SPEAKING OF HER IN THIS MANNER.
PLEASE... DON'T START THAT SHIT WITH ME.
TAKE YOUR SHOT.
WELL?!
I'LL MAKE IT EASY ON YOU.
WHAT ARE YOU WAITING FOR?!
MAY THE GODDESS OF WINTER GREET YOU AT THE FROZEN GATES.

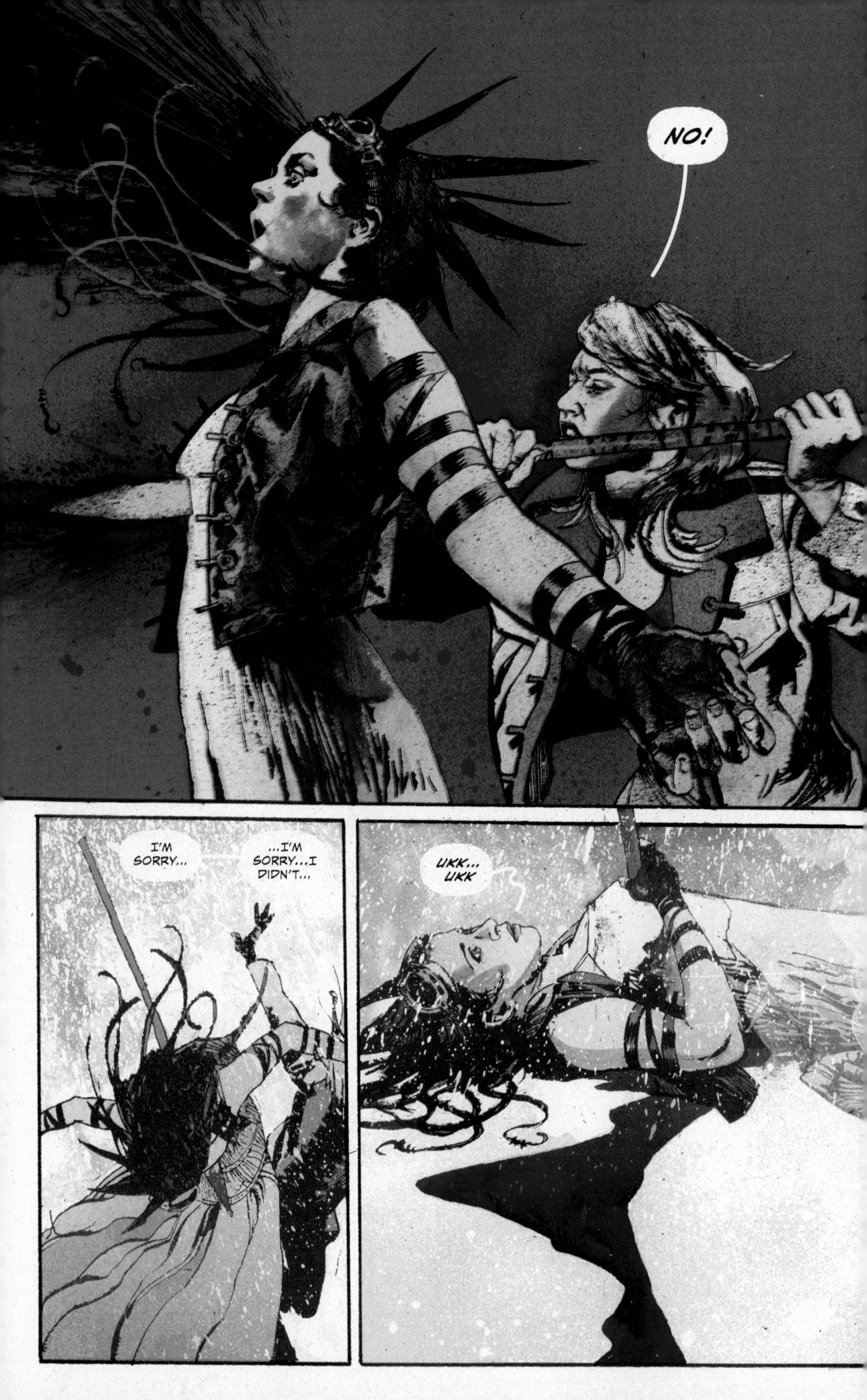
NO!
I'M SORRY...
...I'M SORRY...I DIDN'T...
UKK... UKK

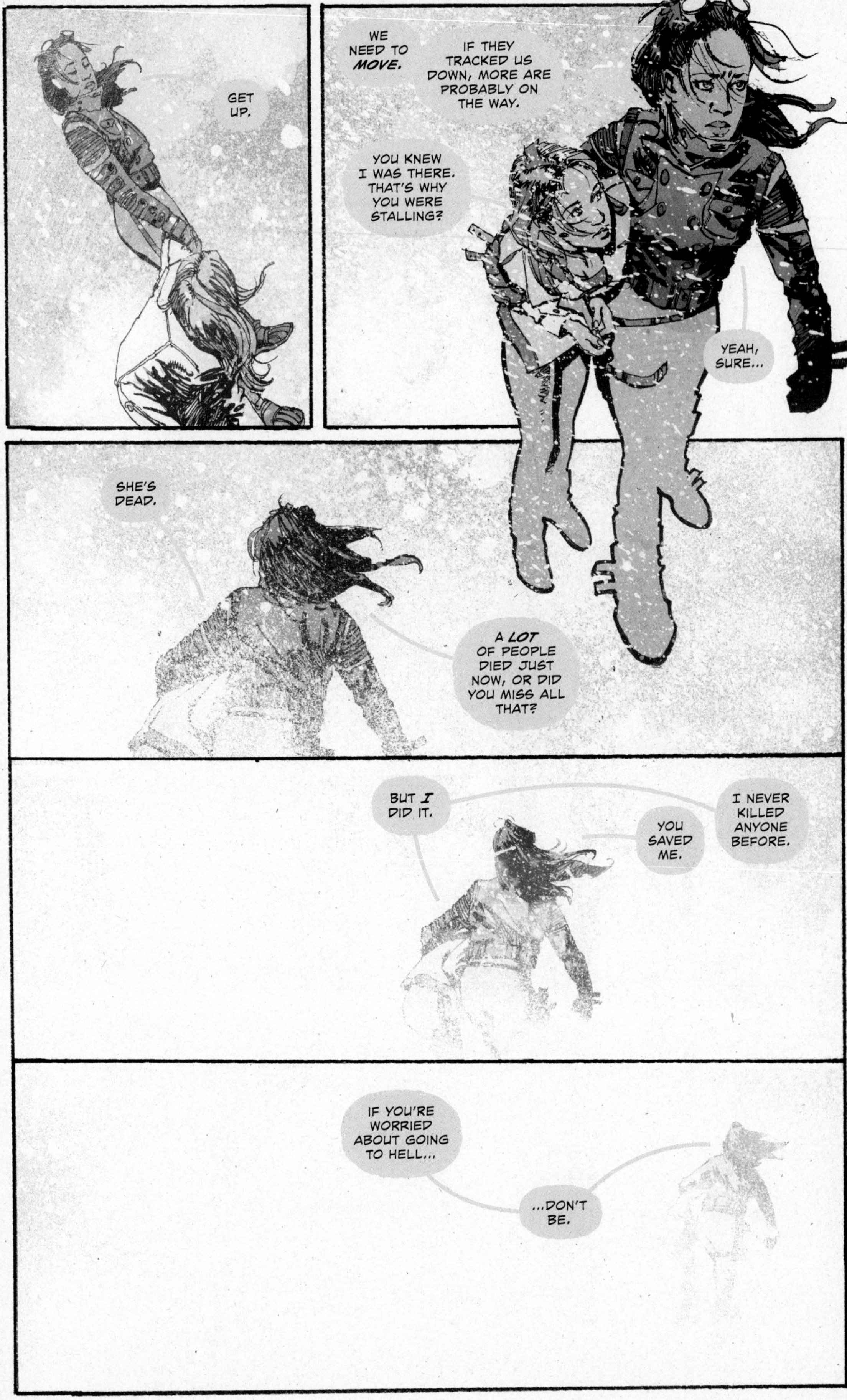
GET UP.
WE NEED TO *MOVE.*
IF THEY TRACKED US DOWN, MORE ARE PROBABLY ON THE WAY.
YOU KNEW I WAS THERE. THAT'S WHY YOU WERE STALLING?
YEAH, SURE...
SHE'S DEAD.
A *LOT* OF PEOPLE DIED JUST NOW, OR DID YOU MISS ALL THAT?
BUT *I* DID IT.
I NEVER KILLED ANYONE BEFORE.
YOU SAVED ME.
IF YOU'RE WORRIED ABOUT GOING TO HELL...
...DON'T BE.

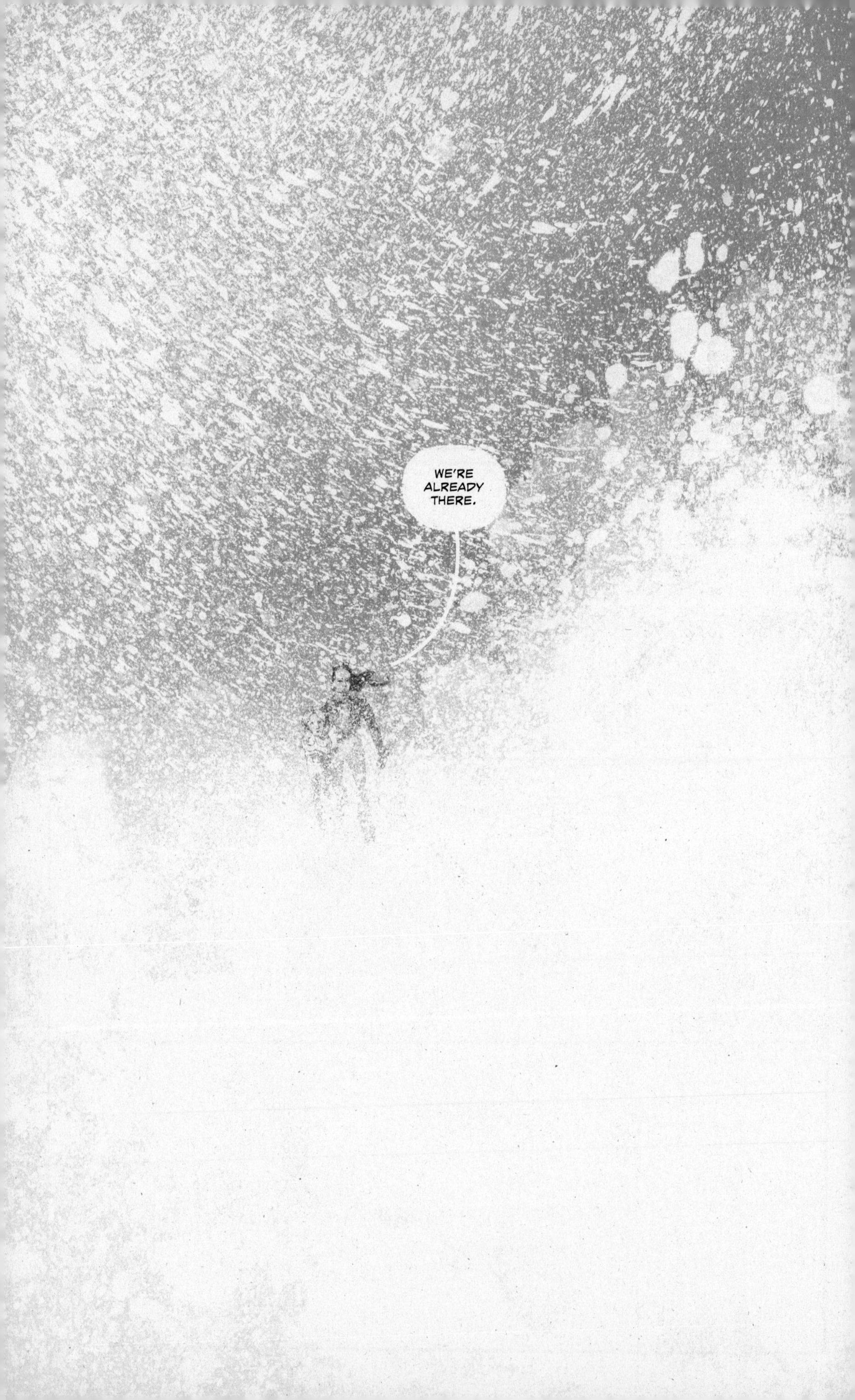
WE'RE ALREADY THERE.

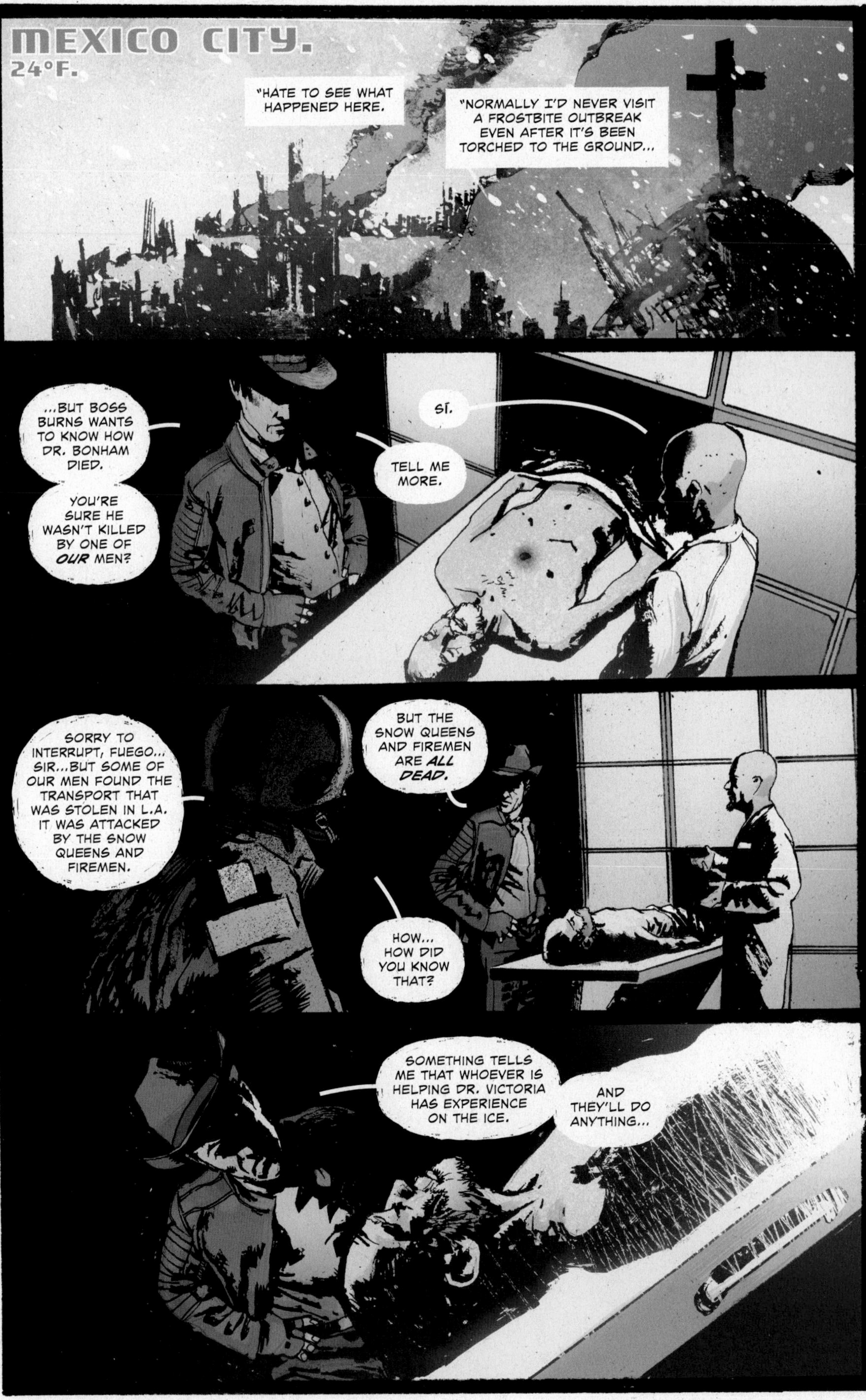
MEXICO CITY.
24°F.
"HATE TO SEE WHAT HAPPENED HERE.
"NORMALLY I'D NEVER VISIT A FROSTBITE OUTBREAK EVEN AFTER IT'S BEEN TORCHED TO THE GROUND...
...BUT BOSS BURNS WANTS TO KNOW HOW DR. BONHAM DIED.
YOU'RE SURE HE WASN'T KILLED BY ONE OF *OUR* MEN?
SÍ.
TELL ME MORE.
SORRY TO INTERRUPT, FUEGO... SIR...BUT SOME OF OUR MEN FOUND THE TRANSPORT THAT WAS STOLEN IN L.A. IT WAS ATTACKED BY THE SNOW QUEENS AND FIREMEN.
BUT THE SNOW QUEENS AND FIREMEN ARE ***ALL DEAD.***
HOW... HOW DID YOU KNOW THAT?
SOMETHING TELLS ME THAT WHOEVER IS HELPING DR. VICTORIA HAS EXPERIENCE ON THE ICE.
AND THEY'LL DO ANYTHING...

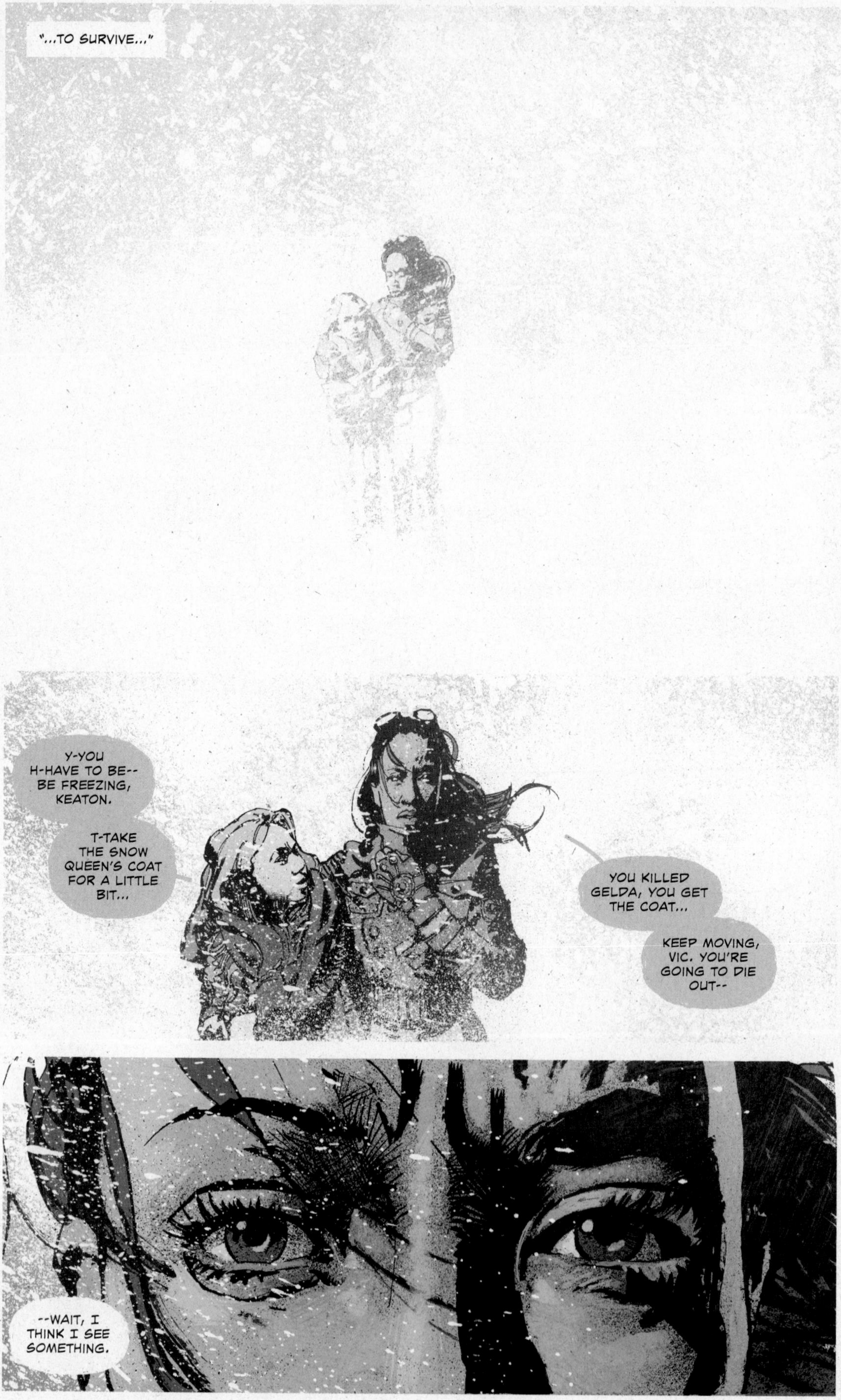
"...TO SURVIVE..."
Y-YOU H-HAVE TO BE-- BE FREEZING, KEATON.
T-TAKE THE SNOW QUEEN'S COAT FOR A LITTLE BIT...
YOU KILLED GELDA, YOU GET THE COAT...
KEEP MOVING, VIC. YOU'RE GOING TO DIE OUT--
--WAIT, I THINK I SEE SOMETHING.

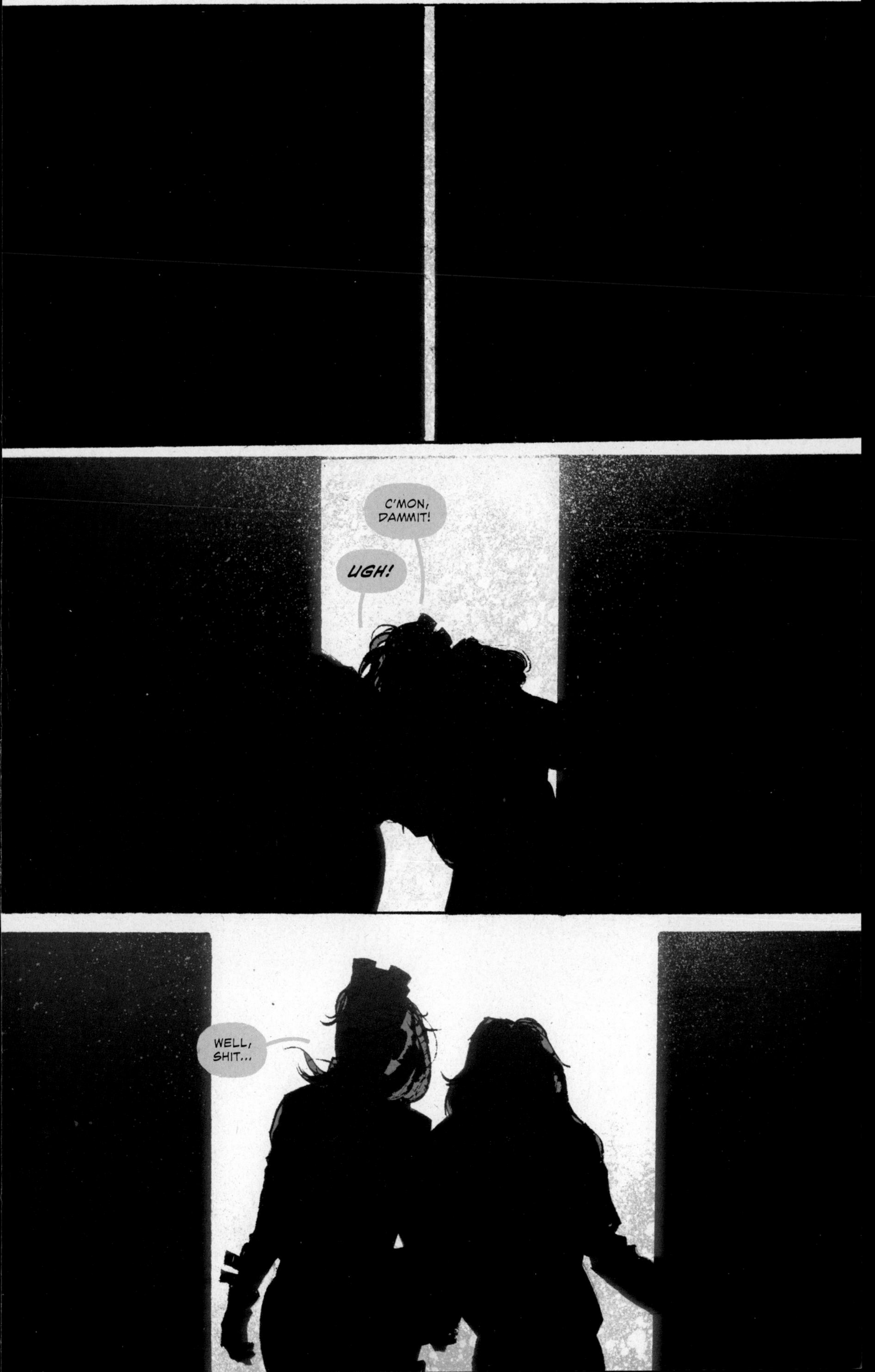
C'MON, DAMMIT!
UGH!
WELL, SHIT...

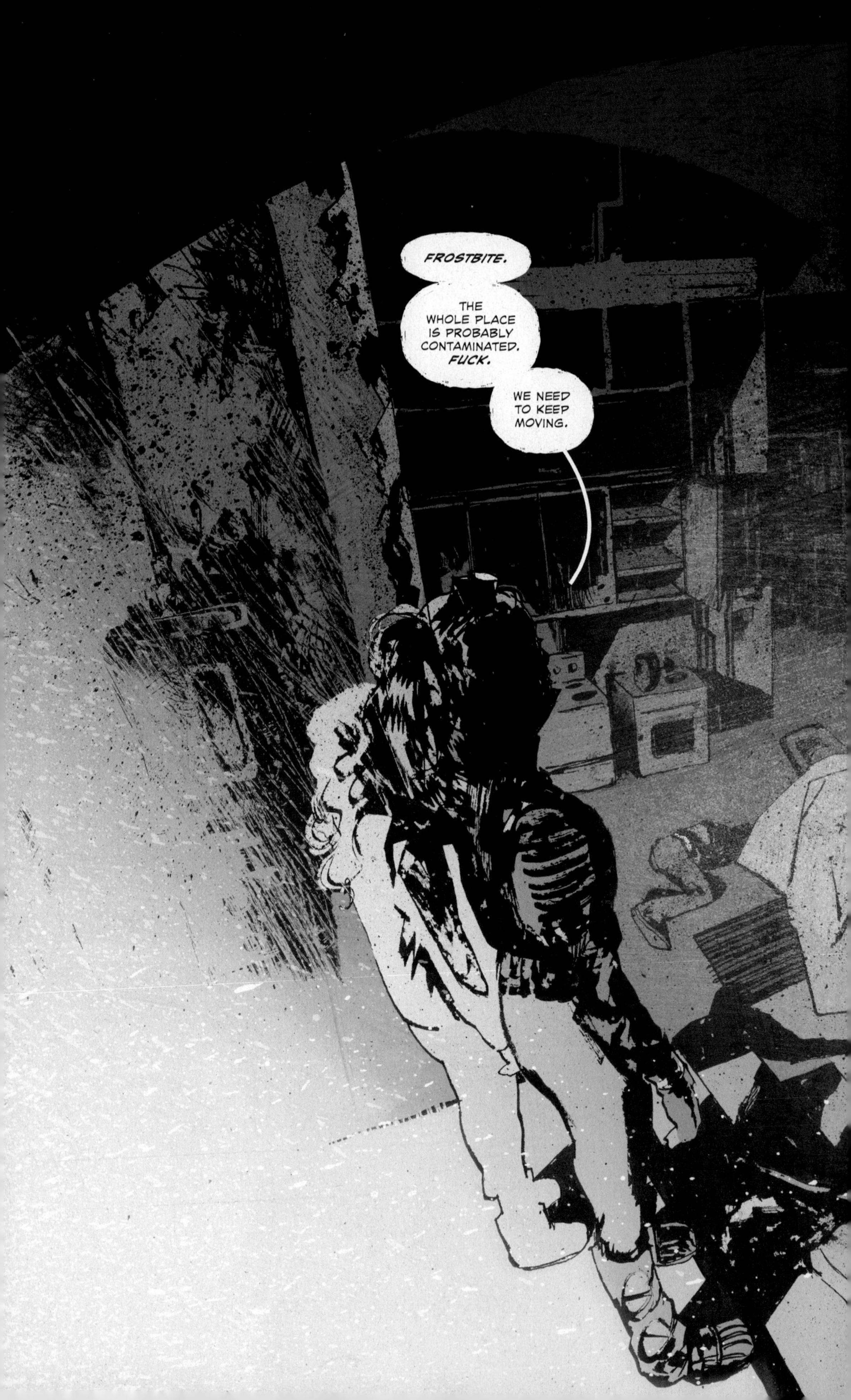
FROSTBITE.
THE WHOLE PLACE IS PROBABLY CONTAMINATED. FUCK.
WE NEED TO KEEP MOVING.

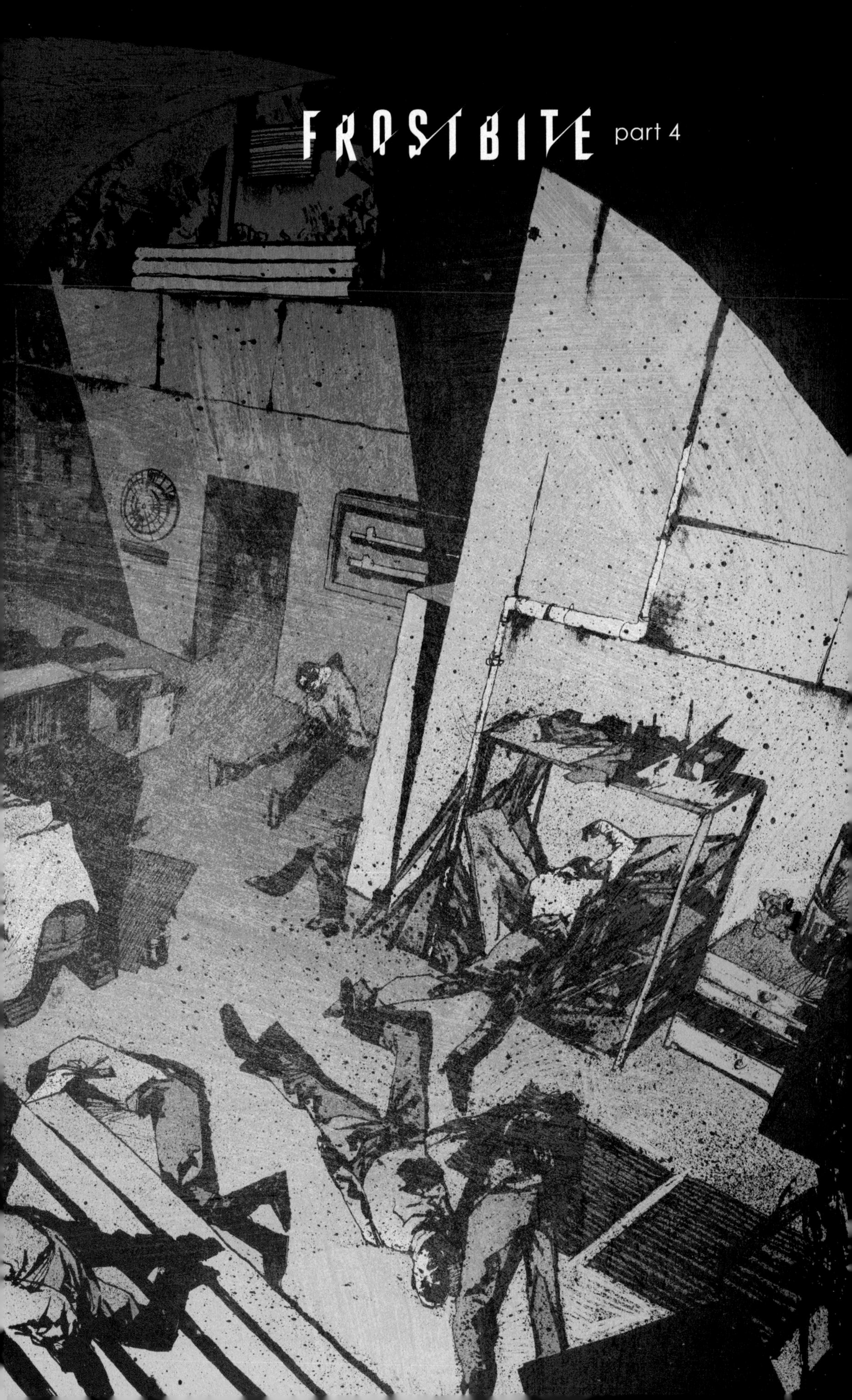
FROSTBITE part 4

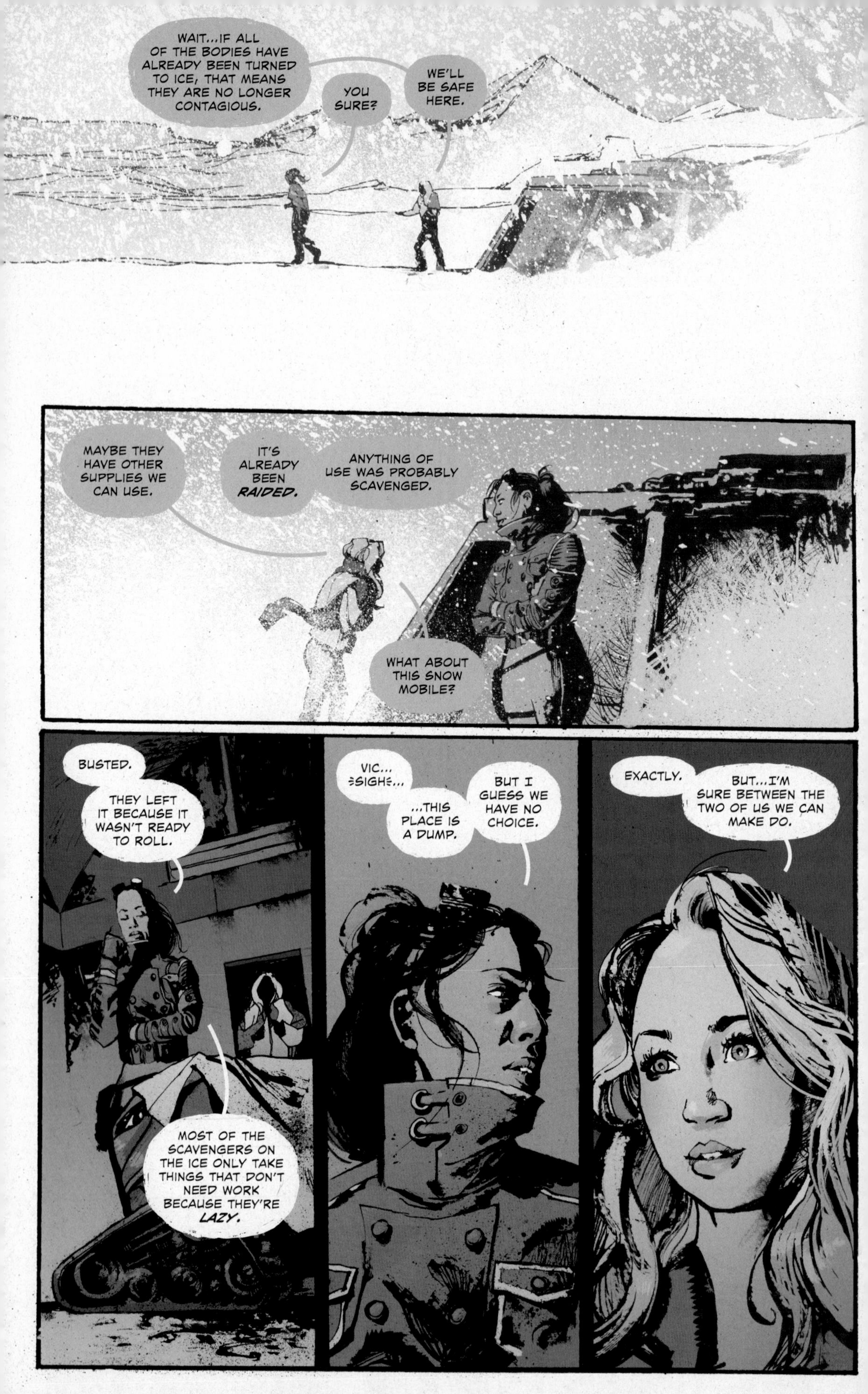
WAIT...IF ALL OF THE BODIES HAVE ALREADY BEEN TURNED TO ICE, THAT MEANS THEY ARE NO LONGER CONTAGIOUS.
YOU SURE?
WE'LL BE SAFE HERE.
MAYBE THEY HAVE OTHER SUPPLIES WE CAN USE.
IT'S ALREADY BEEN *RAIDED.*
ANYTHING OF USE WAS PROBABLY SCAVENGED.
WHAT ABOUT THIS SNOW MOBILE?
BUSTED.
THEY LEFT IT BECAUSE IT WASN'T READY TO ROLL.
MOST OF THE SCAVENGERS ON THE ICE ONLY TAKE THINGS THAT DON'T NEED WORK BECAUSE THEY'RE *LAZY.*
VIC... =SIGH=...
...THIS PLACE IS A DUMP.
BUT I GUESS WE HAVE NO CHOICE.
EXACTLY.
BUT...I'M SURE BETWEEN THE TWO OF US WE CAN MAKE DO.

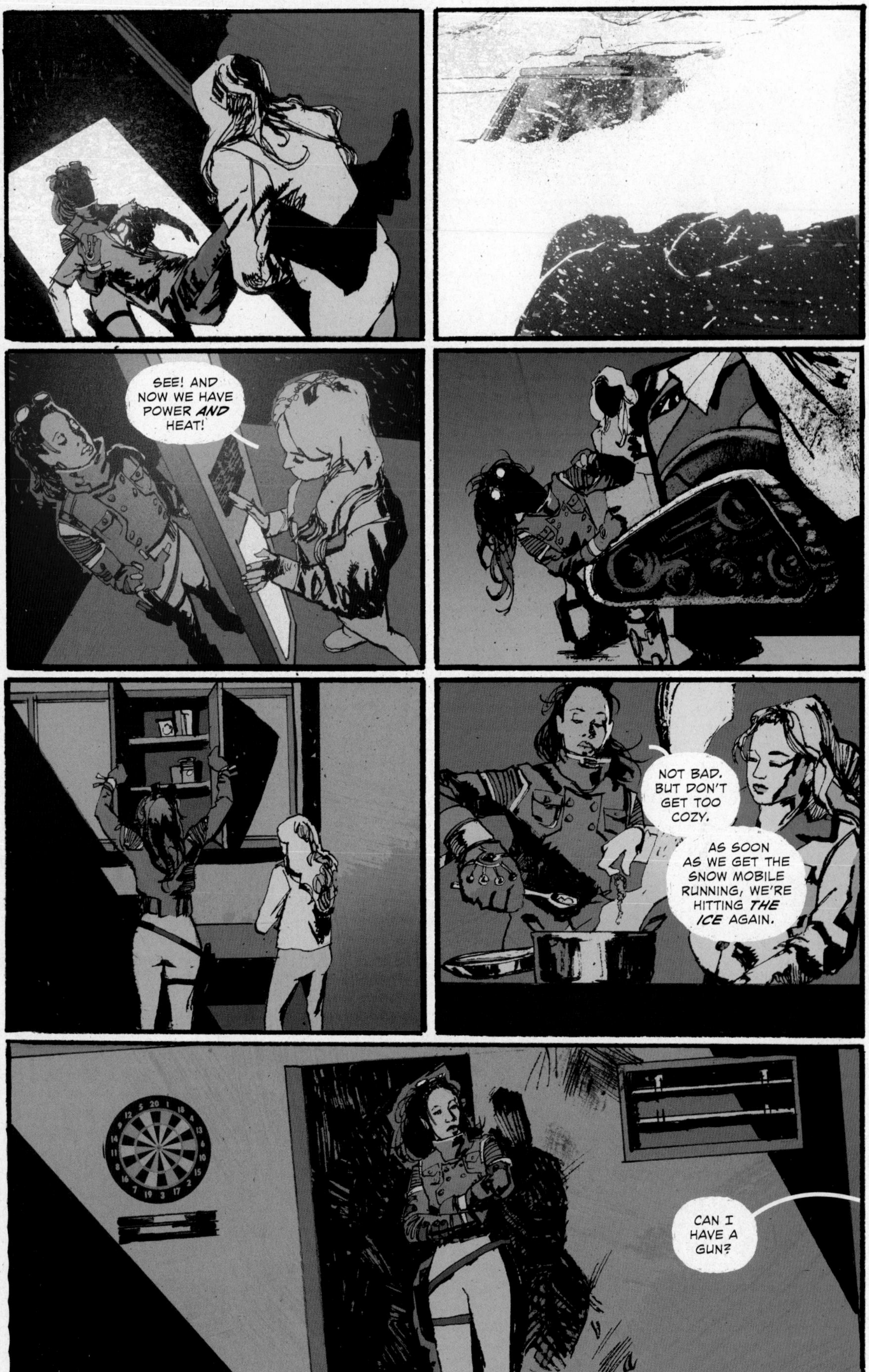
SEE! AND NOW WE HAVE POWER *AND* HEAT!
NOT BAD. BUT DON'T GET TOO COZY.
AS SOON AS WE GET THE SNOW MOBILE RUNNING, WE'RE HITTING *THE ICE* AGAIN.
CAN I HAVE A GUN?

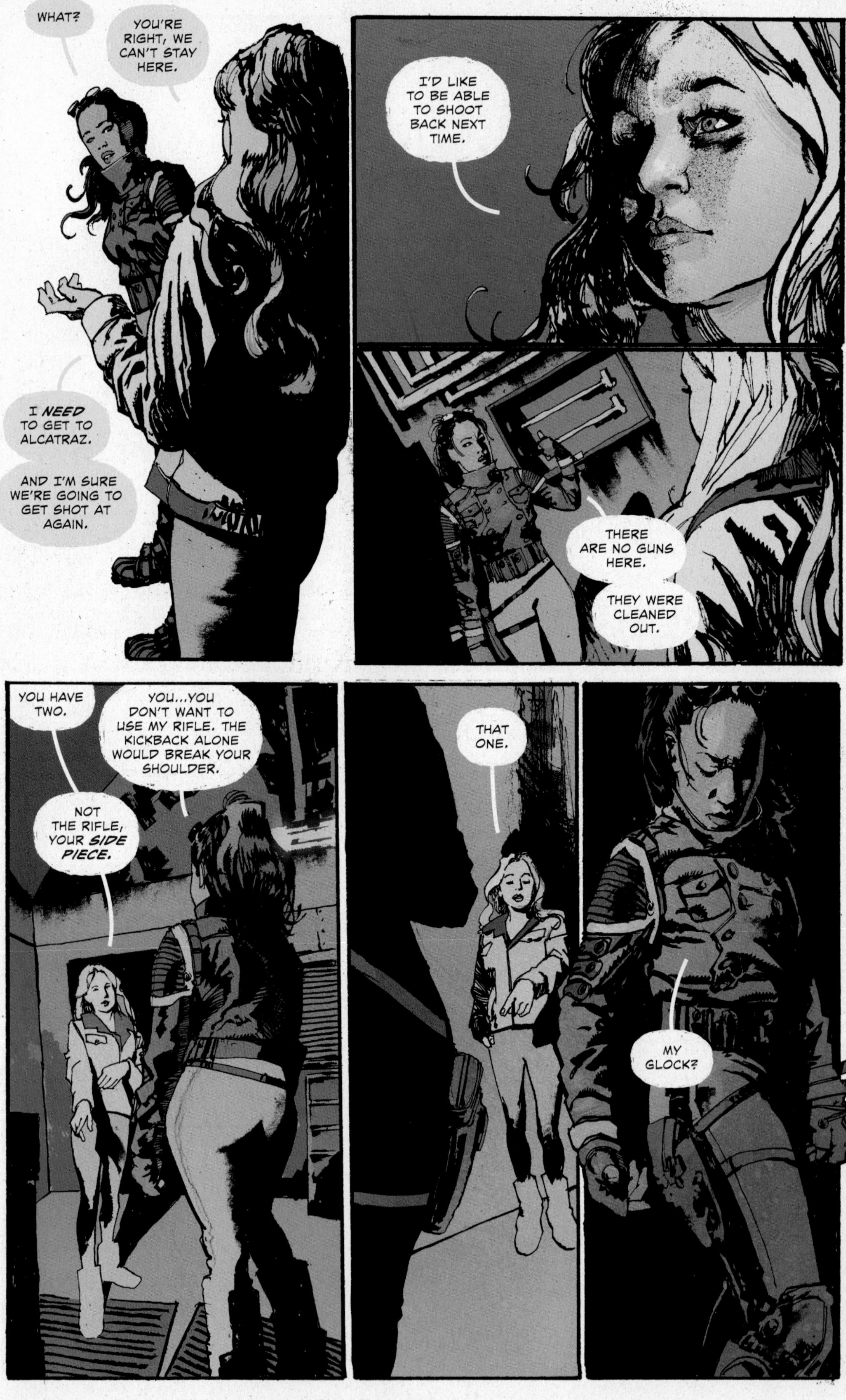
WHAT?
YOU'RE RIGHT, WE CAN'T STAY HERE.
I'D LIKE TO BE ABLE TO SHOOT BACK NEXT TIME.
I *NEED* TO GET TO ALCATRAZ.
AND I'M SURE WE'RE GOING TO GET SHOT AT AGAIN.
THERE ARE NO GUNS HERE.
THEY WERE CLEANED OUT.
YOU HAVE TWO.
YOU...YOU DON'T WANT TO USE MY RIFLE. THE KICKBACK ALONE WOULD BREAK YOUR SHOULDER.
NOT THE RIFLE, YOUR *SIDE PIECE.*
THAT ONE.
MY GLOCK?

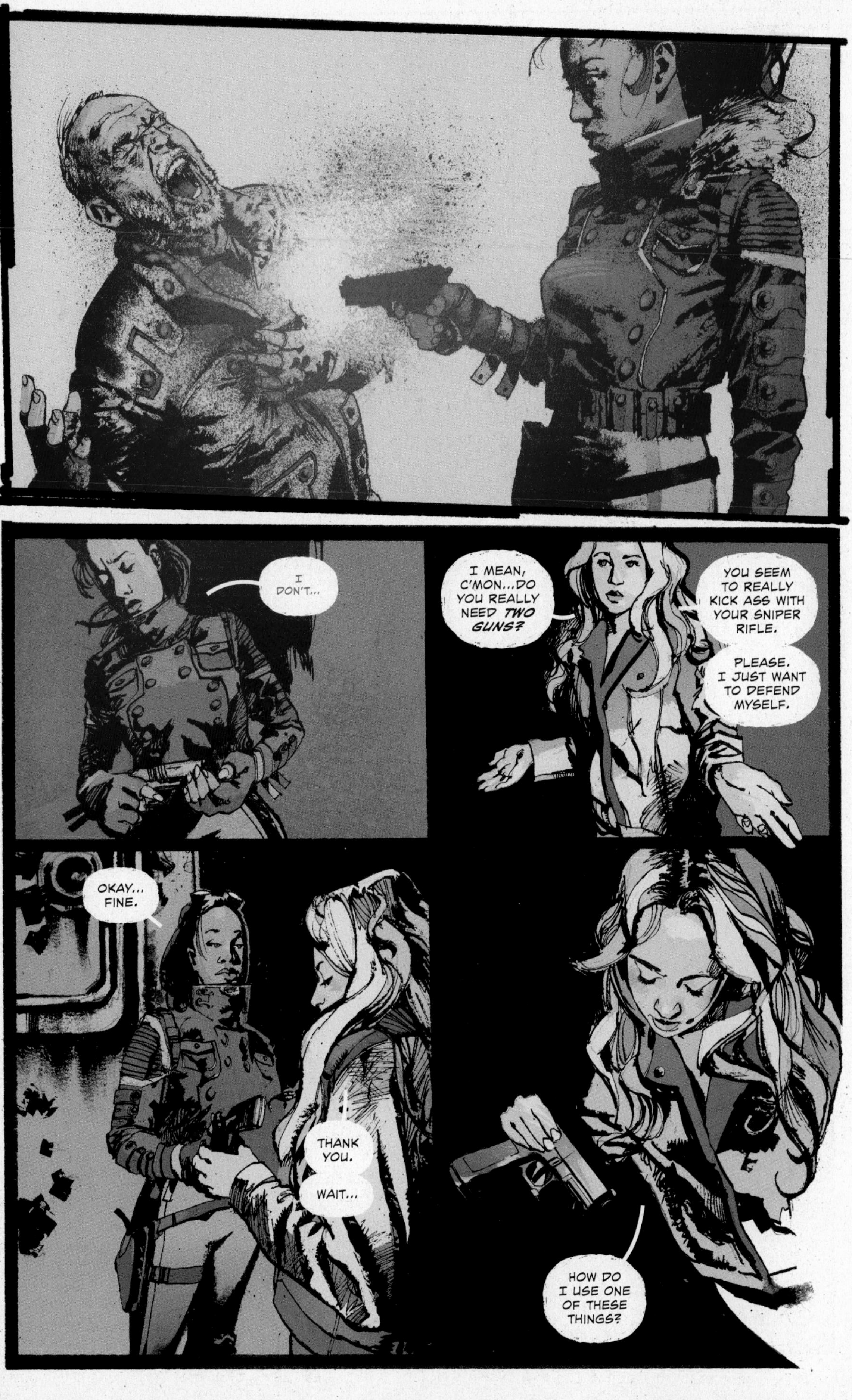
I DON'T...
I MEAN, C'MON...DO YOU REALLY NEED *TWO GUNS?*
YOU SEEM TO REALLY KICK ASS WITH YOUR SNIPER RIFLE.
PLEASE. I JUST WANT TO DEFEND MYSELF.
OKAY... FINE.
THANK YOU.
WAIT...
HOW DO I USE ONE OF THESE THINGS?

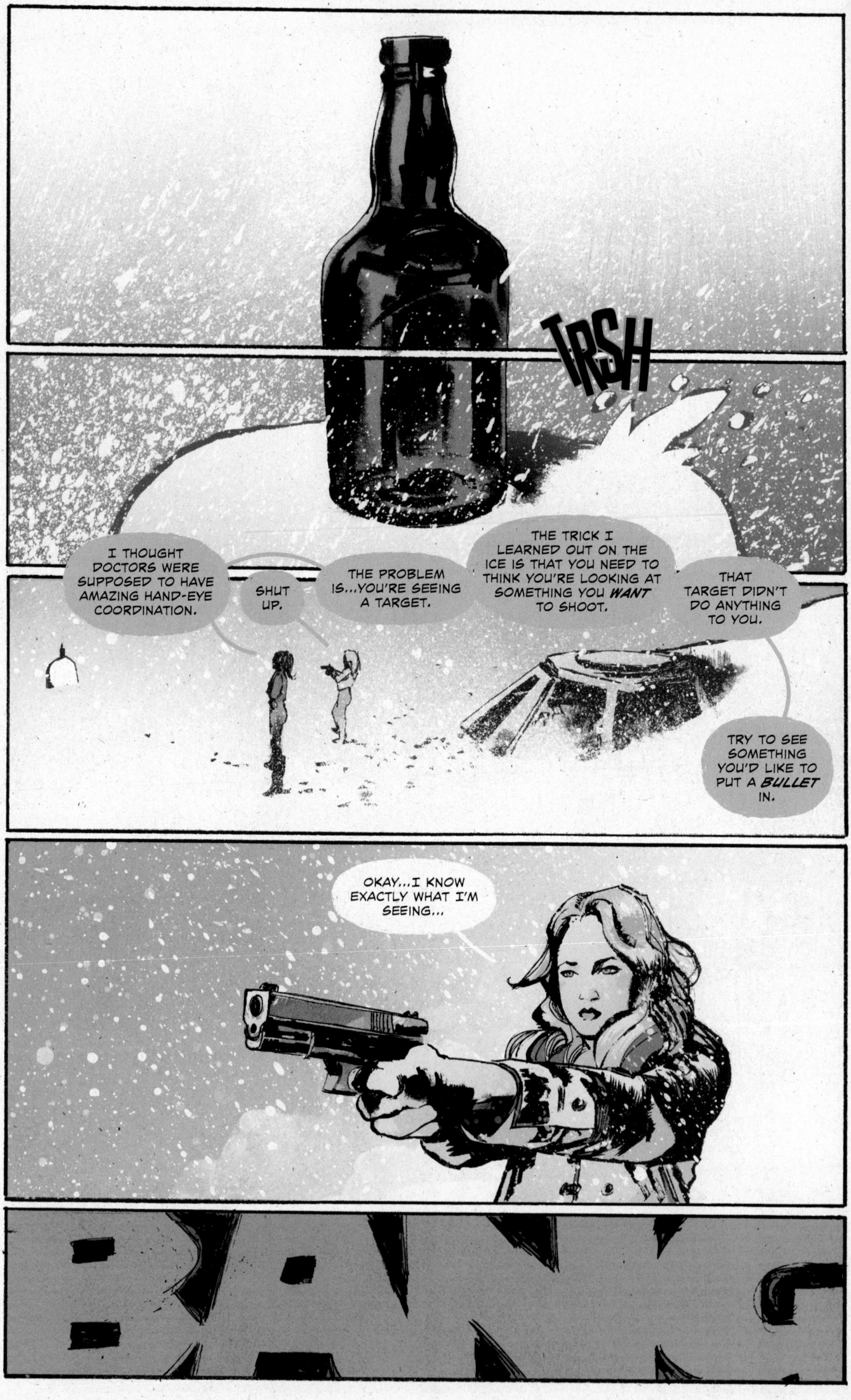
TRSH
I THOUGHT DOCTORS WERE SUPPOSED TO HAVE AMAZING HAND-EYE COORDINATION.
SHUT UP.
THE PROBLEM IS...YOU'RE SEEING A TARGET.
THE TRICK I LEARNED OUT ON THE ICE IS THAT YOU NEED TO THINK YOU'RE LOOKING AT SOMETHING YOU *WANT* TO SHOOT.
THAT TARGET DIDN'T DO ANYTHING TO YOU.
TRY TO SEE SOMETHING YOU'D LIKE TO PUT A *BULLET* IN.
OKAY...I KNOW EXACTLY WHAT I'M SEEING...

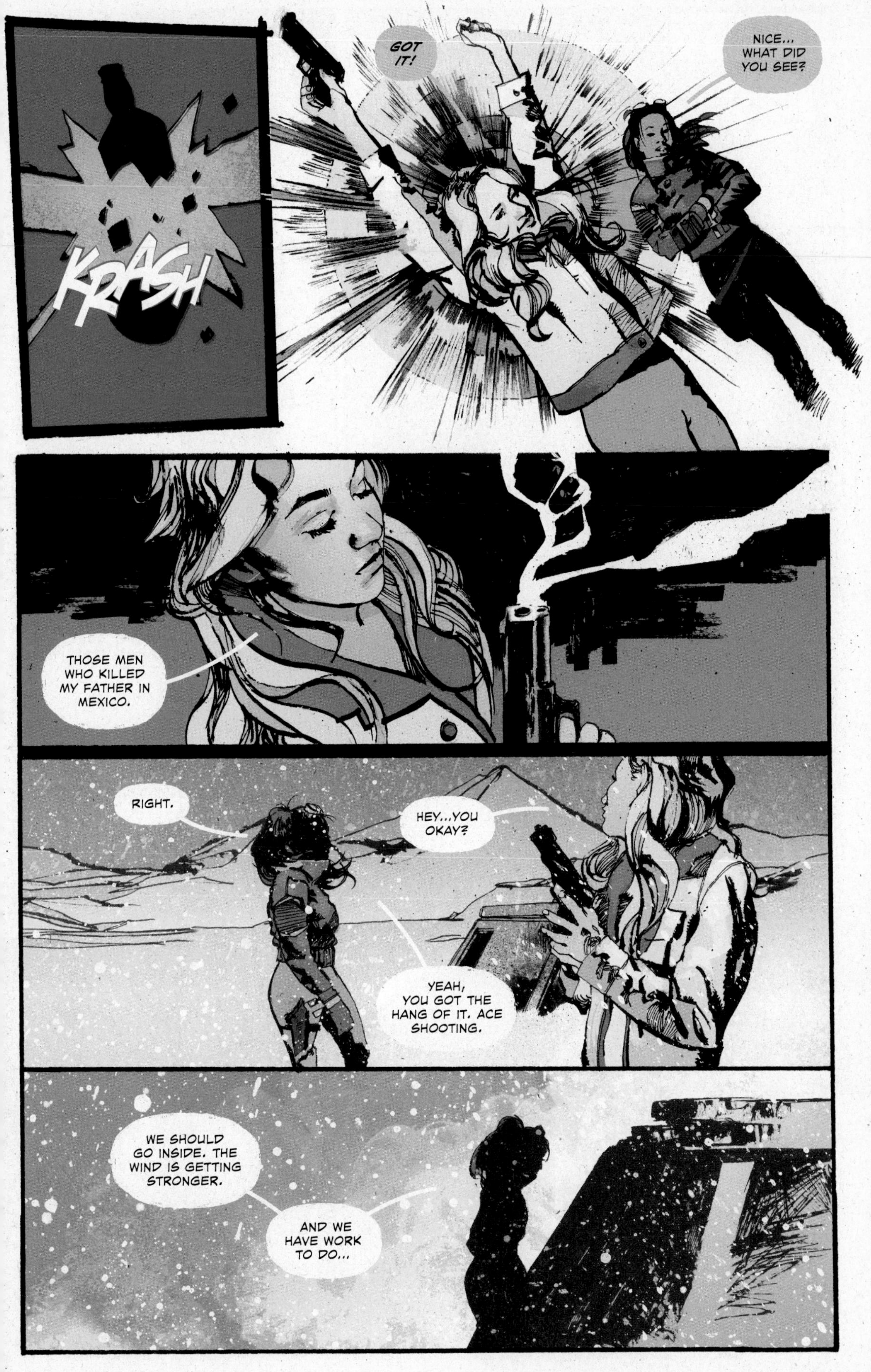
KRASH
GOT IT!
NICE... WHAT DID YOU SEE?
THOSE MEN WHO KILLED MY FATHER IN MEXICO.
RIGHT.
HEY...YOU OKAY?
YEAH, YOU GOT THE HANG OF IT. ACE SHOOTING.
WE SHOULD GO INSIDE. THE WIND IS GETTING STRONGER.
AND WE HAVE WORK TO DO...

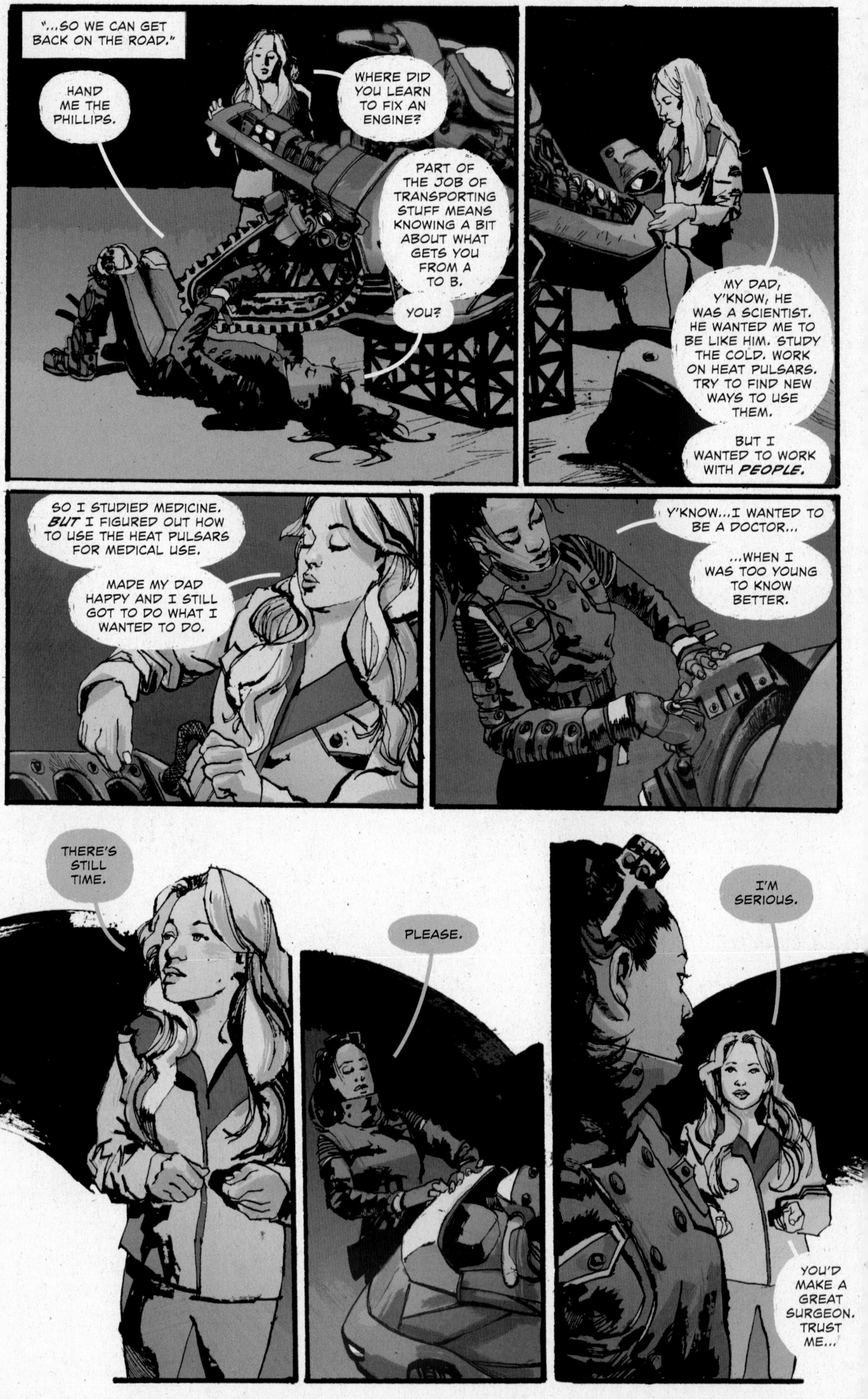
"...SO WE CAN GET BACK ON THE ROAD."
HAND ME THE PHILLIPS.
WHERE DID YOU LEARN TO FIX AN ENGINE?
PART OF THE JOB OF TRANSPORTING STUFF MEANS KNOWING A BIT ABOUT WHAT GETS YOU FROM A TO B.
YOU?
MY DAD, Y'KNOW, HE WAS A SCIENTIST. HE WANTED ME TO BE LIKE HIM. STUDY THE COLD. WORK ON HEAT PULSARS. TRY TO FIND NEW WAYS TO USE THEM.
BUT I WANTED TO WORK WITH *PEOPLE.*
SO I STUDIED MEDICINE. *BUT* I FIGURED OUT HOW TO USE THE HEAT PULSARS FOR MEDICAL USE.
MADE MY DAD HAPPY AND I STILL GOT TO DO WHAT I WANTED TO DO.
Y'KNOW...I WANTED TO BE A DOCTOR...
...WHEN I WAS TOO YOUNG TO KNOW BETTER.
THERE'S STILL TIME.
PLEASE.
I'M SERIOUS.
YOU'D MAKE A GREAT SURGEON. TRUST ME...

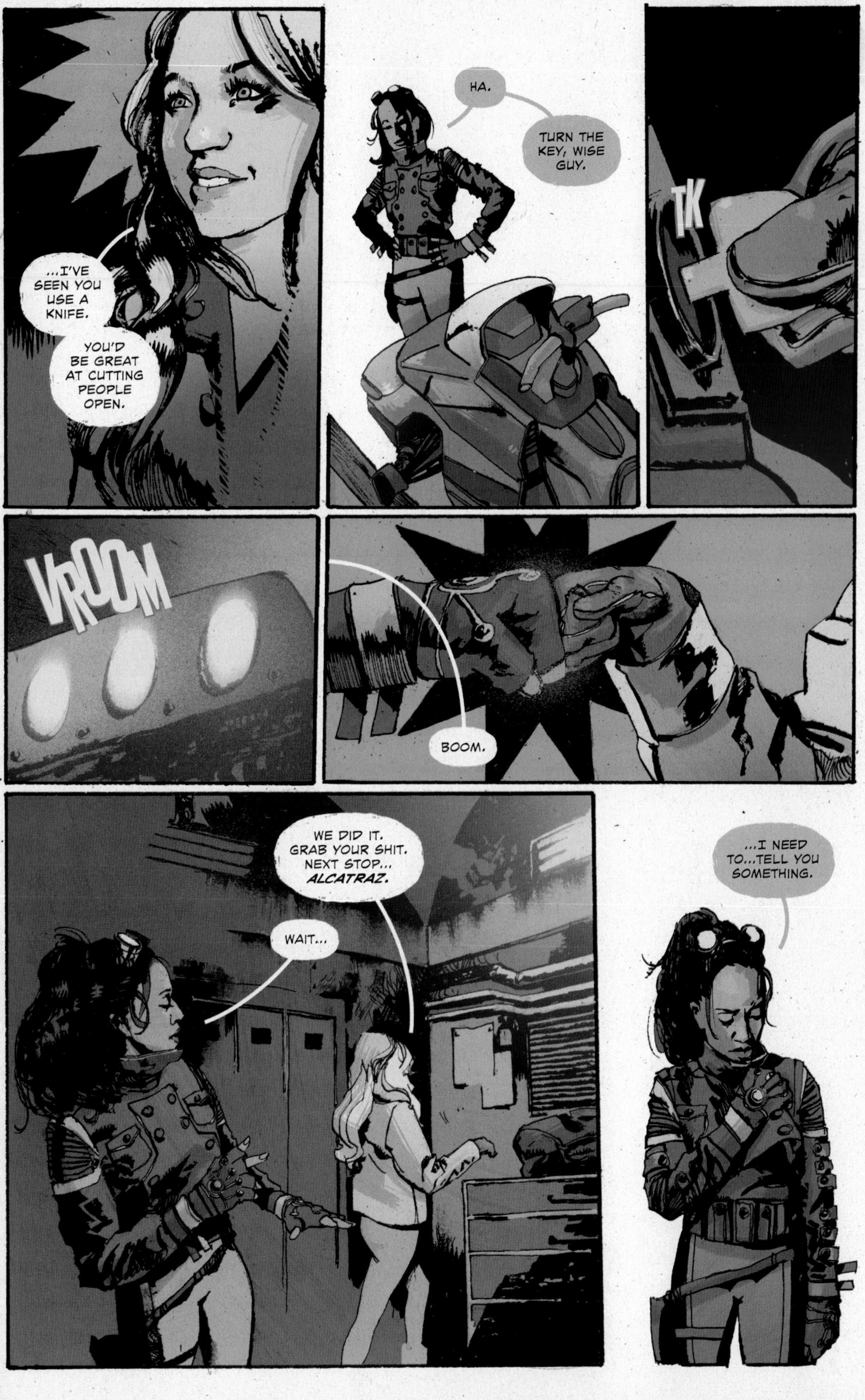
...I'VE SEEN YOU USE A KNIFE.
YOU'D BE GREAT AT CUTTING PEOPLE OPEN.
HA.
TURN THE KEY, WISE GUY.
TK
VROOM
BOOM.
WE DID IT. GRAB YOUR SHIT. NEXT STOP... *ALCATRAZ.*
WAIT...
...I NEED TO...TELL YOU SOMETHING.

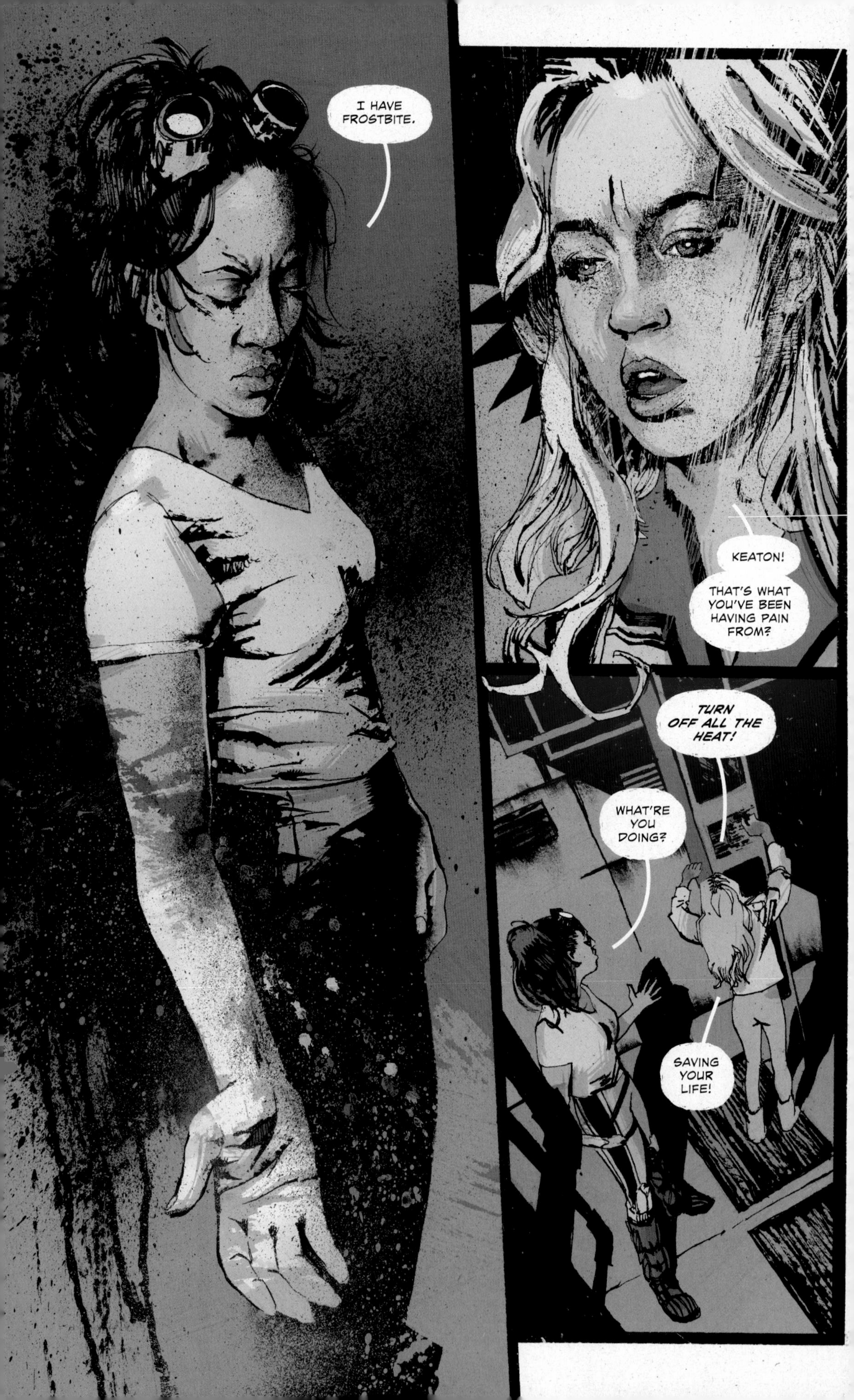
I HAVE FROSTBITE.
KEATON!
THAT'S WHAT YOU'VE BEEN HAVING PAIN FROM?
TURN OFF ALL THE HEAT!
WHAT'RE YOU DOING?
SAVING YOUR LIFE!

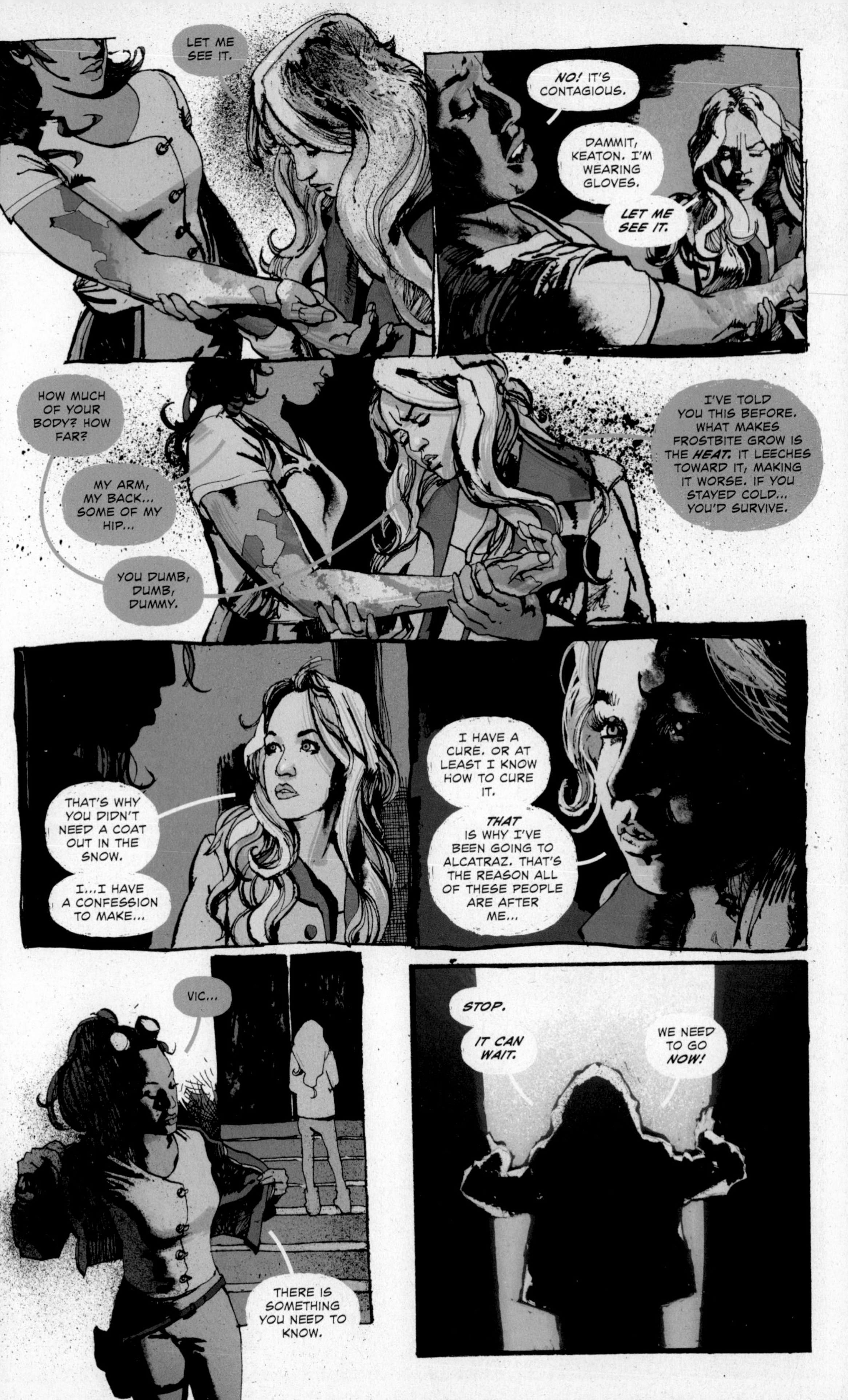
LET ME SEE IT.
NO! IT'S CONTAGIOUS.
DAMMIT, KEATON. I'M WEARING GLOVES.
LET ME SEE IT.
HOW MUCH OF YOUR BODY? HOW FAR?
MY ARM, MY BACK... SOME OF MY HIP...
YOU DUMB, DUMB, DUMMY.
I'VE TOLD YOU THIS BEFORE. WHAT MAKES FROSTBITE GROW IS THE HEAT. IT LEECHES TOWARD IT, MAKING IT WORSE. IF YOU STAYED COLD... YOU'D SURVIVE.
THAT'S WHY YOU DIDN'T NEED A COAT OUT IN THE SNOW.
I...I HAVE A CONFESSION TO MAKE...
I HAVE A CURE. OR AT LEAST I KNOW HOW TO CURE IT.
THAT IS WHY I'VE BEEN GOING TO ALCATRAZ. THAT'S THE REASON ALL OF THESE PEOPLE ARE AFTER ME...
VIC...
THERE IS SOMETHING YOU NEED TO KNOW.
STOP.
IT CAN WAIT.
WE NEED TO GO NOW!

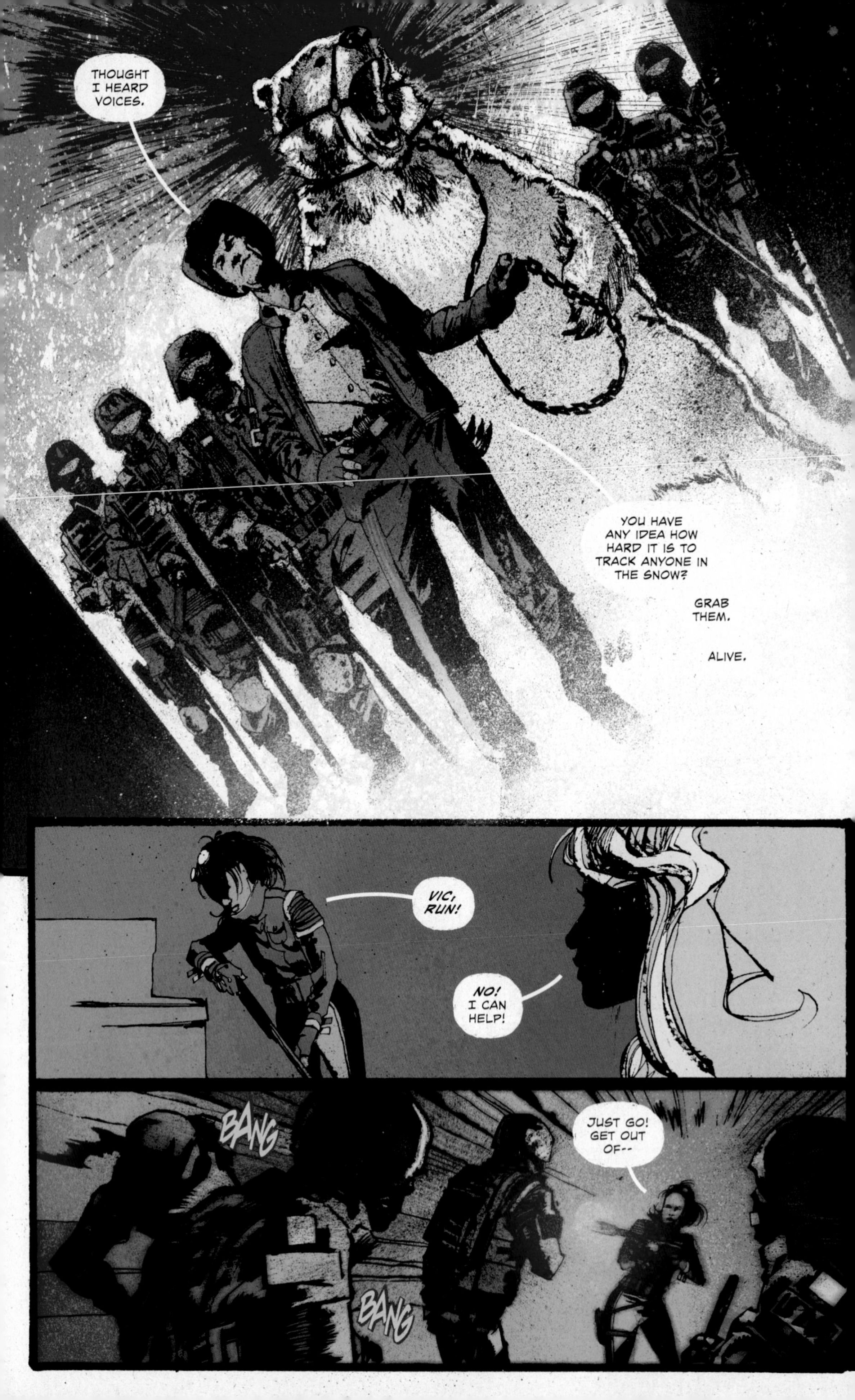
THOUGHT I HEARD VOICES.
YOU HAVE ANY IDEA HOW HARD IT IS TO TRACK ANYONE IN THE SNOW?
GRAB THEM.
ALIVE.
VIC, RUN!
NO! I CAN HELP!
BANG
JUST GO! GET OUT OF--
BANG

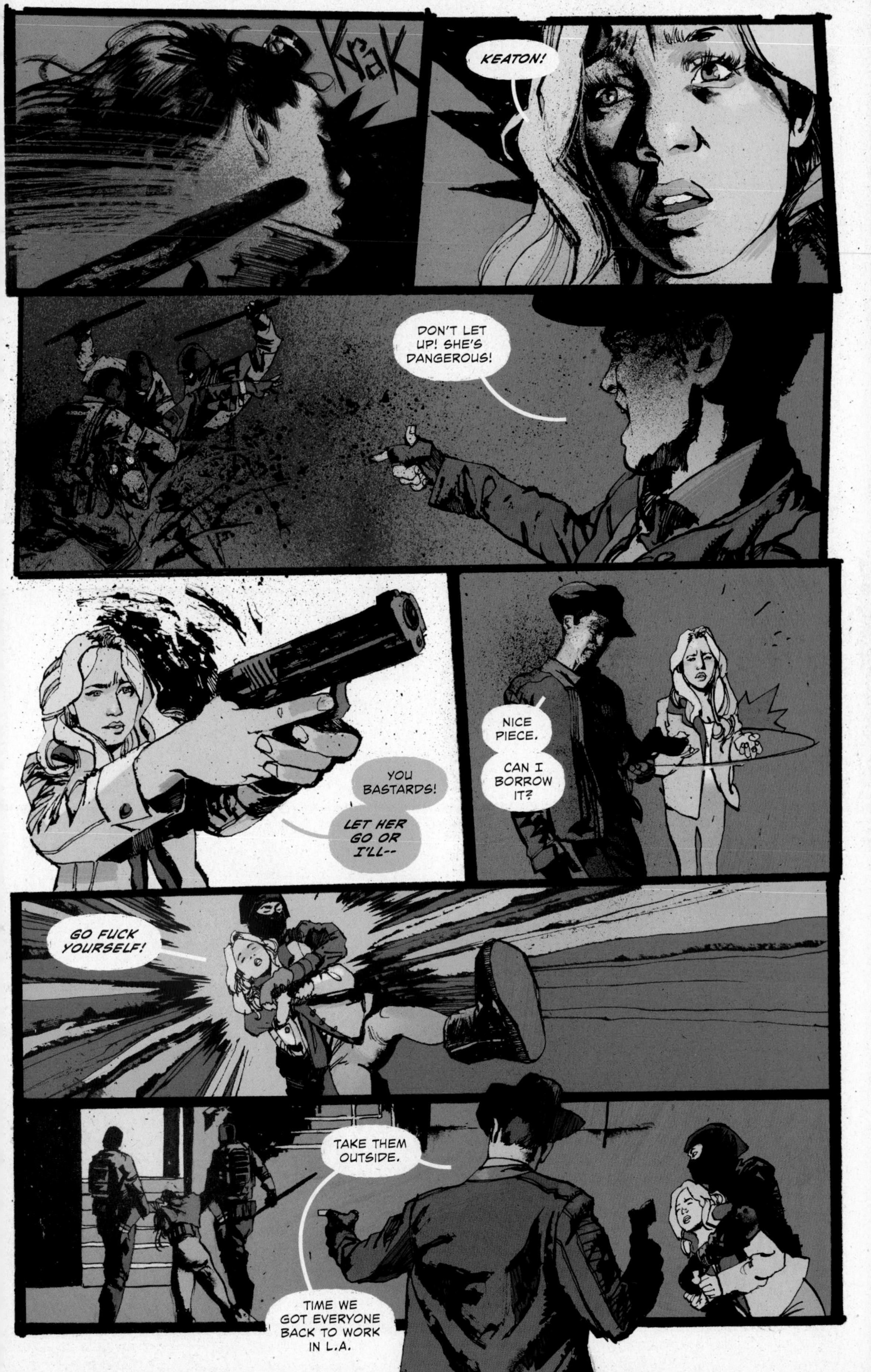
KRAK
KEATON!
DON'T LET UP! SHE'S DANGEROUS!
YOU BASTARDS!
LET HER GO OR I'LL--
NICE PIECE.
CAN I BORROW IT?
GO FUCK YOURSELF!
TAKE THEM OUTSIDE.
TIME WE GOT EVERYONE BACK TO WORK IN L.A.

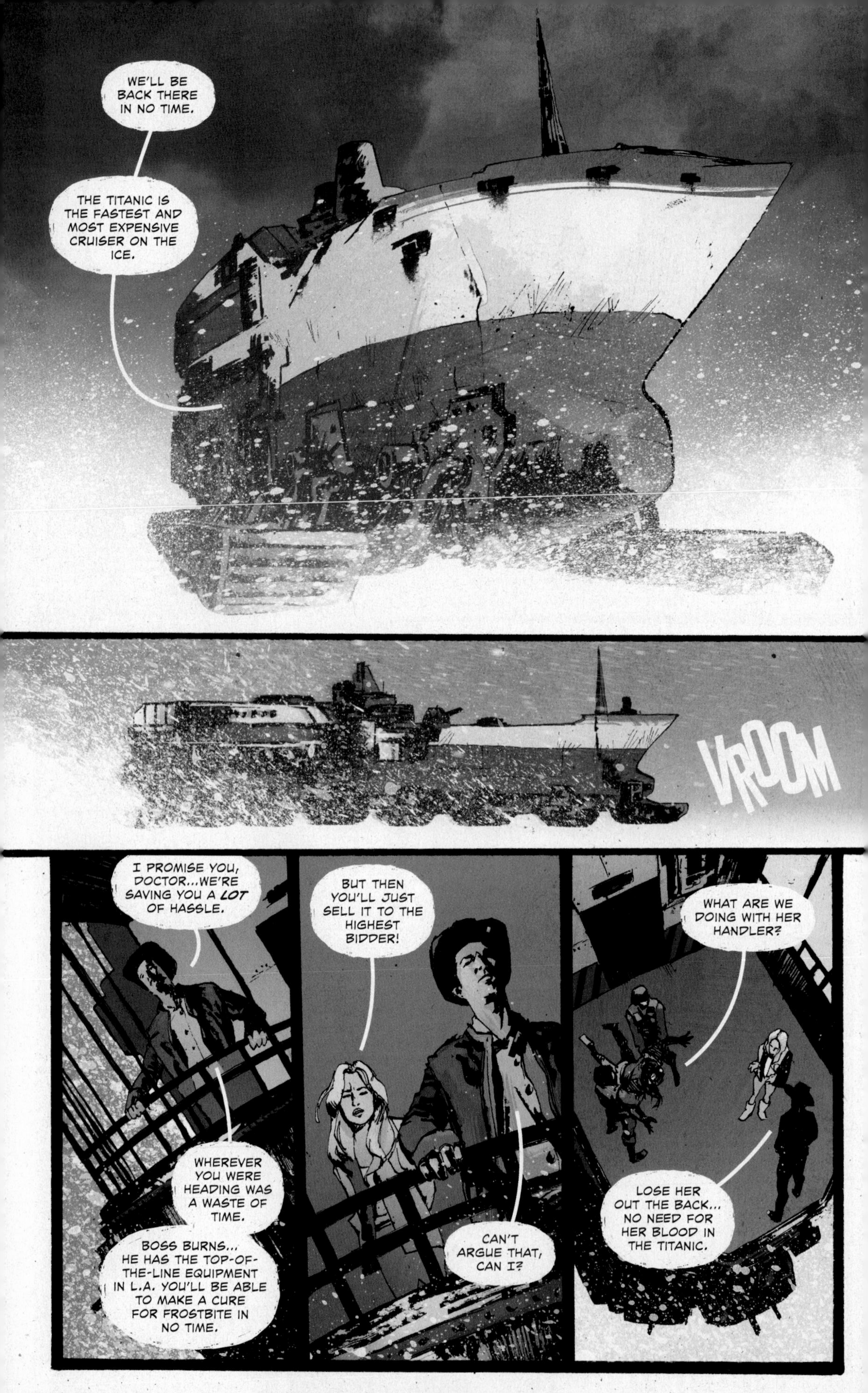
WE'LL BE BACK THERE IN NO TIME.
THE TITANIC IS THE FASTEST AND MOST EXPENSIVE CRUISER ON THE ICE.
VROOM
I PROMISE YOU, DOCTOR...WE'RE SAVING YOU A *LOT* OF HASSLE.
WHEREVER YOU WERE HEADING WAS A WASTE OF TIME.
BOSS BURNS... HE HAS THE TOP-OF-THE-LINE EQUIPMENT IN L.A. YOU'LL BE ABLE TO MAKE A CURE FOR FROSTBITE IN NO TIME.
BUT THEN YOU'LL JUST SELL IT TO THE HIGHEST BIDDER!
CAN'T ARGUE THAT, CAN I?
WHAT ARE WE DOING WITH HER HANDLER?
LOSE HER OUT THE BACK... NO NEED FOR HER BLOOD IN THE TITANIC.

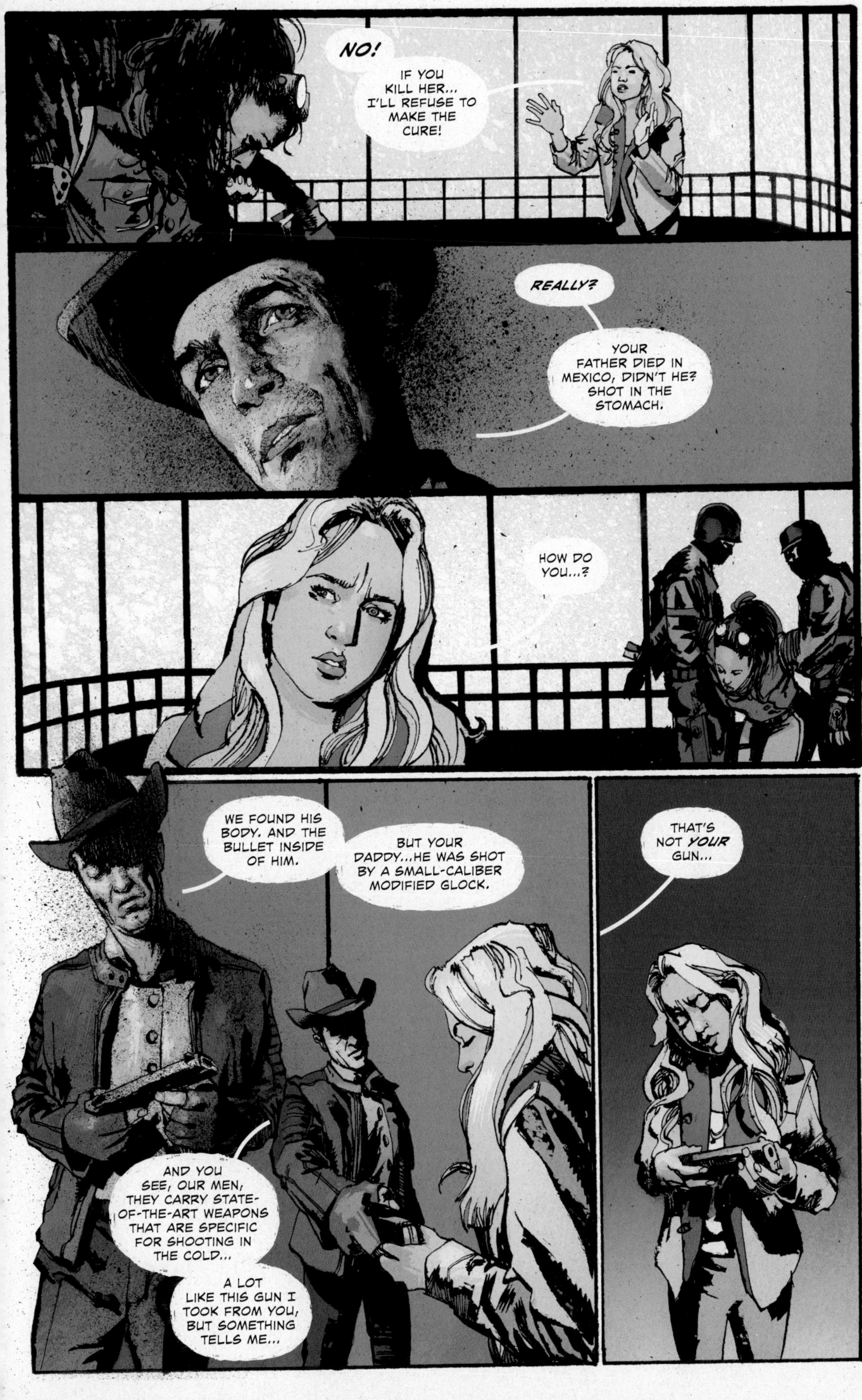
NO!
IF YOU KILL HER... I'LL REFUSE TO MAKE THE CURE!
REALLY?
YOUR FATHER DIED IN MEXICO, DIDN'T HE? SHOT IN THE STOMACH.
HOW DO YOU...?
WE FOUND HIS BODY. AND THE BULLET INSIDE OF HIM.
BUT YOUR DADDY...HE WAS SHOT BY A SMALL-CALIBER MODIFIED GLOCK.
AND YOU SEE, OUR MEN, THEY CARRY STATE-OF-THE-ART WEAPONS THAT ARE SPECIFIC FOR SHOOTING IN THE COLD...
A LOT LIKE THIS GUN I TOOK FROM YOU, BUT SOMETHING TELLS ME...
THAT'S NOT YOUR GUN...

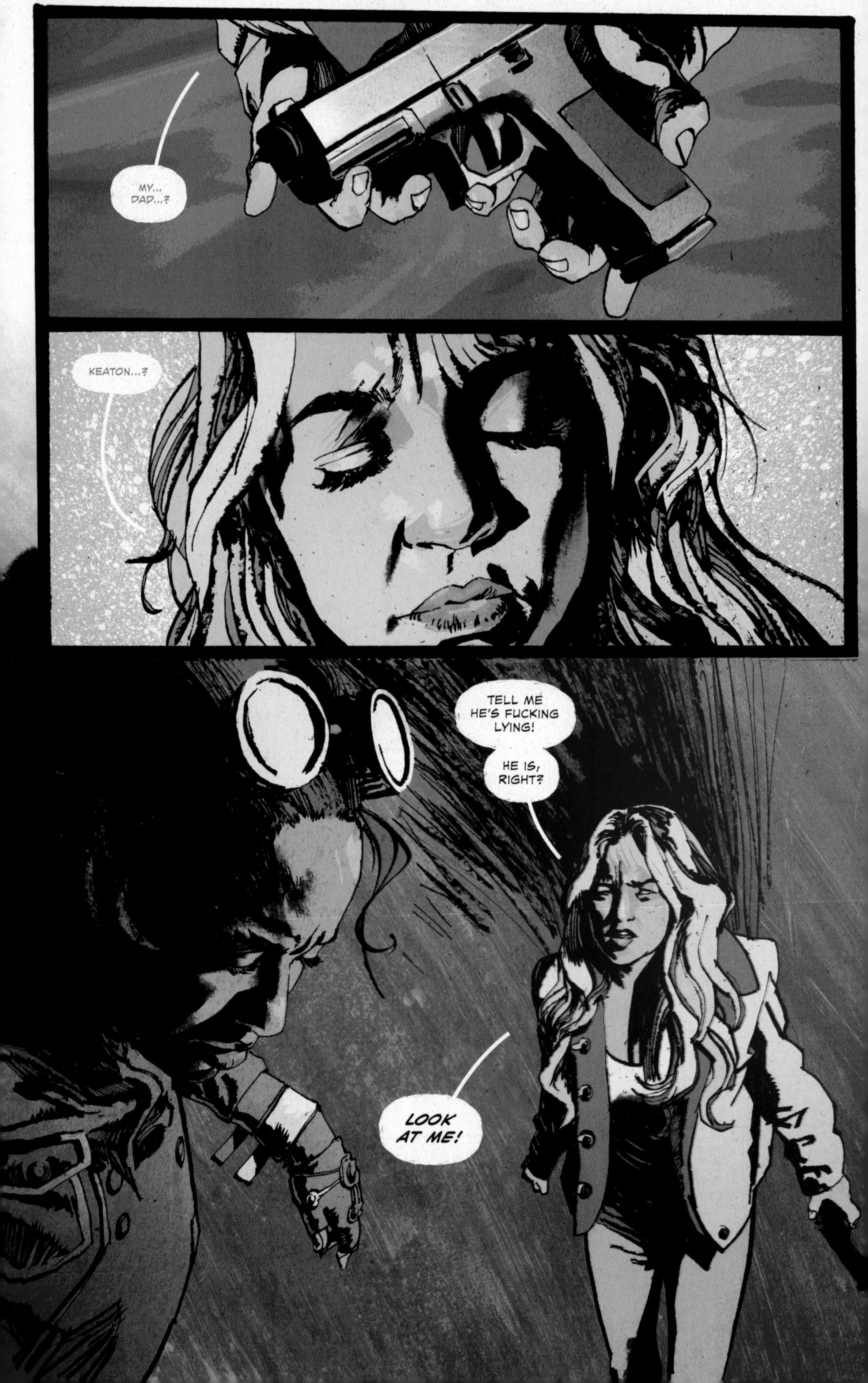

MY... DAD...?
KEATON...?
TELL ME HE'S FUCKING LYING!
HE IS, RIGHT?
LOOK AT ME!

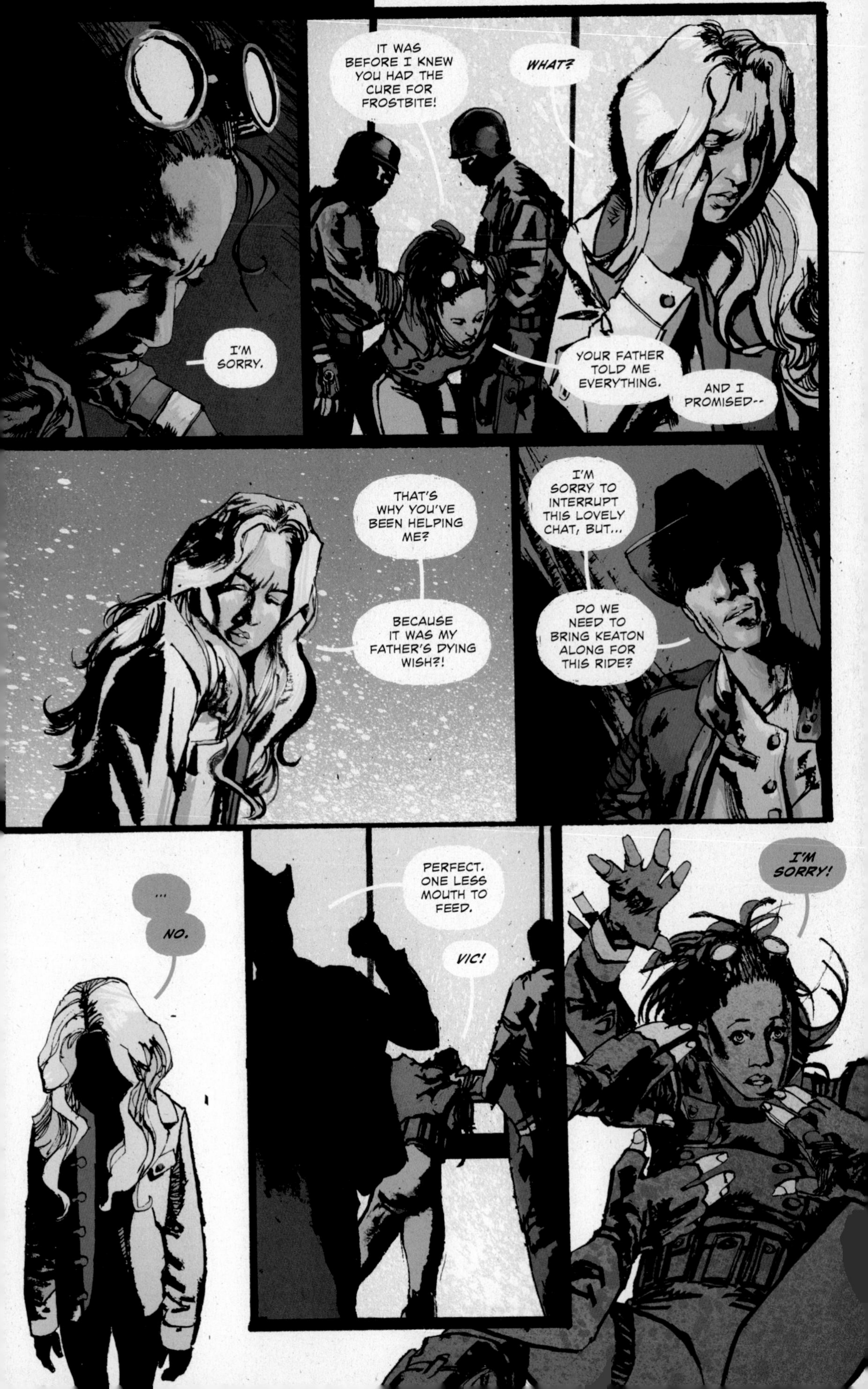
I'M SORRY.
IT WAS BEFORE I KNEW YOU HAD THE CURE FOR FROSTBITE!
WHAT?
YOUR FATHER TOLD ME EVERYTHING.
AND I PROMISED--
THAT'S WHY YOU'VE BEEN HELPING ME?
BECAUSE IT WAS MY FATHER'S DYING WISH?!
I'M SORRY TO INTERRUPT THIS LOVELY CHAT, BUT...
DO WE NEED TO BRING KEATON ALONG FOR THIS RIDE?
...
NO.
PERFECT. ONE LESS MOUTH TO FEED.
VIC!
I'M SORRY!

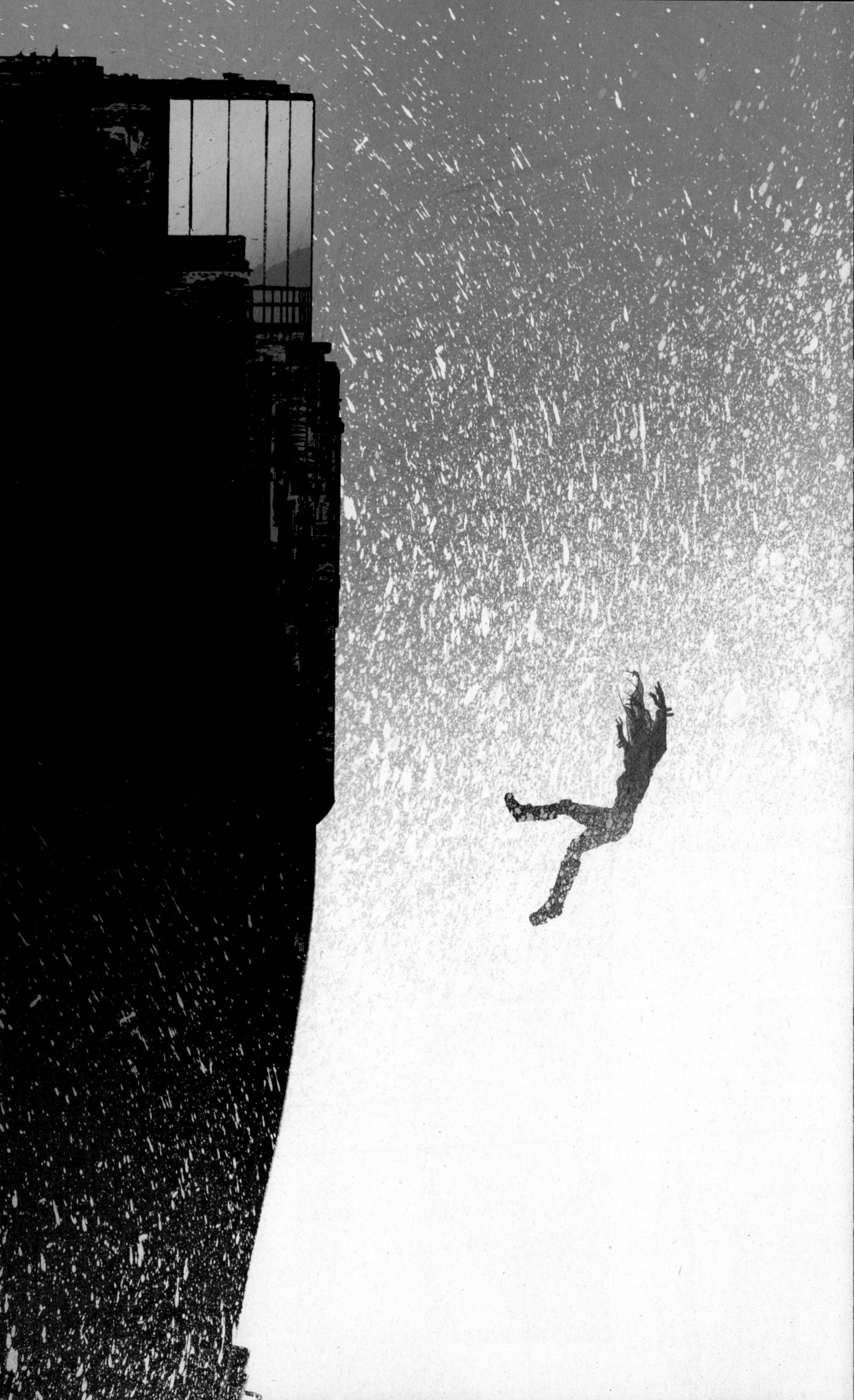

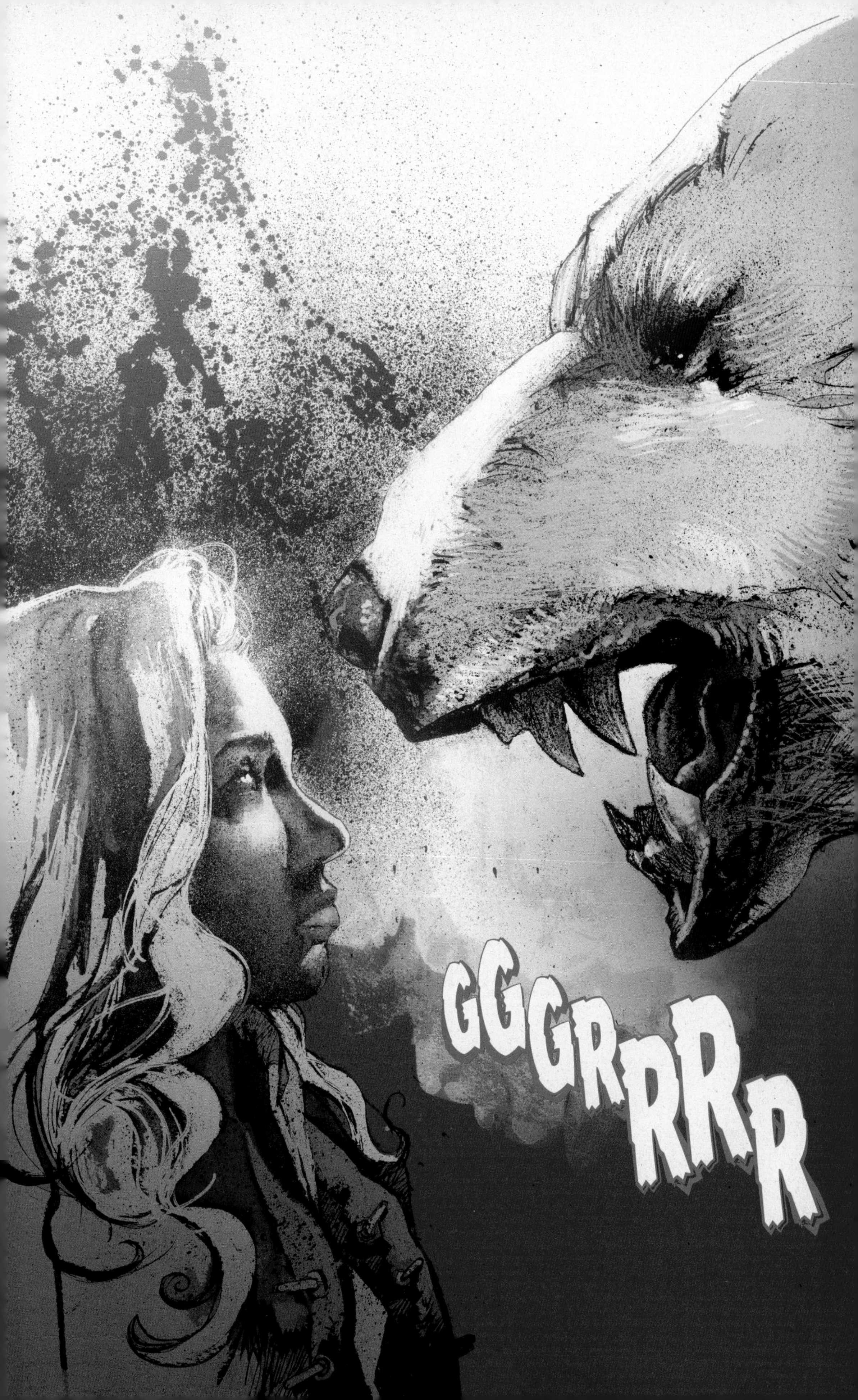
GGGRRRR

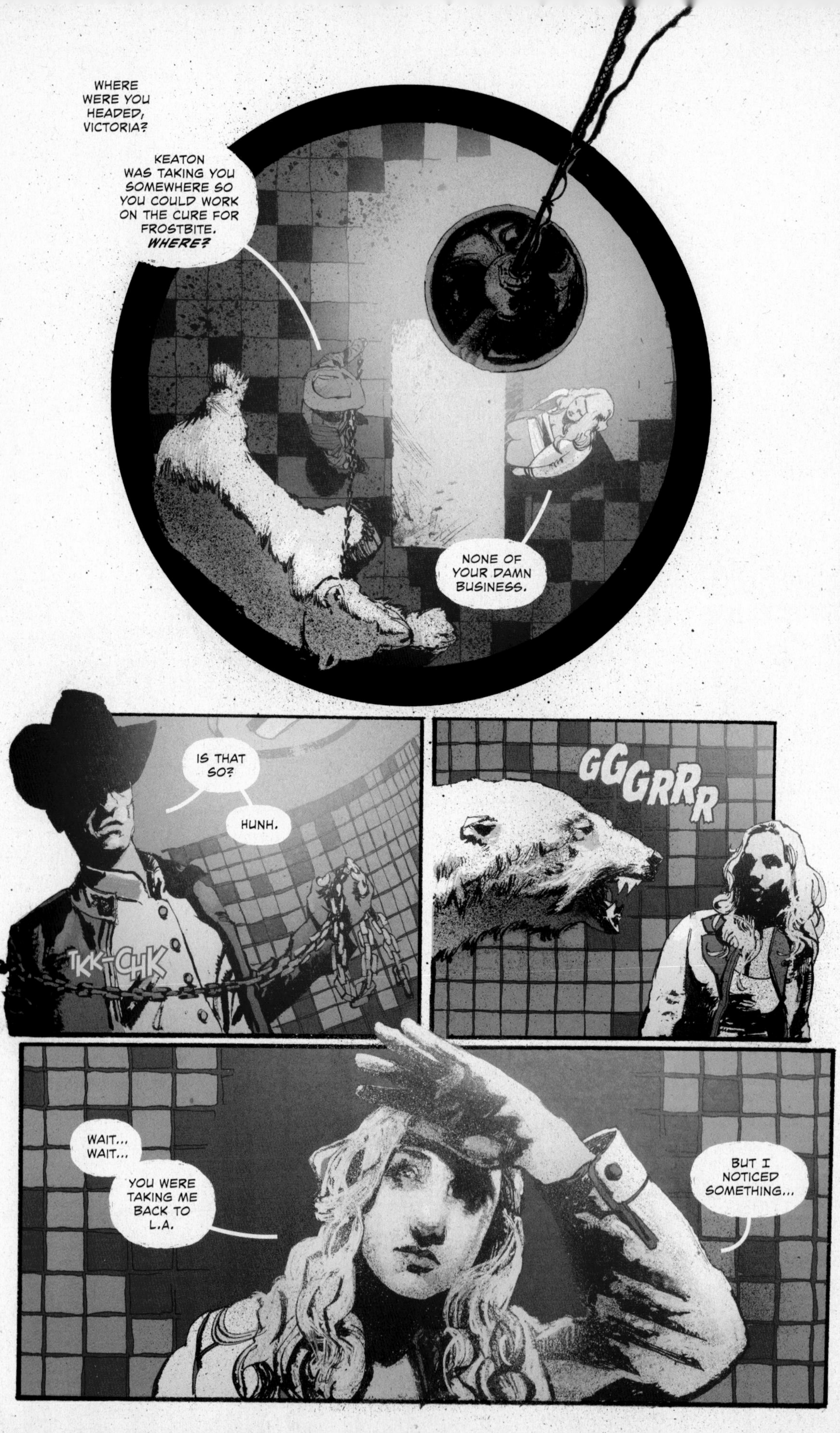
WHERE WERE YOU HEADED, VICTORIA?
KEATON WAS TAKING YOU SOMEWHERE SO YOU COULD WORK ON THE CURE FOR FROSTBITE. WHERE?
NONE OF YOUR DAMN BUSINESS.
IS THAT SO?
HUNH.
TKK-CHK
GGGRRRR
WAIT... WAIT...
YOU WERE TAKING ME BACK TO L.A.
BUT I NOTICED SOMETHING...

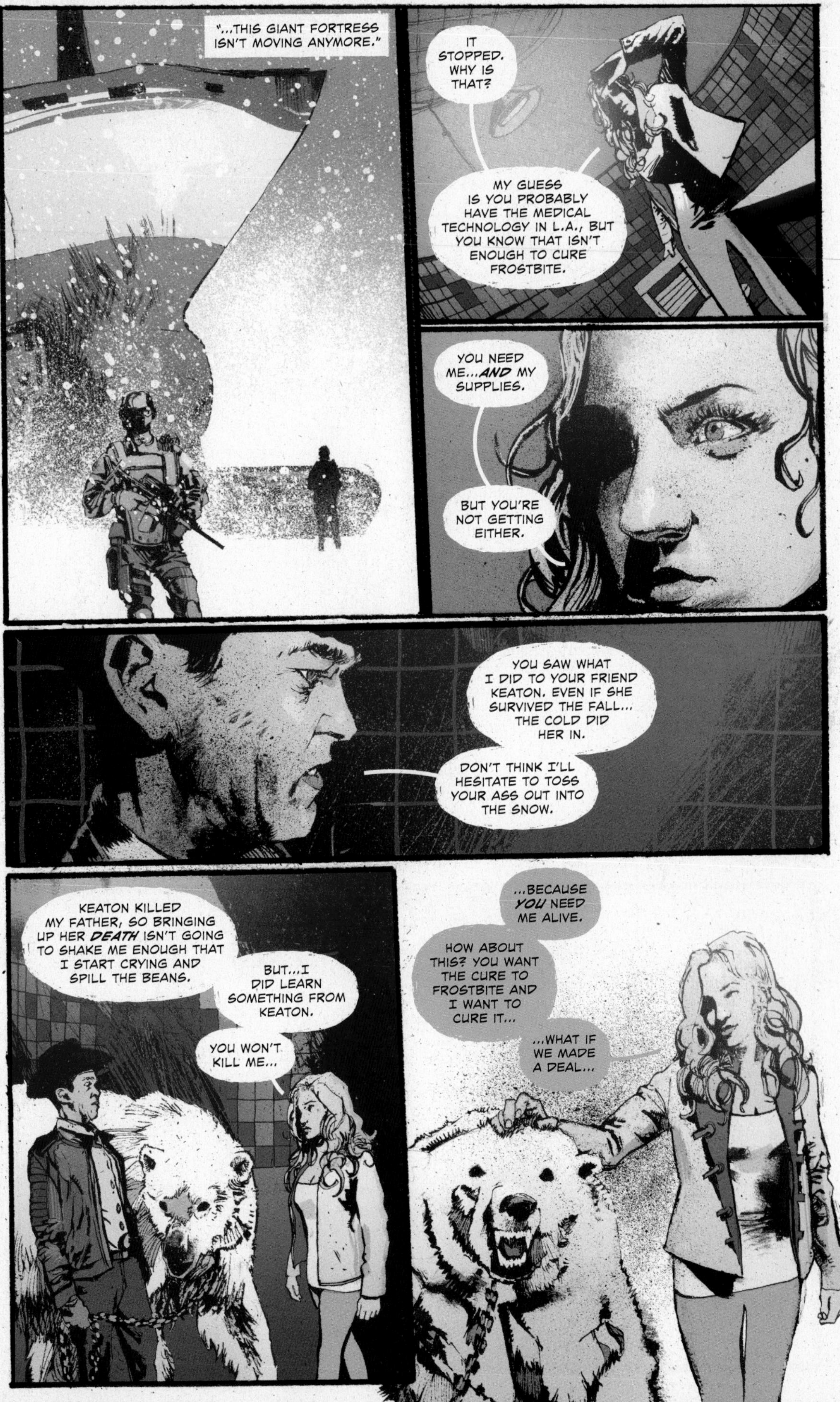
"...THIS GIANT FORTRESS ISN'T MOVING ANYMORE."
IT STOPPED. WHY IS THAT?
MY GUESS IS YOU PROBABLY HAVE THE MEDICAL TECHNOLOGY IN L.A., BUT YOU KNOW THAT ISN'T ENOUGH TO CURE FROSTBITE.
YOU NEED ME...AND MY SUPPLIES.
BUT YOU'RE NOT GETTING EITHER.
YOU SAW WHAT I DID TO YOUR FRIEND KEATON. EVEN IF SHE SURVIVED THE FALL... THE COLD DID HER IN.
DON'T THINK I'LL HESITATE TO TOSS YOUR ASS OUT INTO THE SNOW.
KEATON KILLED MY FATHER, SO BRINGING UP HER DEATH ISN'T GOING TO SHAKE ME ENOUGH THAT I START CRYING AND SPILL THE BEANS.
BUT...I DID LEARN SOMETHING FROM KEATON.
YOU WON'T KILL ME...
...BECAUSE YOU NEED ME ALIVE.
HOW ABOUT THIS? YOU WANT THE CURE TO FROSTBITE AND I WANT TO CURE IT...
...WHAT IF WE MADE A DEAL...

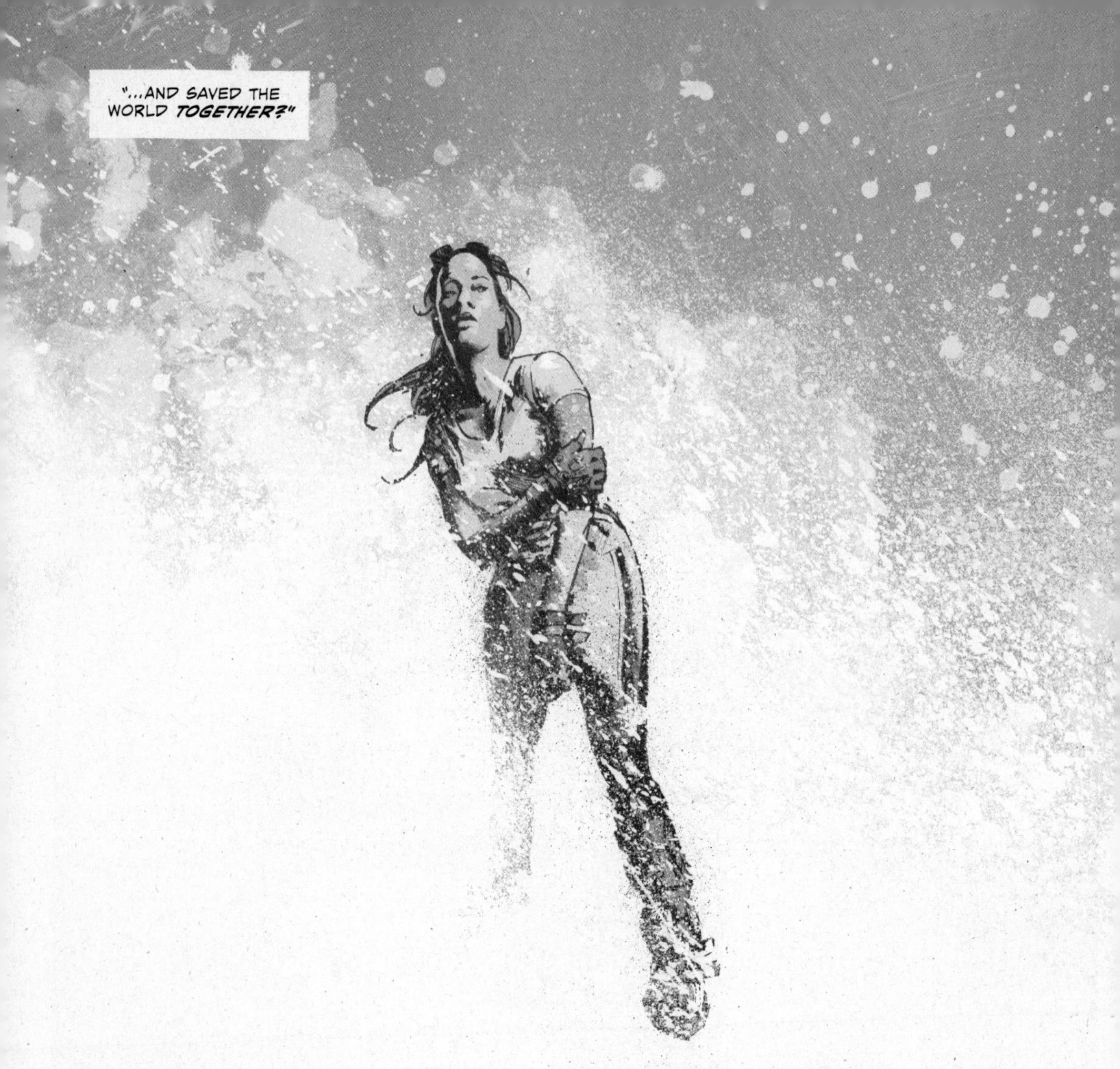
"...AND SAVED THE WORLD TOGETHER?"

## FROSTBITE part 5

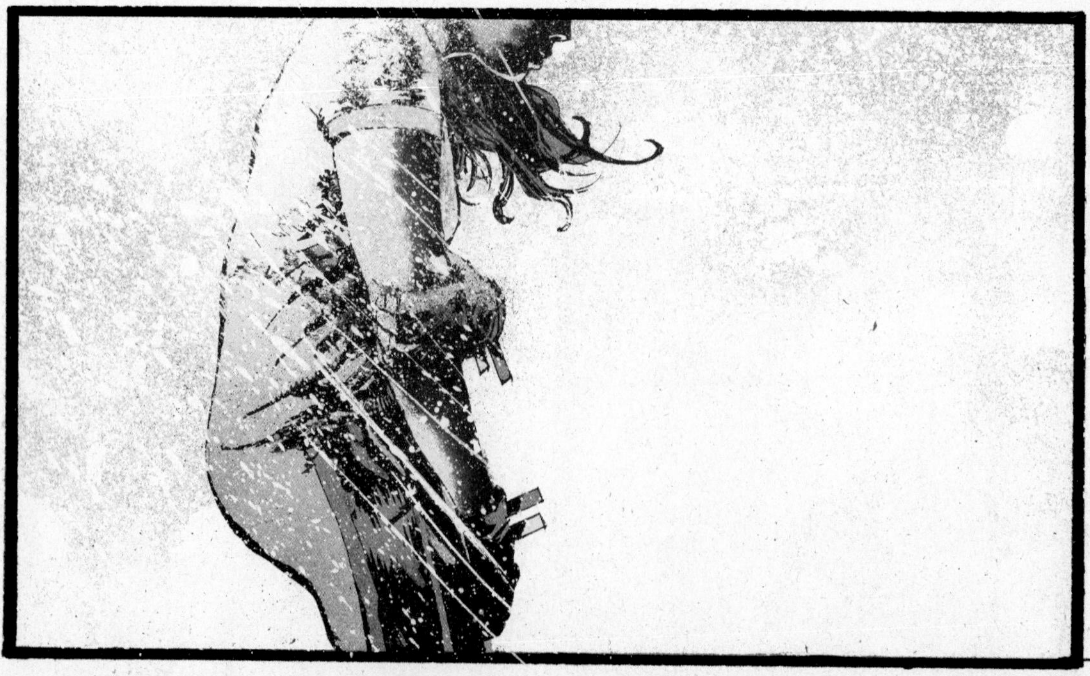

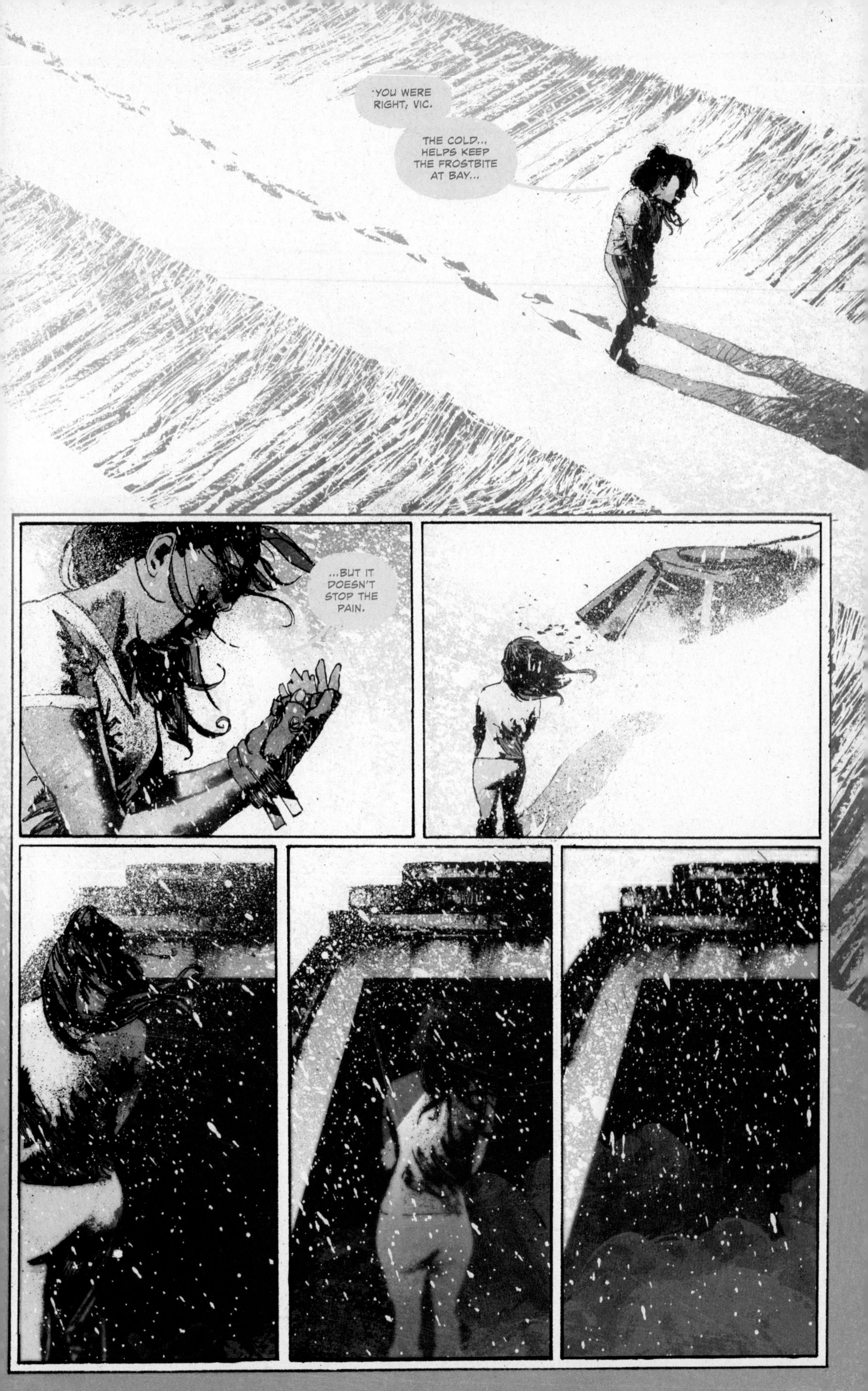
YOU WERE RIGHT, VIC.
THE COLD... HELPS KEEP THE FROSTBITE AT BAY...
...BUT IT DOESN'T STOP THE PAIN.

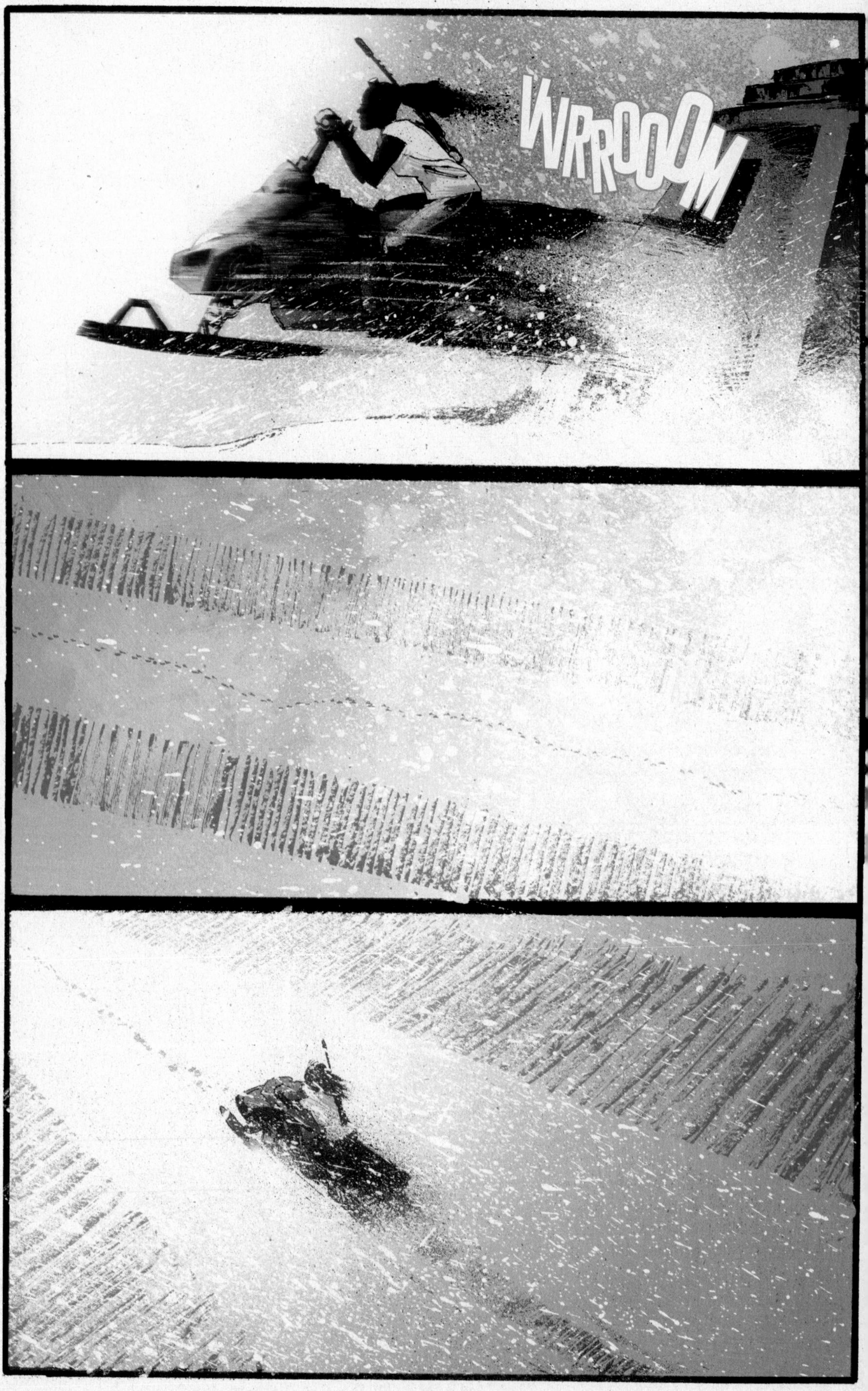
WRROOOM

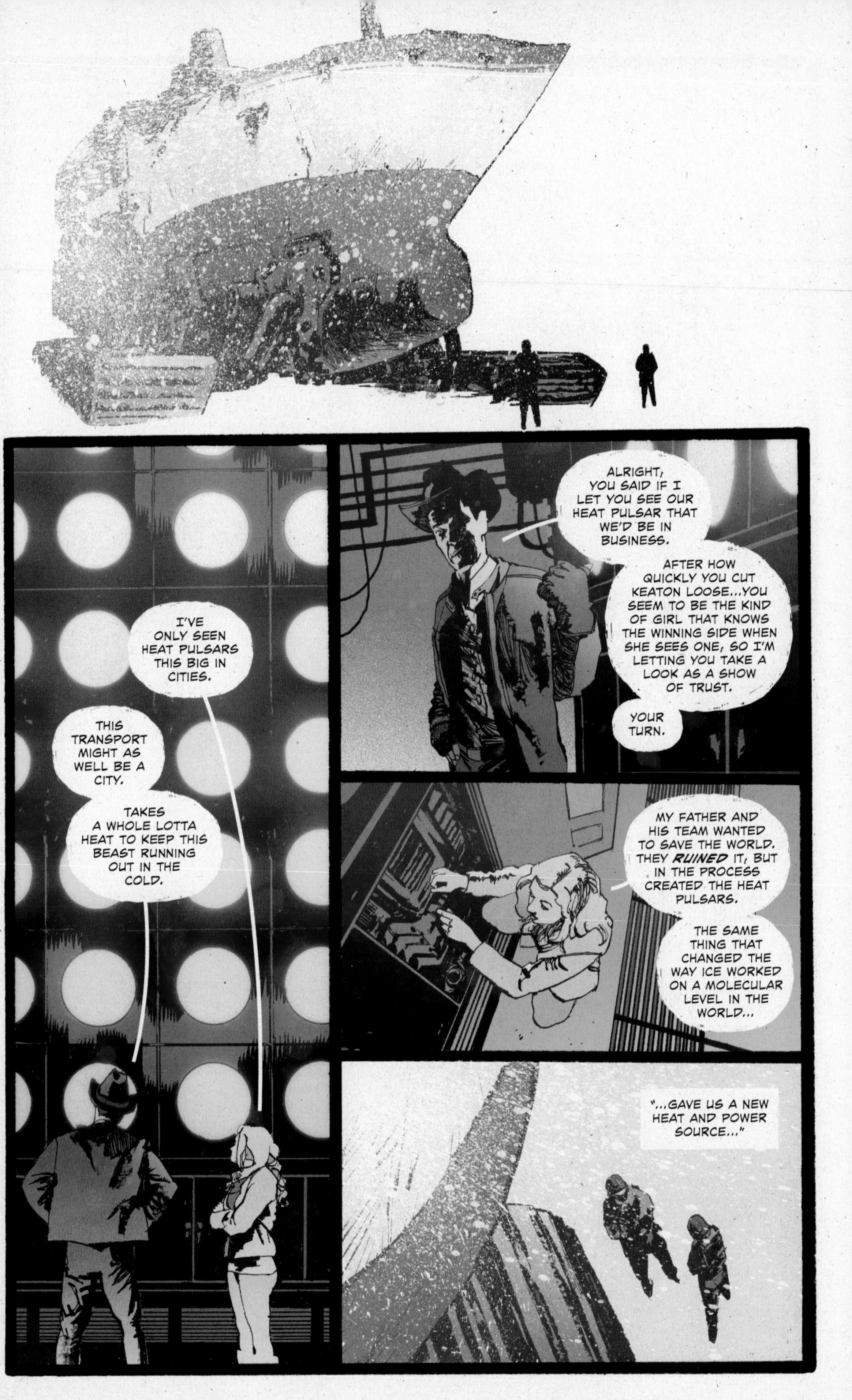
I'VE ONLY SEEN HEAT PULSARS THIS BIG IN CITIES.
THIS TRANSPORT MIGHT AS WELL BE A CITY.
TAKES A WHOLE LOTTA HEAT TO KEEP THIS BEAST RUNNING OUT IN THE COLD.
ALRIGHT, YOU SAID IF I LET YOU SEE OUR HEAT PULSAR THAT WE'D BE IN BUSINESS.
AFTER HOW QUICKLY YOU CUT KEATON LOOSE...YOU SEEM TO BE THE KIND OF GIRL THAT KNOWS THE WINNING SIDE WHEN SHE SEES ONE, SO I'M LETTING YOU TAKE A LOOK AS A SHOW OF TRUST.
YOUR TURN.
MY FATHER AND HIS TEAM WANTED TO SAVE THE WORLD. THEY *RUINED* IT, BUT IN THE PROCESS CREATED THE HEAT PULSARS.
THE SAME THING THAT CHANGED THE WAY ICE WORKED ON A MOLECULAR LEVEL IN THE WORLD...
"...GAVE US A NEW HEAT AND POWER SOURCE..."

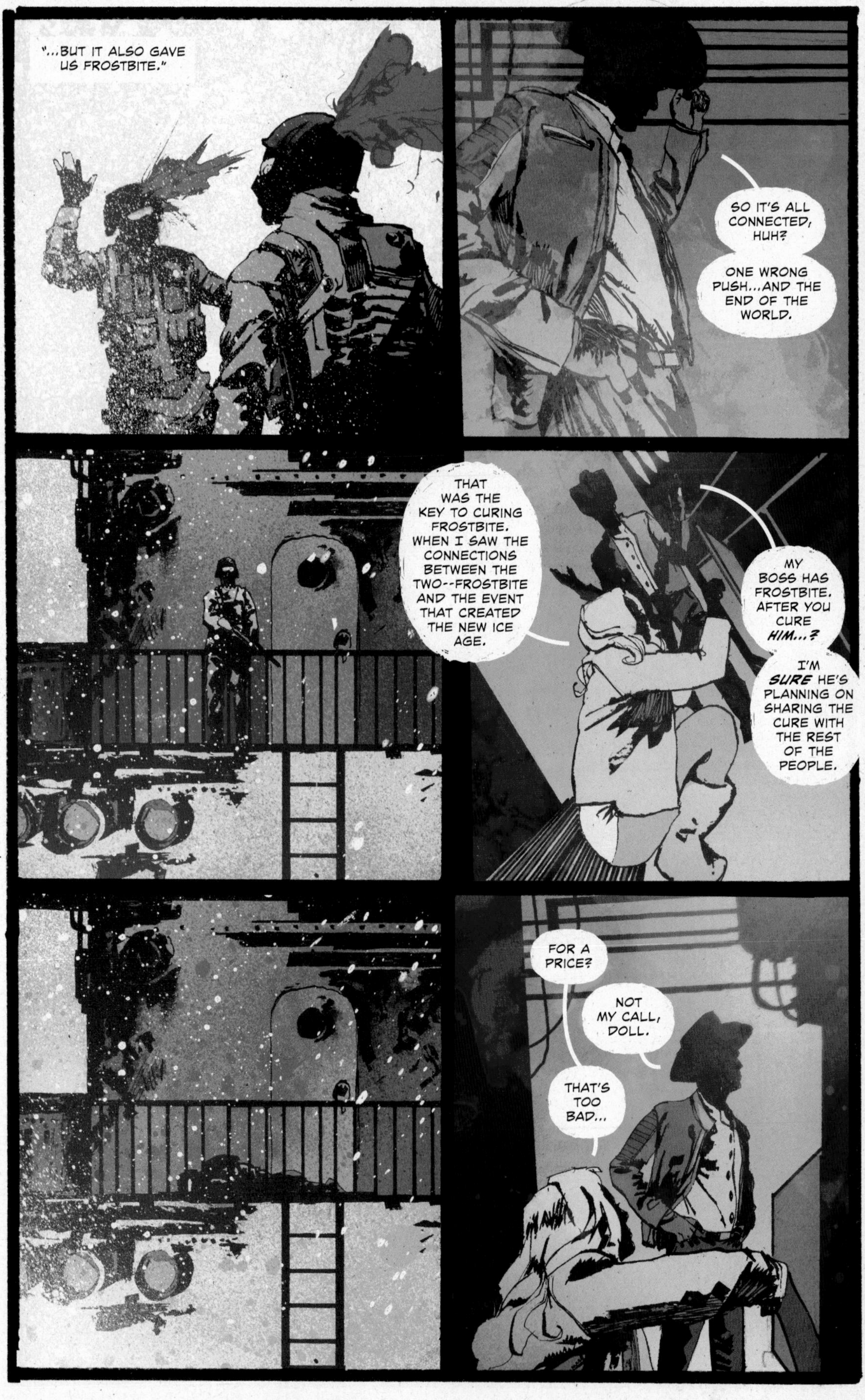
"...BUT IT ALSO GAVE US FROSTBITE."
SO IT'S ALL CONNECTED, HUH?
ONE WRONG PUSH...AND THE END OF THE WORLD.
THAT WAS THE KEY TO CURING FROSTBITE. WHEN I SAW THE CONNECTIONS BETWEEN THE TWO--FROSTBITE AND THE EVENT THAT CREATED THE NEW ICE AGE.
MY BOSS HAS FROSTBITE. AFTER YOU CURE HIM...?
I'M SURE HE'S PLANNING ON SHARING THE CURE WITH THE REST OF THE PEOPLE.
FOR A PRICE?
NOT MY CALL, DOLL.
THAT'S TOO BAD...

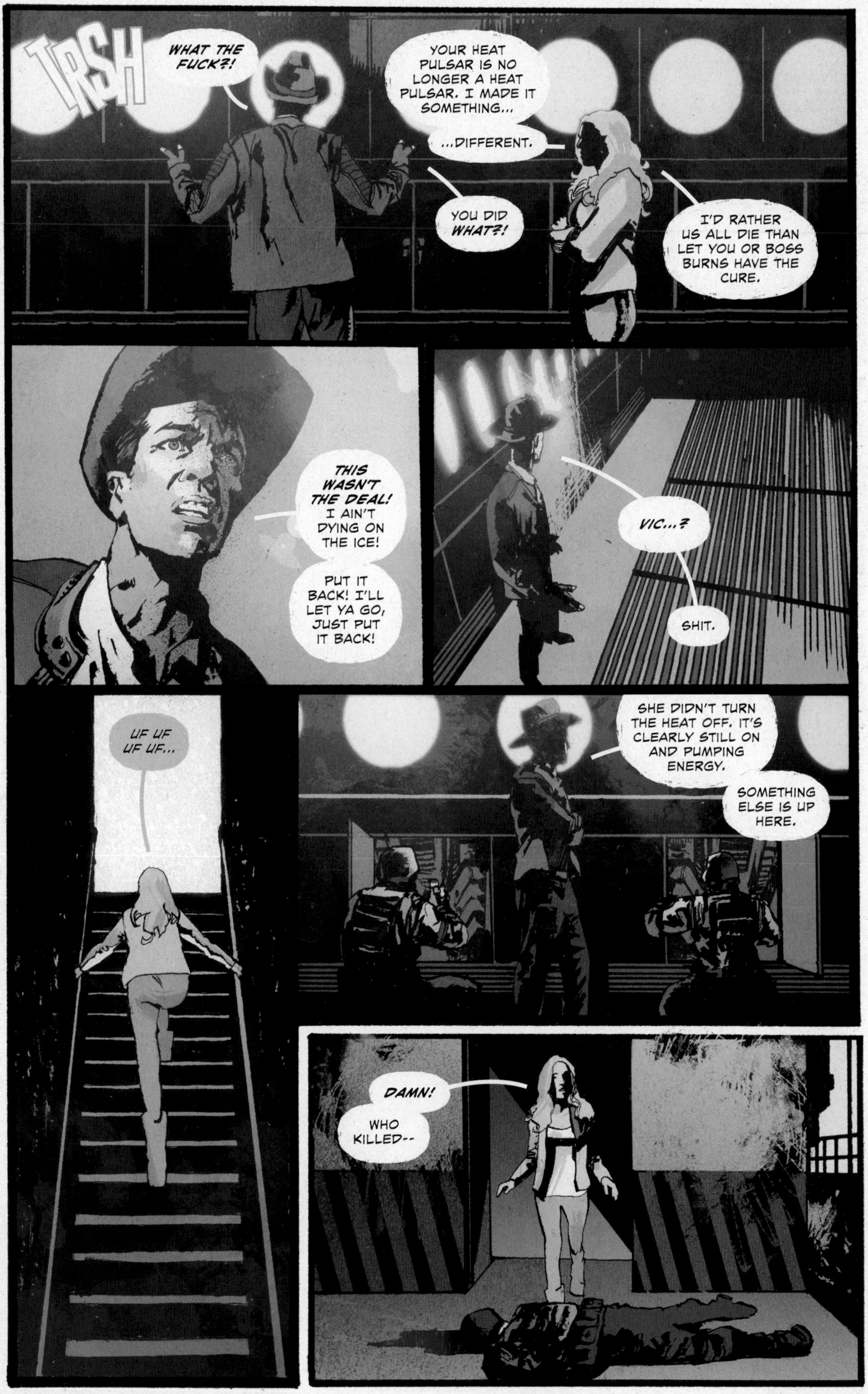
TRSH
WHAT THE FUCK?!
YOUR HEAT PULSAR IS NO LONGER A HEAT PULSAR. I MADE IT SOMETHING...
...DIFFERENT.
YOU DID WHAT?!
I'D RATHER US ALL DIE THAN LET YOU OR BOSS BURNS HAVE THE CURE.
THIS WASN'T THE DEAL! I AIN'T DYING ON THE ICE!
PUT IT BACK! I'LL LET YA GO, JUST PUT IT BACK!
VIC...?
SHIT.
UF UF UF UF...
SHE DIDN'T TURN THE HEAT OFF. IT'S CLEARLY STILL ON AND PUMPING ENERGY.
SOMETHING ELSE IS UP HERE.
DAMN!
WHO KILLED--

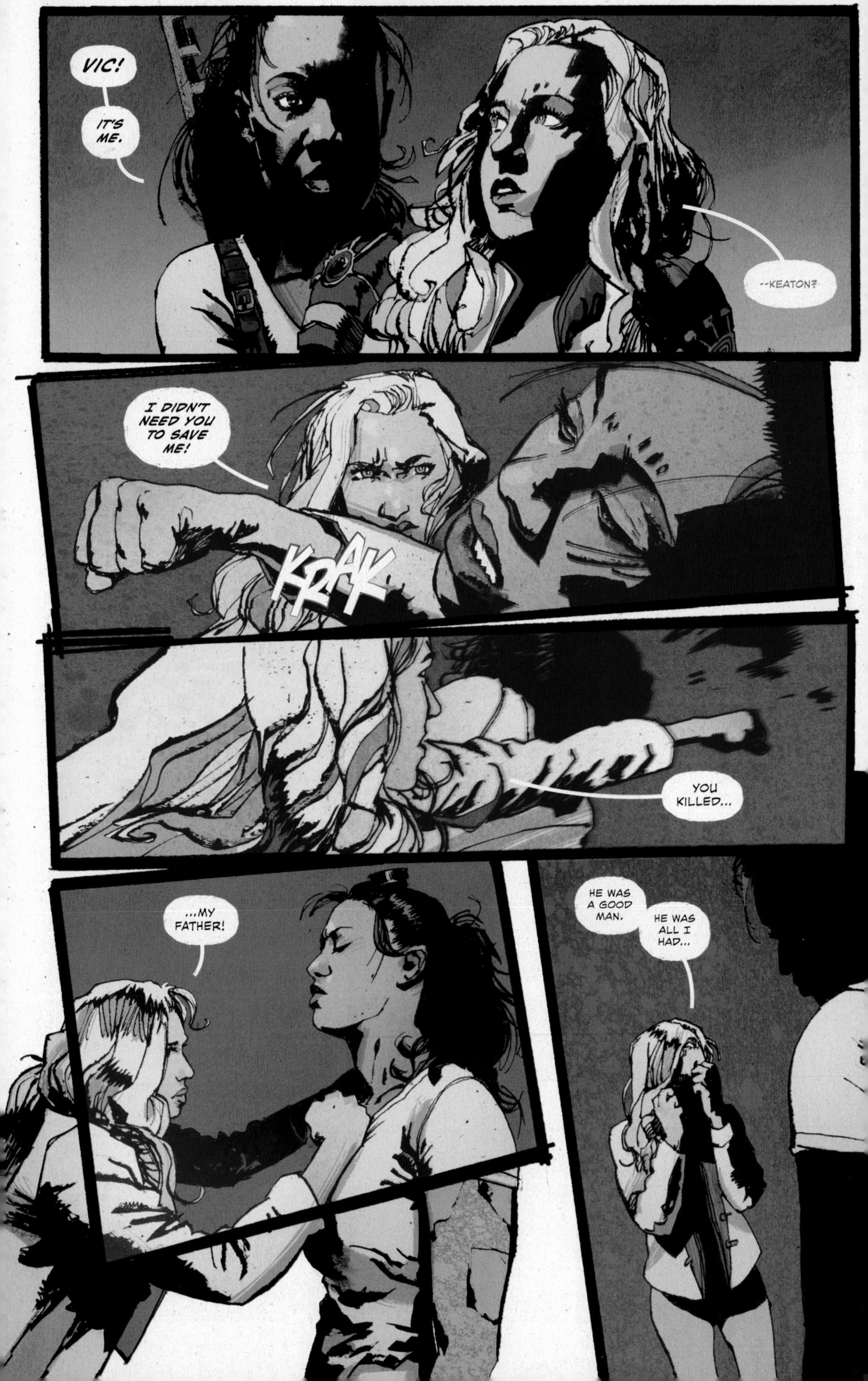
VIC!
IT'S ME.
--KEATON?
I DIDN'T NEED YOU TO SAVE ME!
KRAK
YOU KILLED...
...MY FATHER!
HE WAS A GOOD MAN.
HE WAS ALL I HAD...

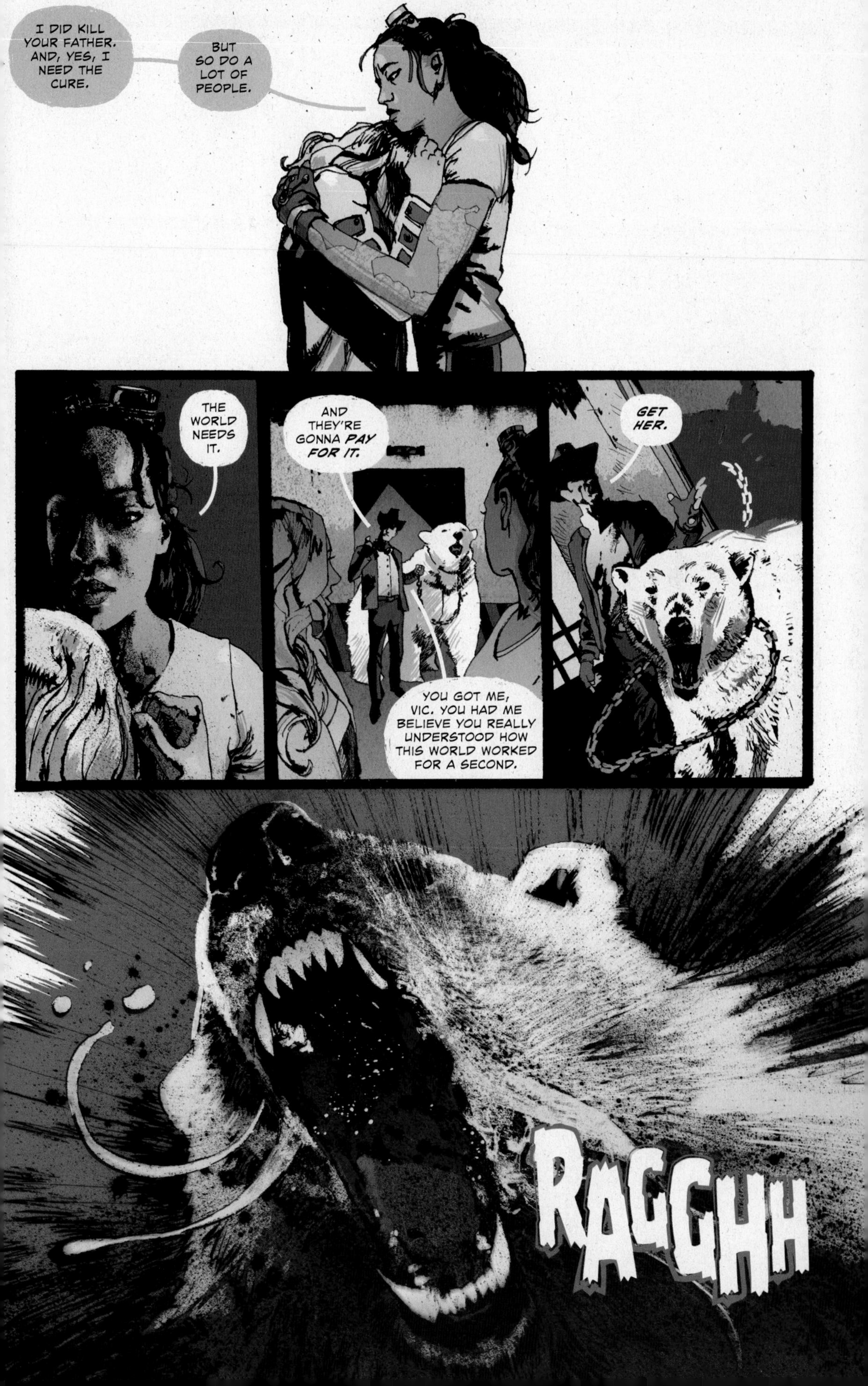
I DID KILL YOUR FATHER. AND, YES, I NEED THE CURE.
BUT SO DO A LOT OF PEOPLE.
THE WORLD NEEDS IT.
AND THEY'RE GONNA *PAY FOR IT.*
YOU GOT ME, VIC. YOU HAD ME BELIEVE YOU REALLY UNDERSTOOD HOW THIS WORLD WORKED FOR A SECOND.
*GET HER.*
RAGGHH

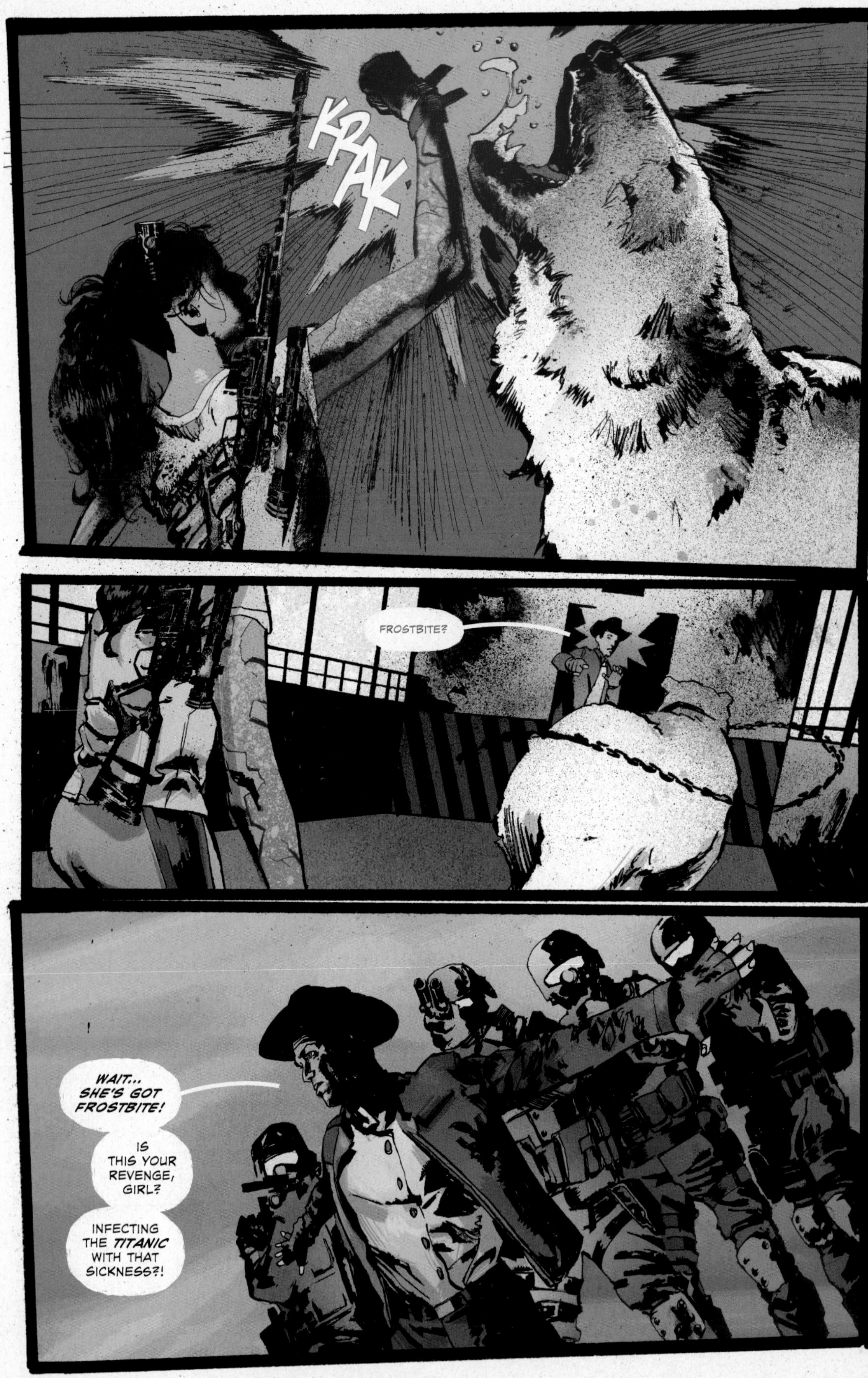
KRAK
FROSTBITE?
WAIT... SHE'S GOT FROSTBITE!
IS THIS YOUR REVENGE, GIRL?
INFECTING THE TITANIC WITH THAT SICKNESS?!

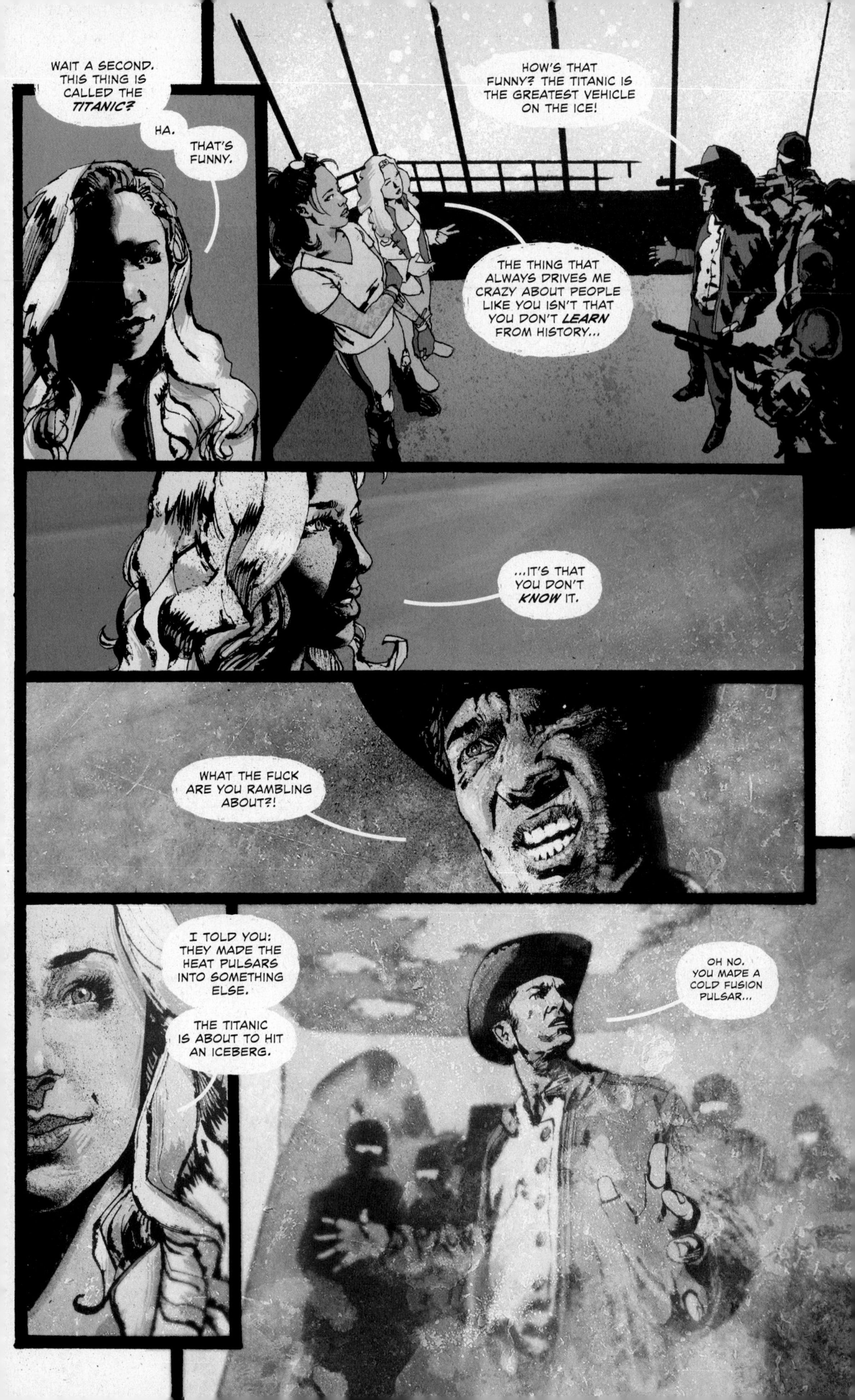
WAIT A SECOND. THIS THING IS CALLED THE TITANIC?
HA.
THAT'S FUNNY.
HOW'S THAT FUNNY? THE TITANIC IS THE GREATEST VEHICLE ON THE ICE!
THE THING THAT ALWAYS DRIVES ME CRAZY ABOUT PEOPLE LIKE YOU ISN'T THAT YOU DON'T LEARN FROM HISTORY...
...IT'S THAT YOU DON'T KNOW IT.
WHAT THE FUCK ARE YOU RAMBLING ABOUT?!
I TOLD YOU: THEY MADE THE HEAT PULSARS INTO SOMETHING ELSE.
THE TITANIC IS ABOUT TO HIT AN ICEBERG.
OH NO. YOU MADE A COLD FUSION PULSAR...

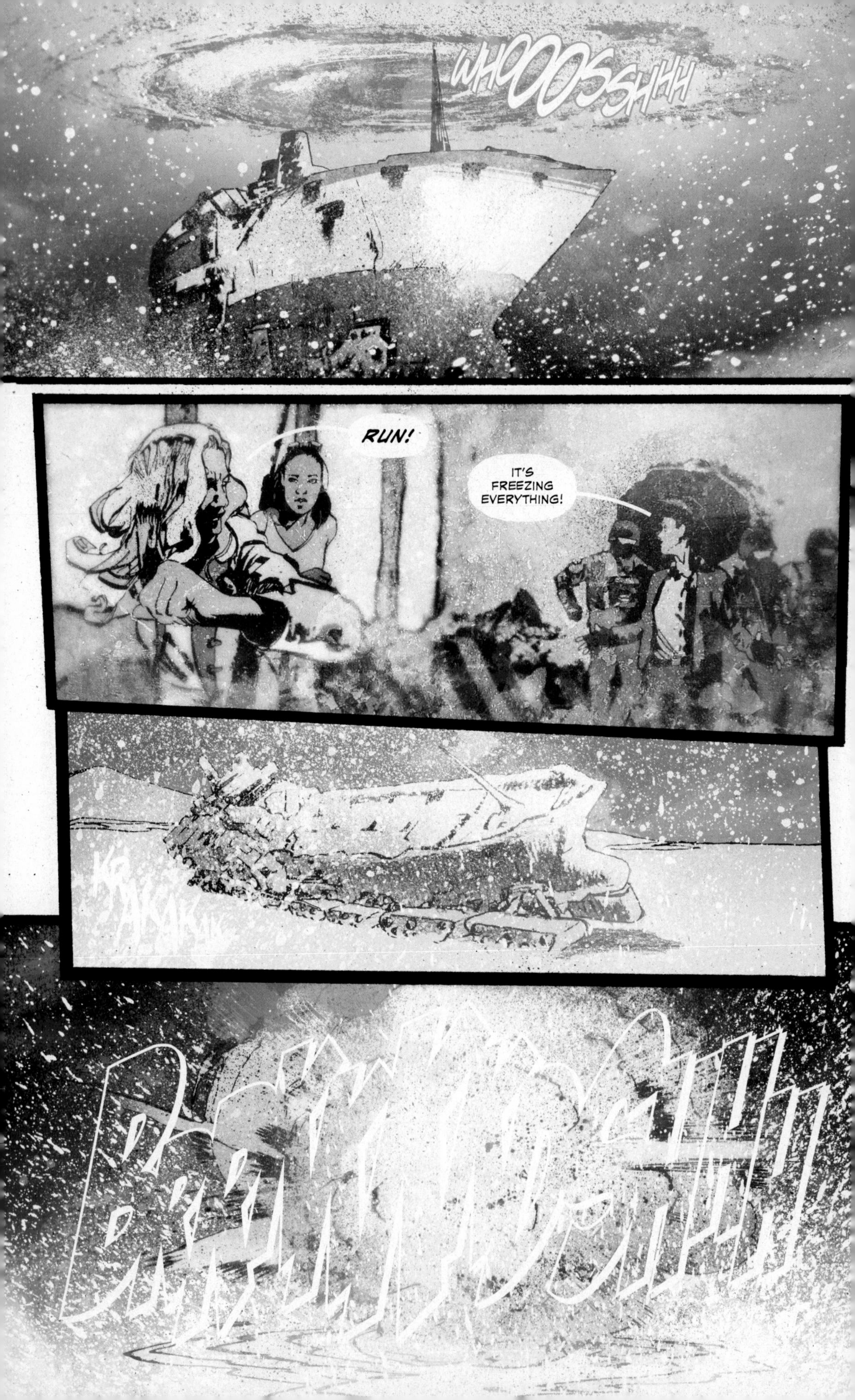
WHOOOSSHHH
RUN!
IT'S FREEZING EVERYTHING!

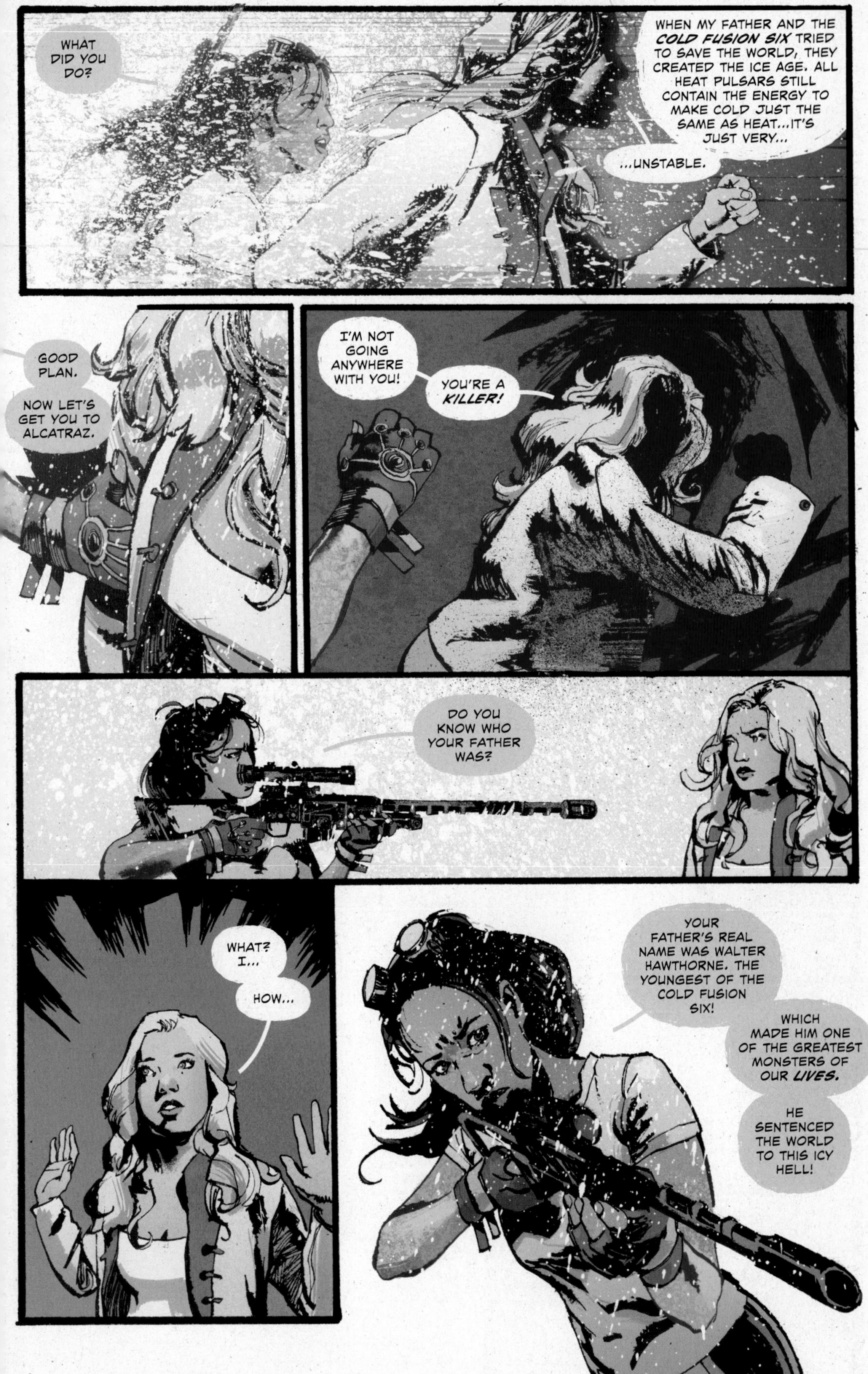

WHAT DID YOU DO?
WHEN MY FATHER AND THE COLD FUSION SIX TRIED TO SAVE THE WORLD, THEY CREATED THE ICE AGE. ALL HEAT PULSARS STILL CONTAIN THE ENERGY TO MAKE COLD JUST THE SAME AS HEAT...IT'S JUST VERY...
...UNSTABLE.
GOOD PLAN.
NOW LET'S GET YOU TO ALCATRAZ.
I'M NOT GOING ANYWHERE WITH YOU!
YOU'RE A KILLER!
DO YOU KNOW WHO YOUR FATHER WAS?
WHAT? I...
HOW...
YOUR FATHER'S REAL NAME WAS WALTER HAWTHORNE. THE YOUNGEST OF THE COLD FUSION SIX!
WHICH MADE HIM ONE OF THE GREATEST MONSTERS OF OUR LIVES.
HE SENTENCED THE WORLD TO THIS ICY HELL!

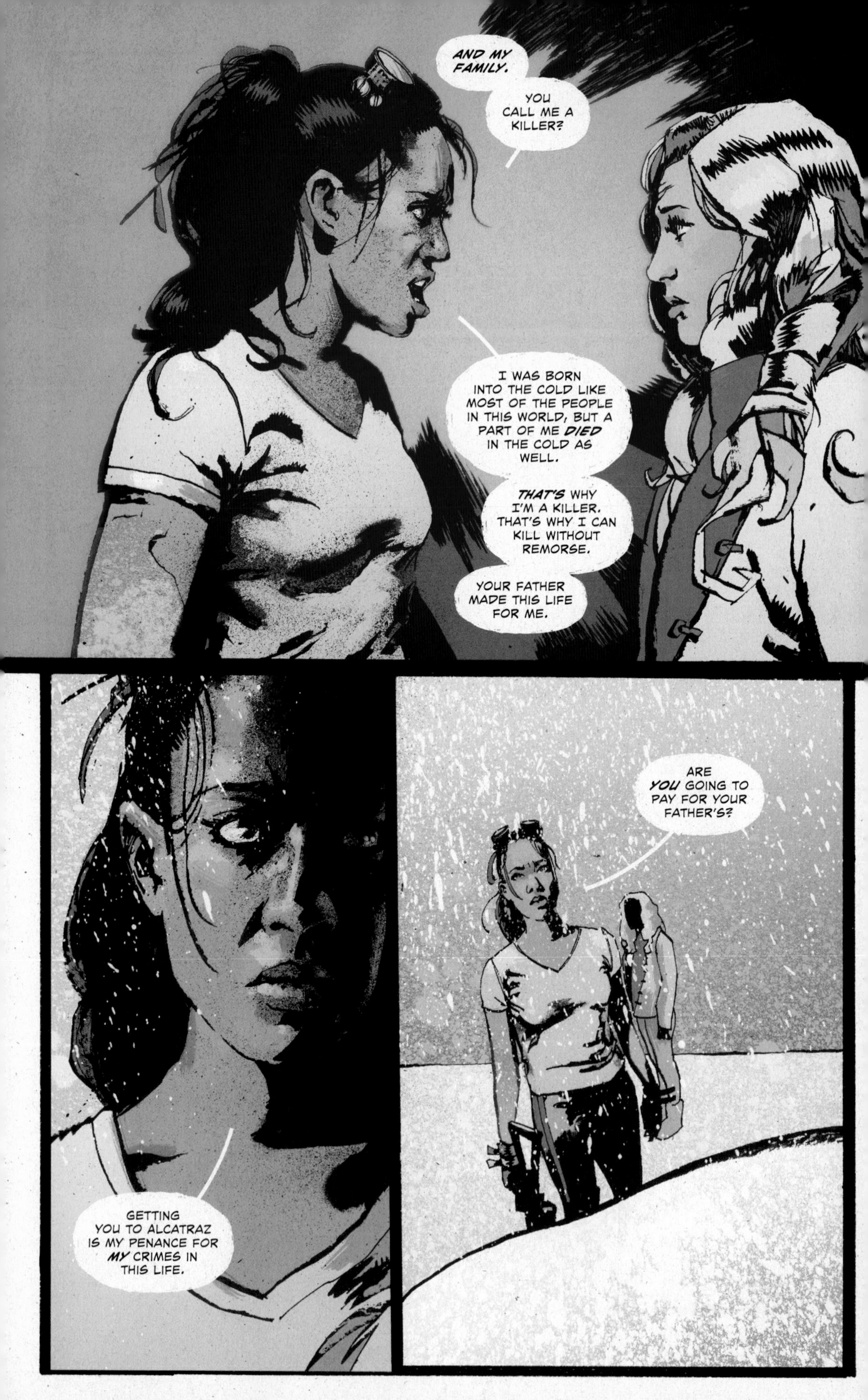
AND MY FAMILY.
YOU CALL ME A KILLER?
I WAS BORN INTO THE COLD LIKE MOST OF THE PEOPLE IN THIS WORLD, BUT A PART OF ME DIED IN THE COLD AS WELL.
THAT'S WHY I'M A KILLER. THAT'S WHY I CAN KILL WITHOUT REMORSE.
YOUR FATHER MADE THIS LIFE FOR ME.
GETTING YOU TO ALCATRAZ IS MY PENANCE FOR MY CRIMES IN THIS LIFE.
ARE YOU GOING TO PAY FOR YOUR FATHER'S?

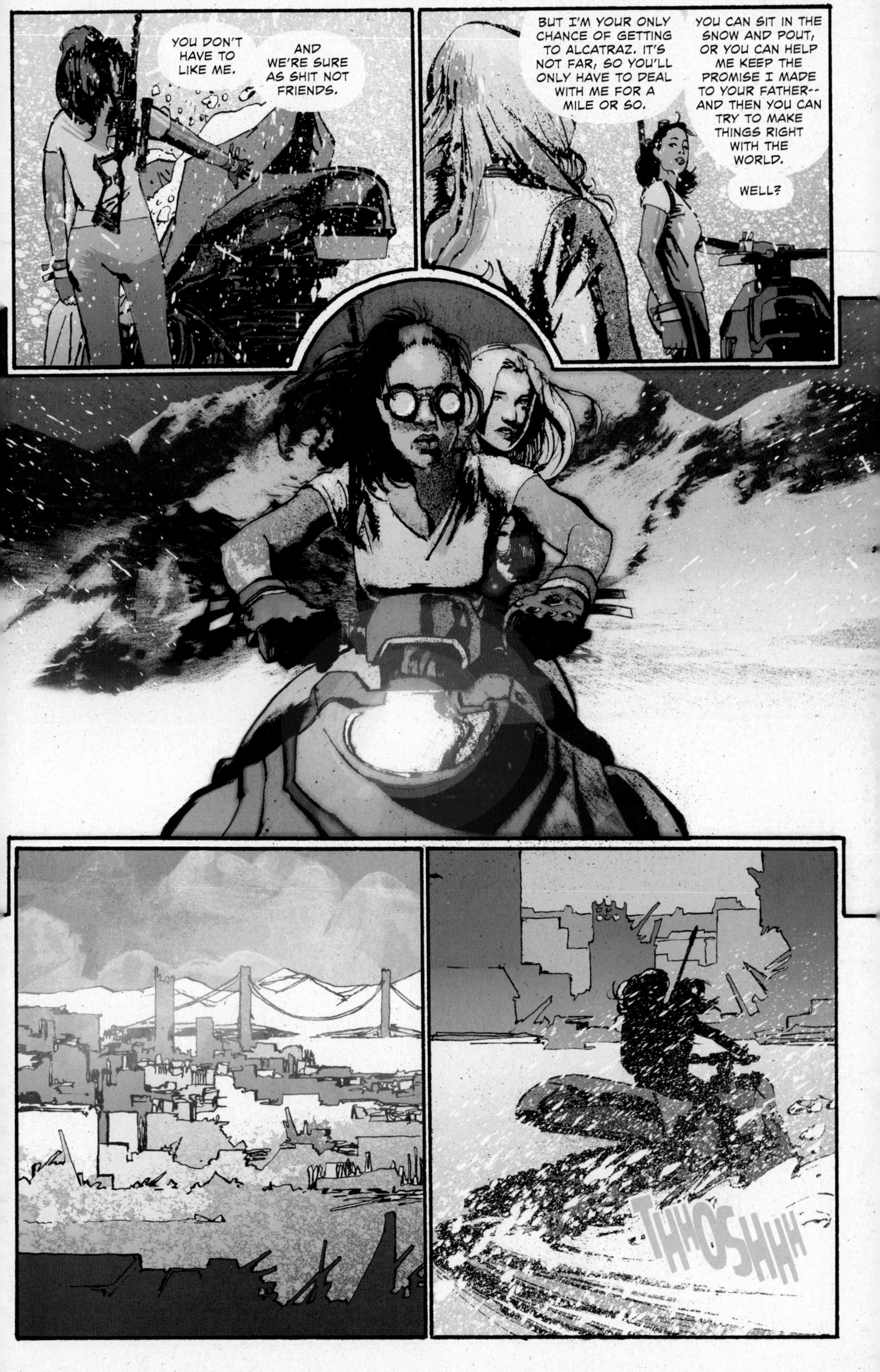
YOU DON'T HAVE TO LIKE ME.
AND WE'RE SURE AS SHIT NOT FRIENDS.
BUT I'M YOUR ONLY CHANCE OF GETTING TO ALCATRAZ. IT'S NOT FAR, SO YOU'LL ONLY HAVE TO DEAL WITH ME FOR A MILE OR SO.
YOU CAN SIT IN THE SNOW AND POUT, OR YOU CAN HELP ME KEEP THE PROMISE I MADE TO YOUR FATHER-- AND THEN YOU CAN TRY TO MAKE THINGS RIGHT WITH THE WORLD.
WELL?
THHOSHHH

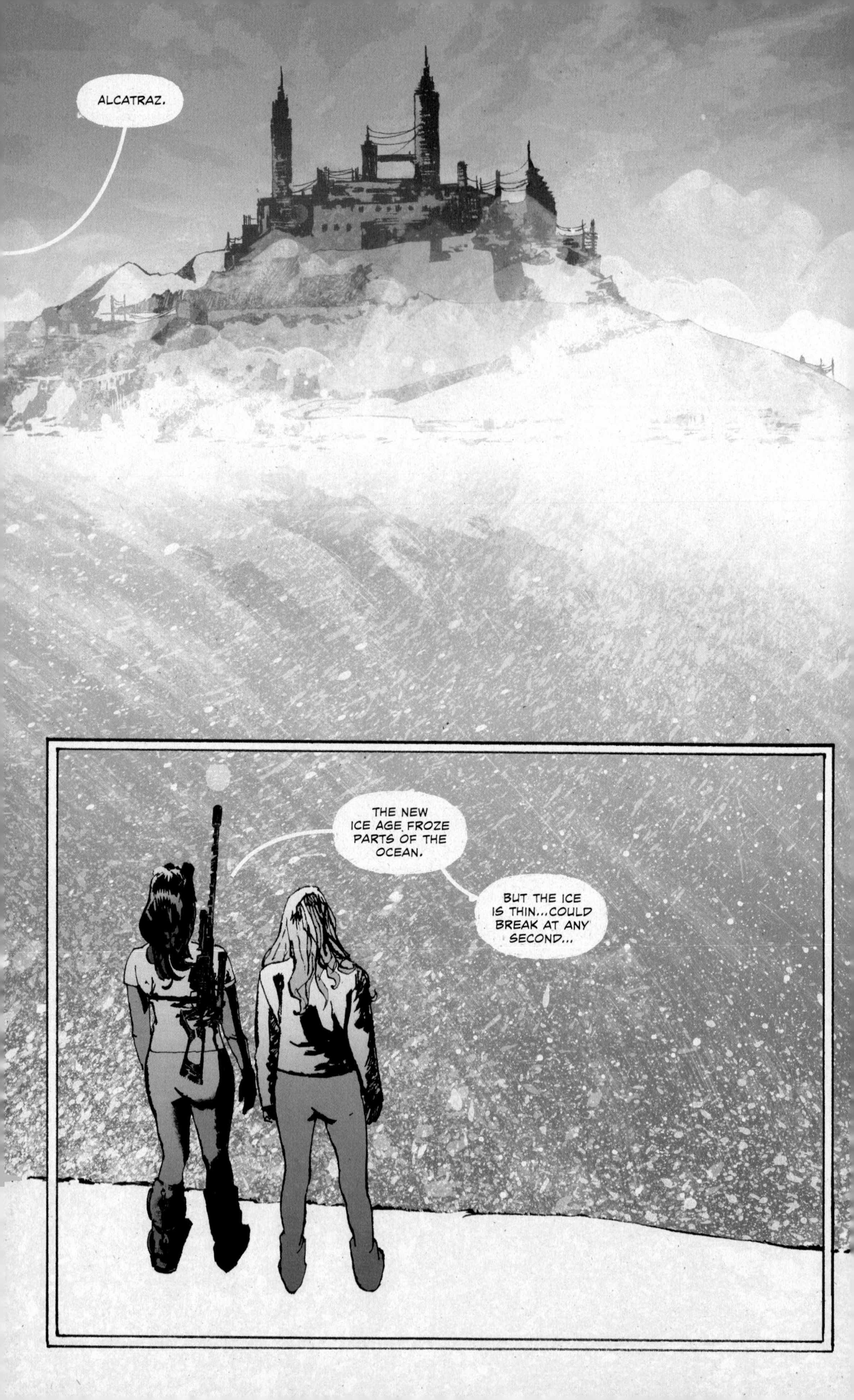
ALCATRAZ.
THE NEW ICE AGE FROZE PARTS OF THE OCEAN.
BUT THE ICE IS THIN...COULD BREAK AT ANY SECOND...

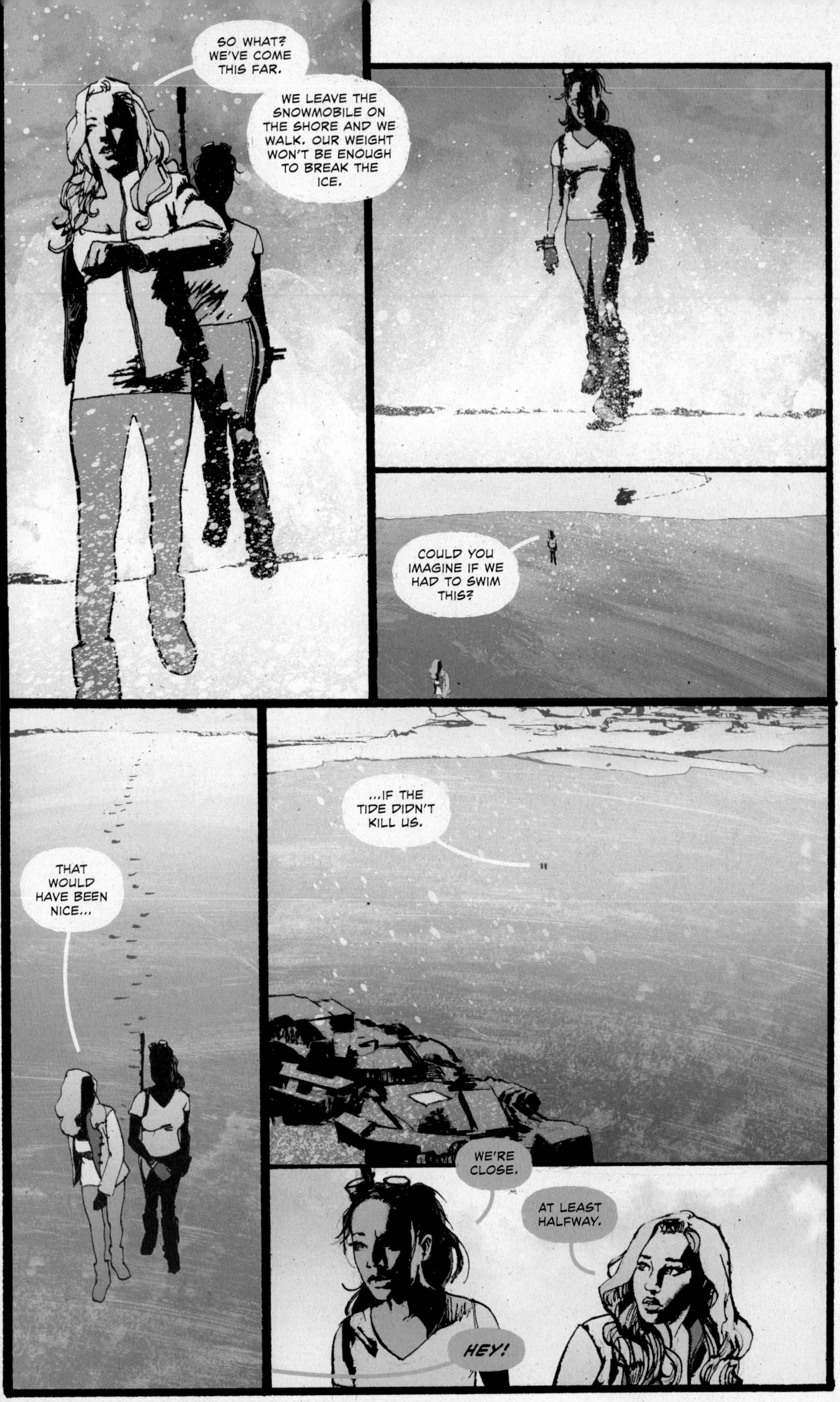
SO WHAT? WE'VE COME THIS FAR.
WE LEAVE THE SNOWMOBILE ON THE SHORE AND WE WALK. OUR WEIGHT WON'T BE ENOUGH TO BREAK THE ICE.
COULD YOU IMAGINE IF WE HAD TO SWIM THIS?
...IF THE TIDE DIDN'T KILL US.
THAT WOULD HAVE BEEN NICE...
WE'RE CLOSE.
AT LEAST HALFWAY.
HEY!

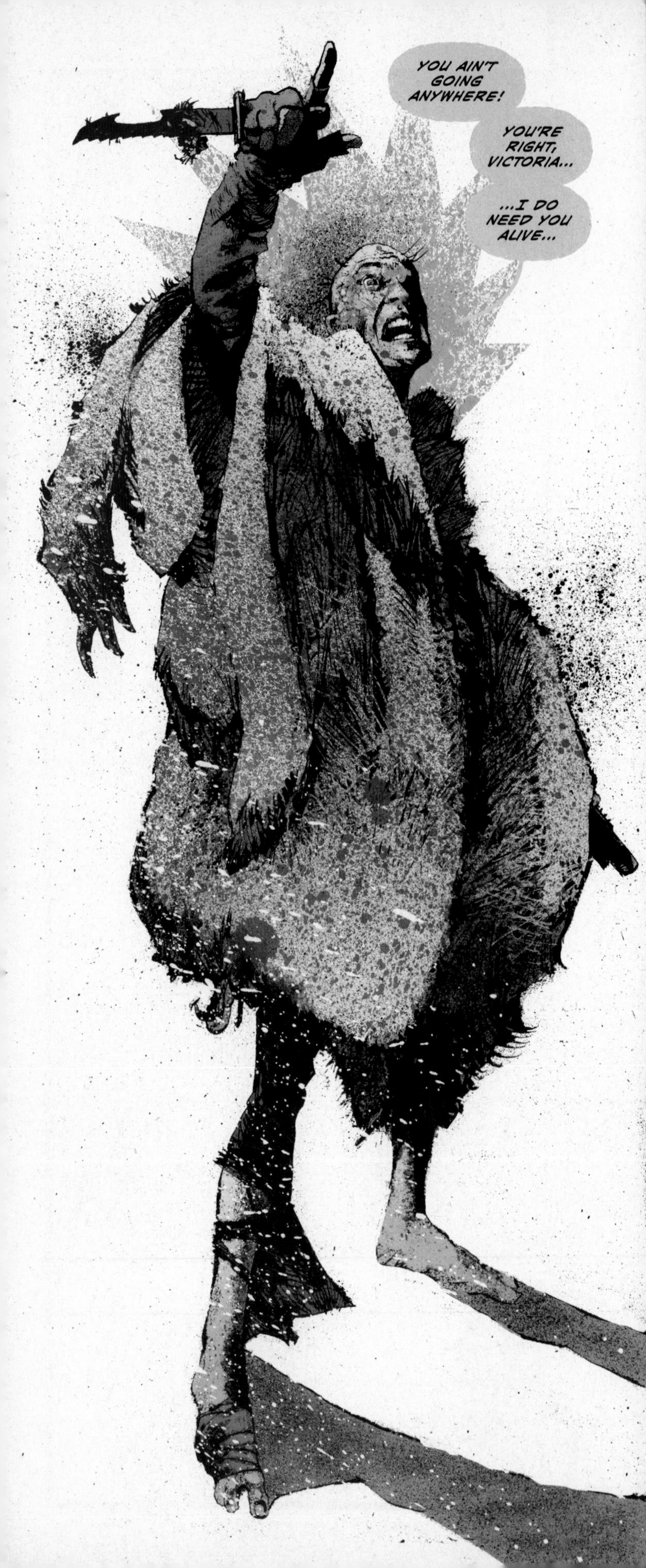
YOU AIN'T GOING ANYWHERE!
YOU'RE RIGHT, VICTORIA...
...I DO NEED YOU ALIVE...

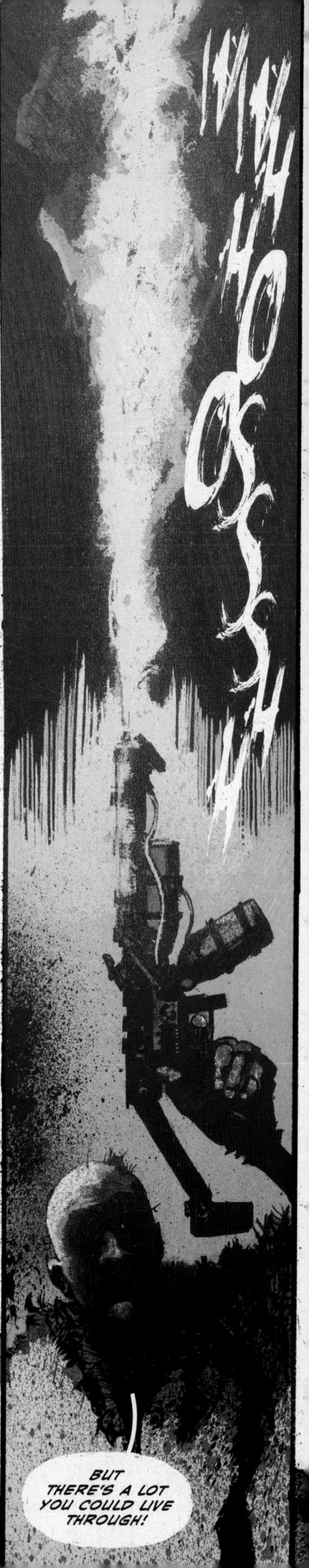
WHOOSHH
BUT THERE'S A LOT YOU COULD LIVE THROUGH!

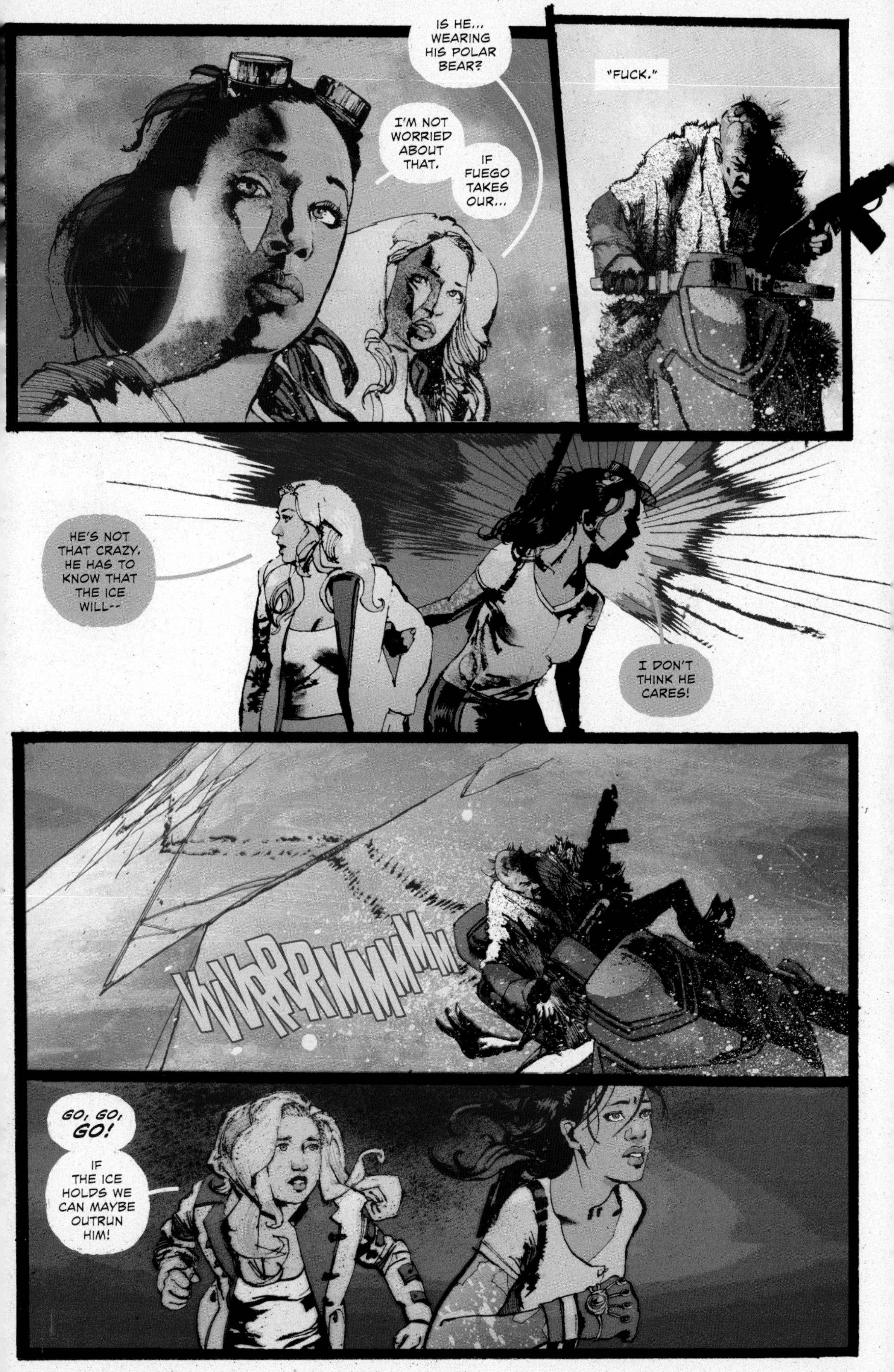
IS HE... WEARING HIS POLAR BEAR?
I'M NOT WORRIED ABOUT THAT.
IF FUEGO TAKES OUR...
"FUCK."
HE'S NOT THAT CRAZY. HE HAS TO KNOW THAT THE ICE WILL--
I DON'T THINK HE CARES!
WVRRRMMMMMM
GO, GO, GO!
IF THE ICE HOLDS WE CAN MAYBE OUTRUN HIM!

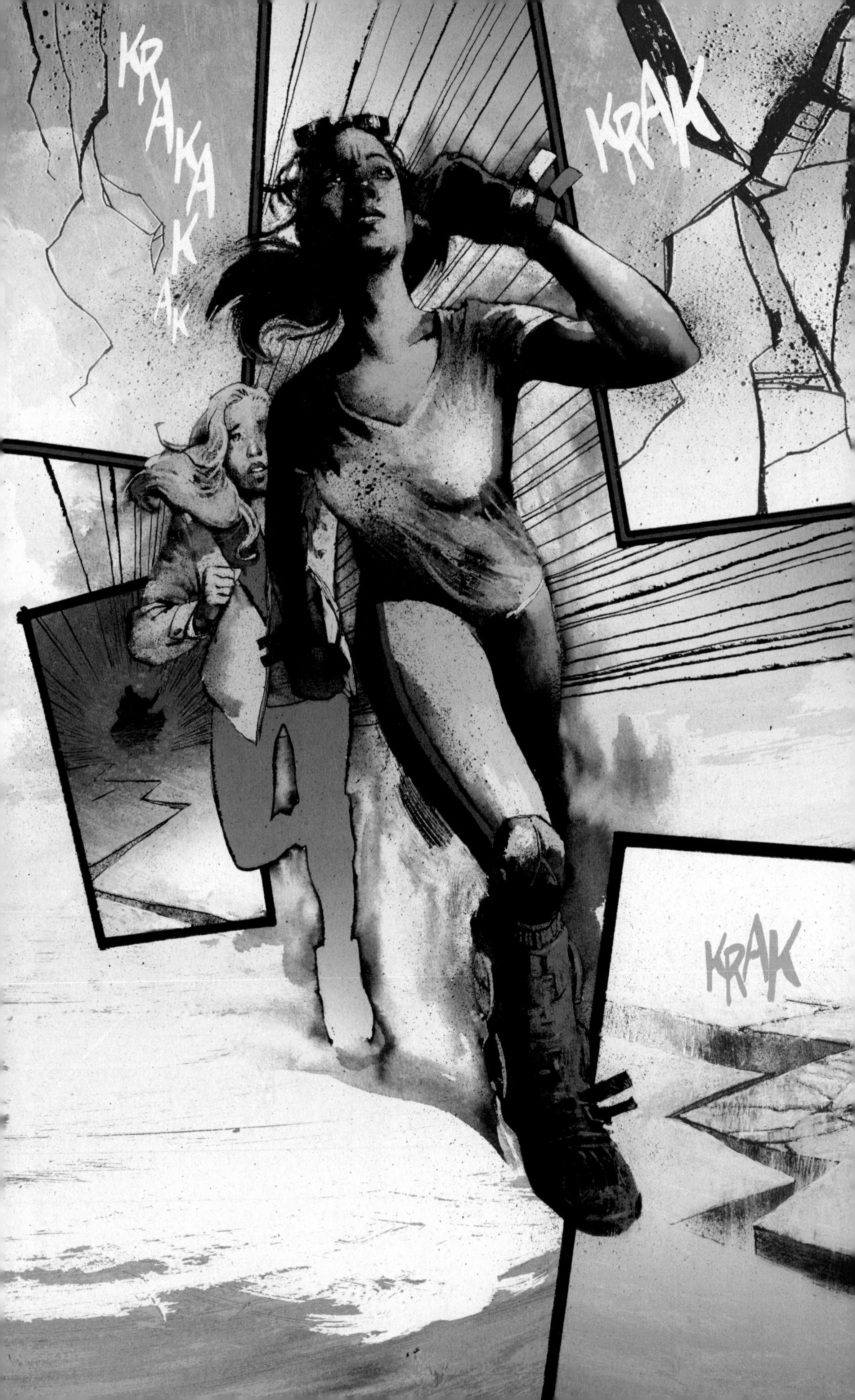
KRAKAKAKAK
KRAK
KRAK

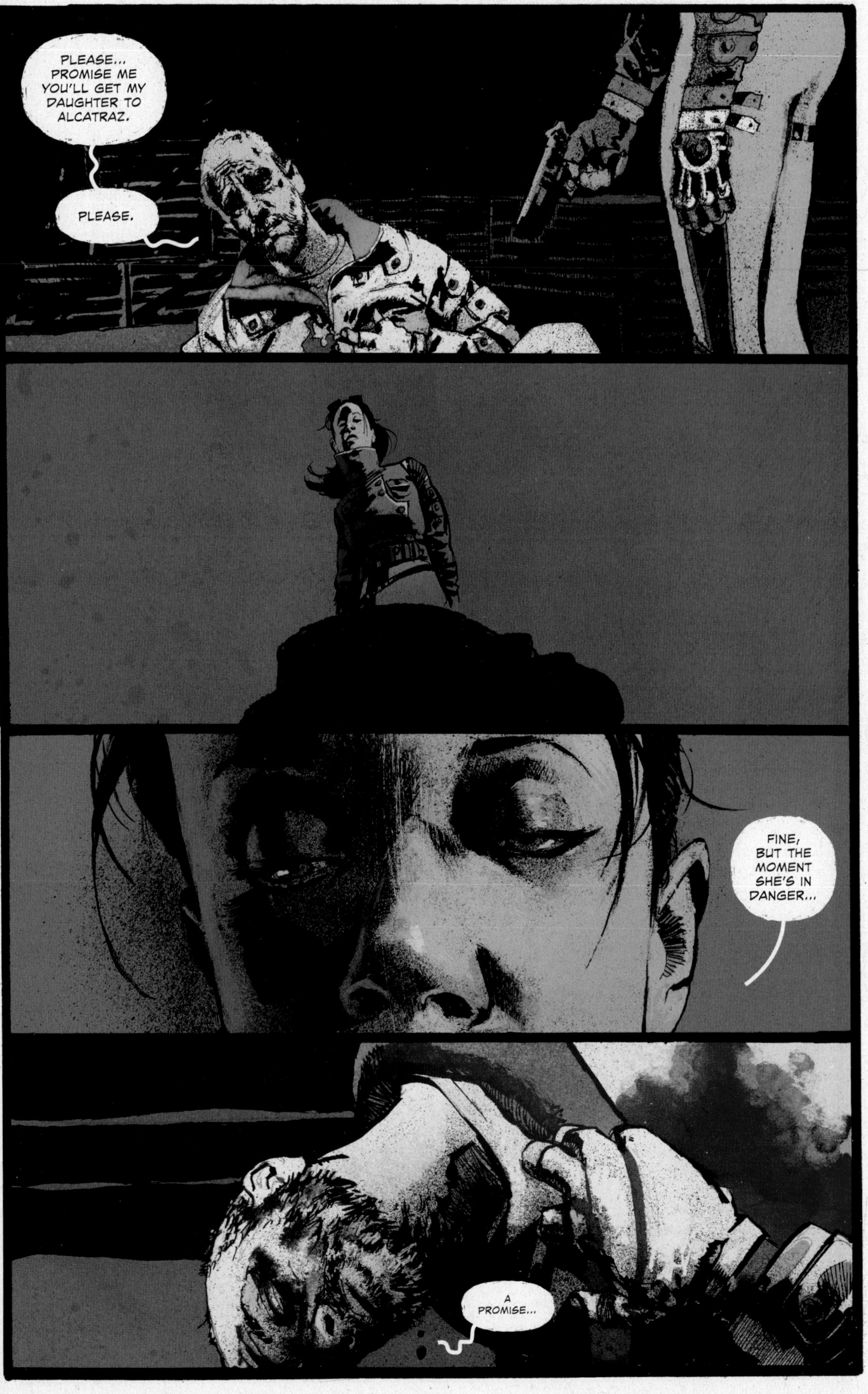
PLEASE... PROMISE ME YOU'LL GET MY DAUGHTER TO ALCATRAZ.
PLEASE.
FINE, BUT THE MOMENT SHE'S IN DANGER...
A PROMISE...

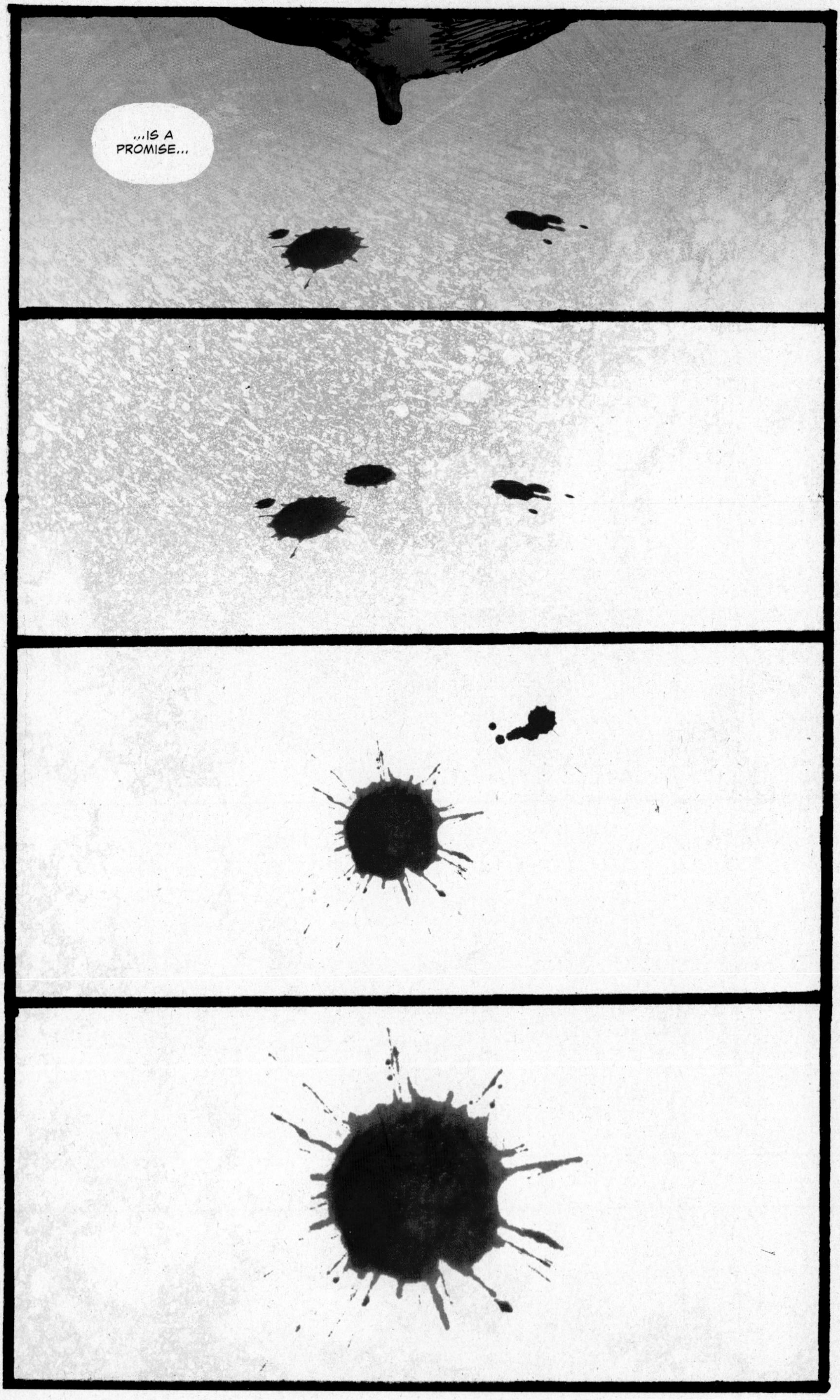
...IS A PROMISE...

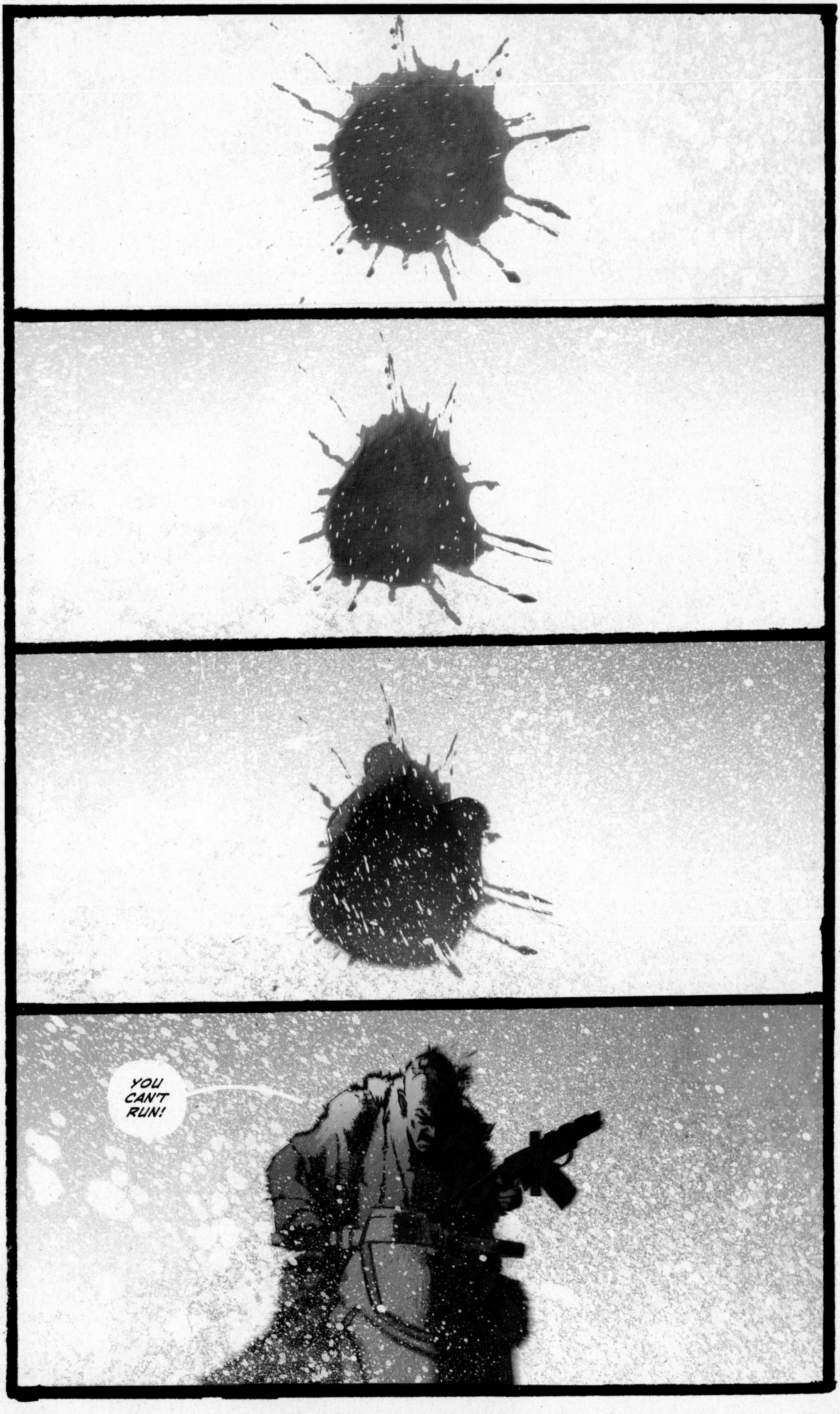
YOU CAN'T RUN!

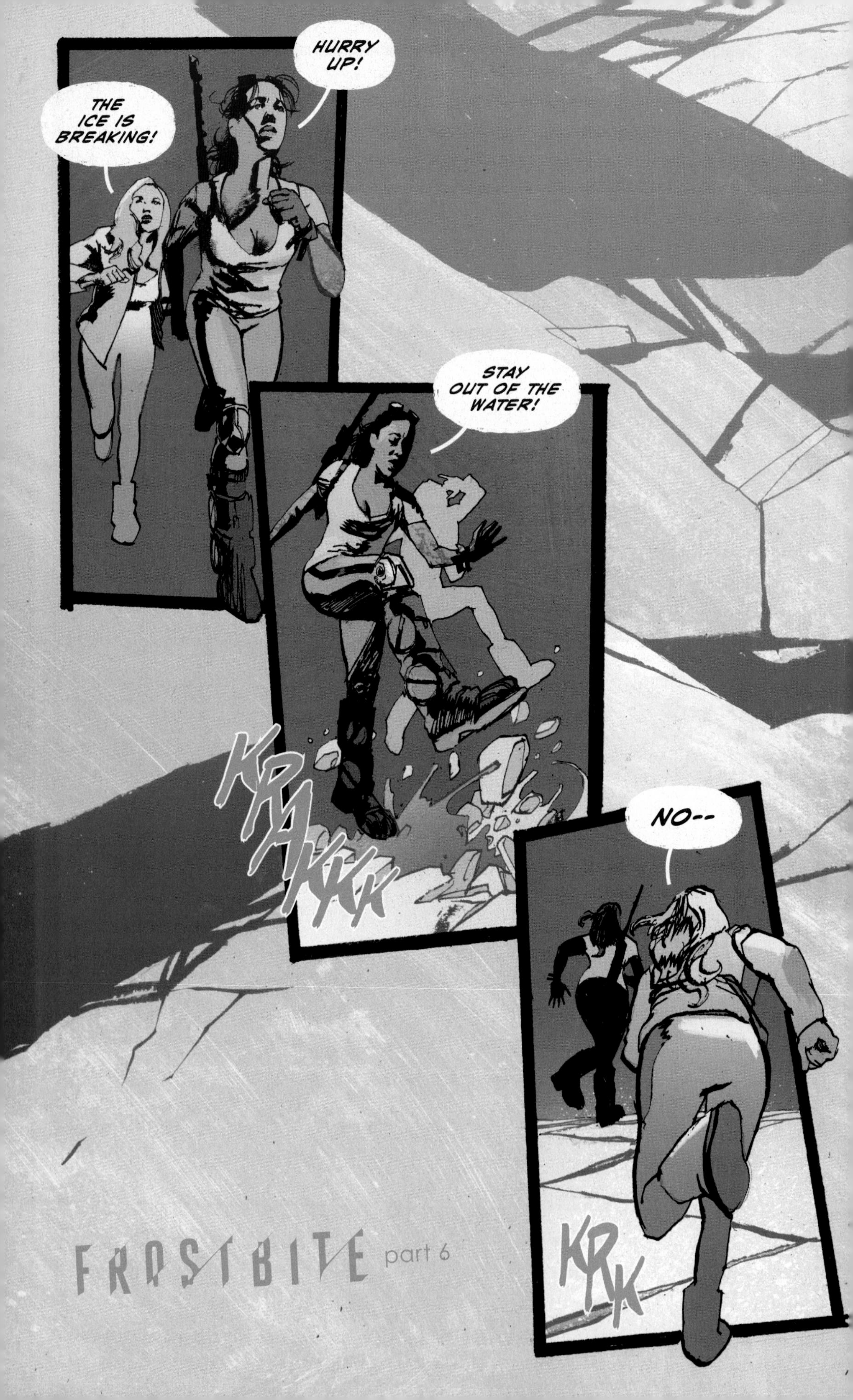
THE ICE IS BREAKING!
HURRY UP!
STAY OUT OF THE WATER!
KRAKKK
NO--
KRK
FROSTBITE part 6

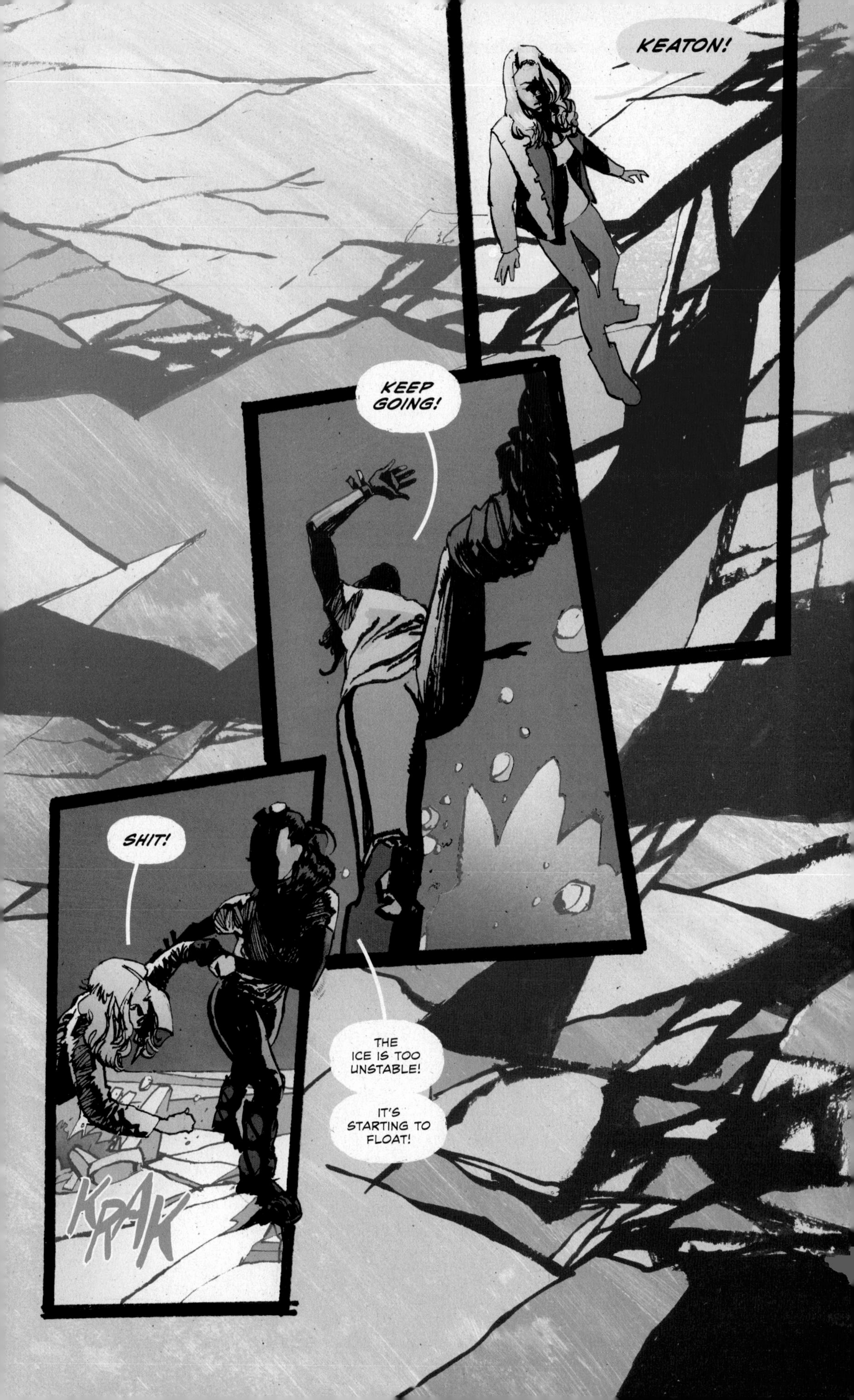
KEATON!
KEEP GOING!
SHIT!
THE ICE IS TOO UNSTABLE!
IT'S STARTING TO FLOAT!
KRAK

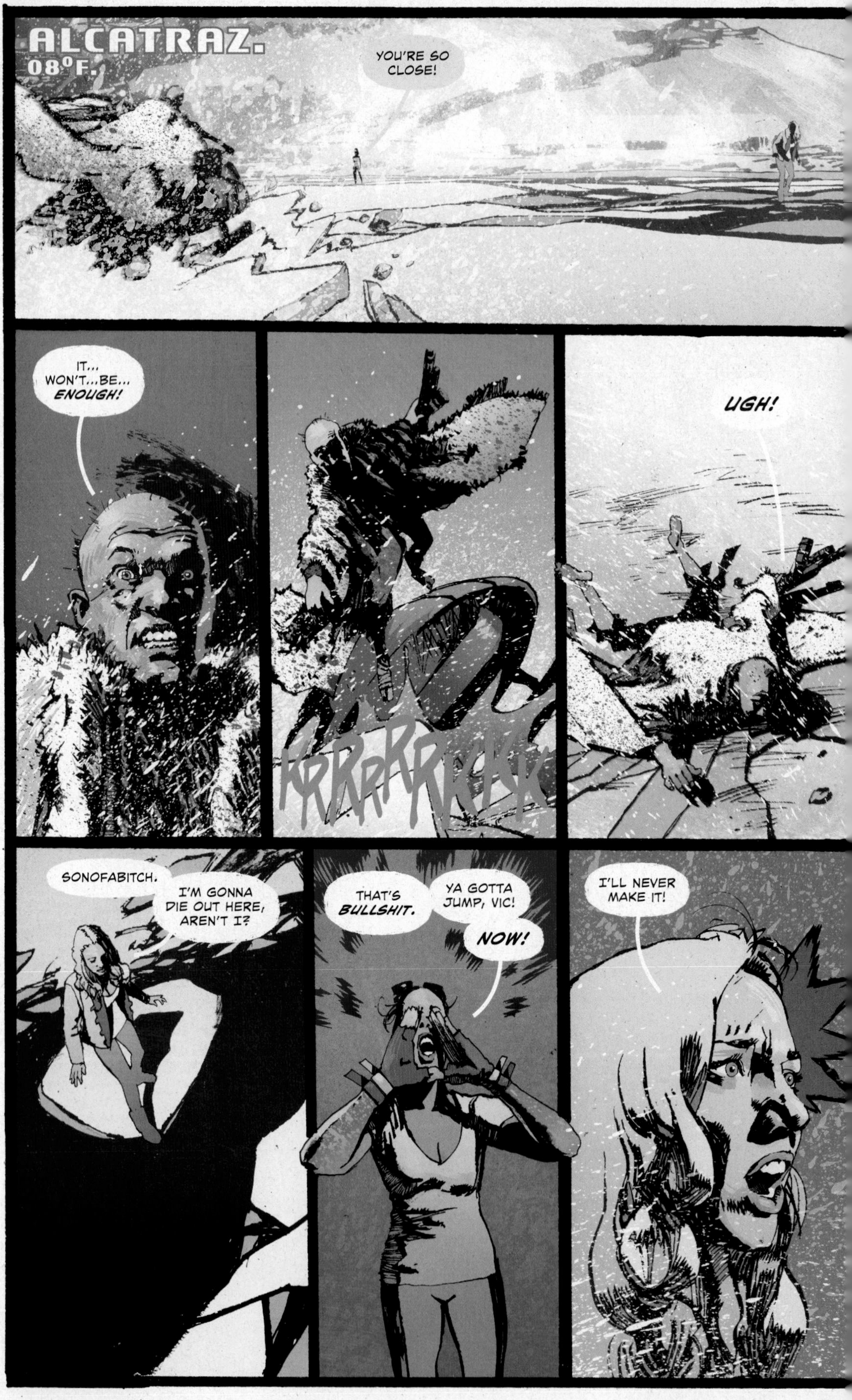
ALCATRAZ.
08°F.
YOU'RE SO CLOSE!
IT... WON'T...BE... ENOUGH!
KRRRRRKKK
UGH!
SONOFABITCH.
I'M GONNA DIE OUT HERE, AREN'T I?
THAT'S BULLSHIT.
YA GOTTA JUMP, VIC!
NOW!
I'LL NEVER MAKE IT!

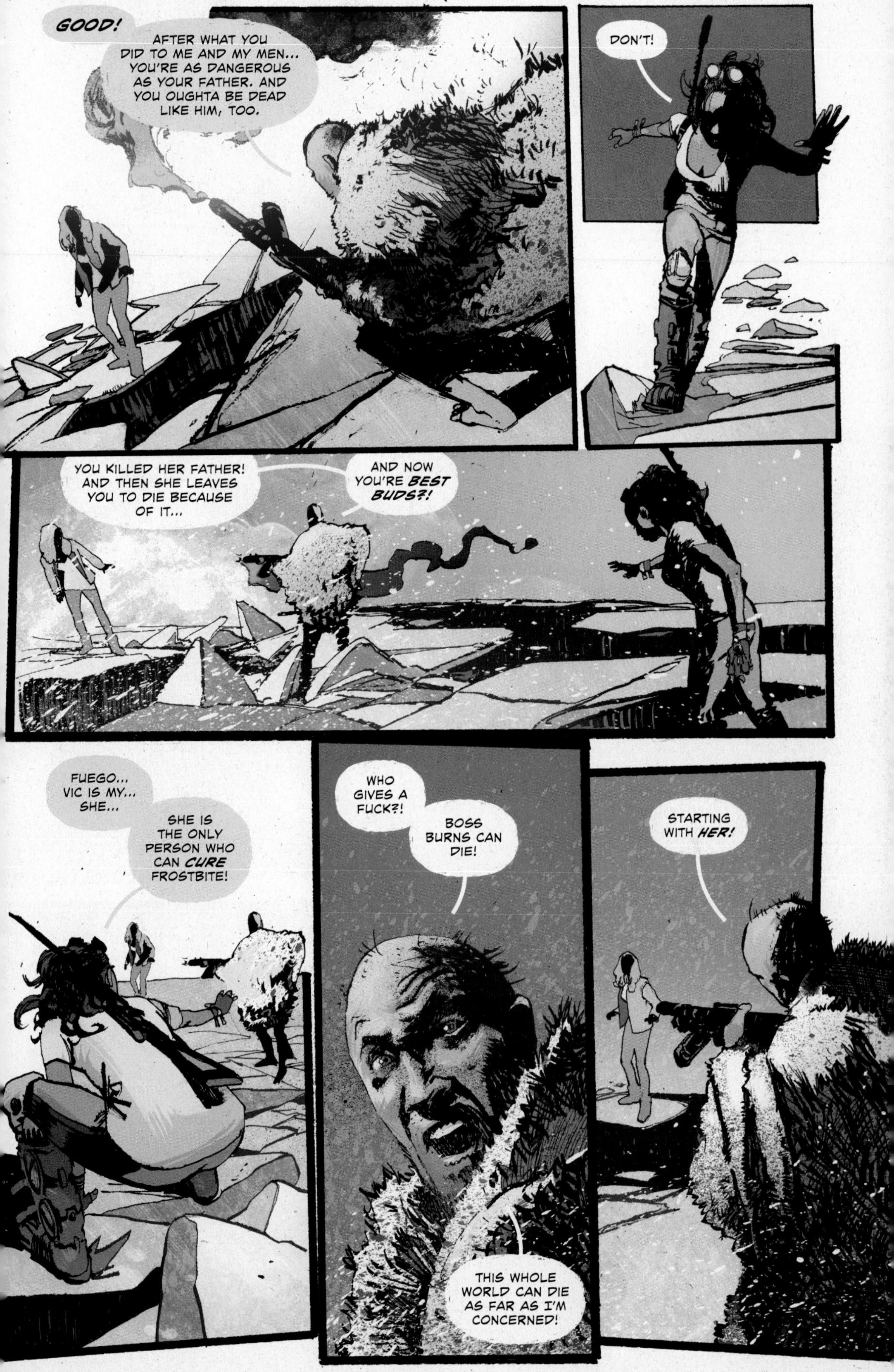
GOOD!
AFTER WHAT YOU DID TO ME AND MY MEN... YOU'RE AS DANGEROUS AS YOUR FATHER. AND YOU OUGHTA BE DEAD LIKE HIM, TOO.
DON'T!
YOU KILLED HER FATHER! AND THEN SHE LEAVES YOU TO DIE BECAUSE OF IT...
AND NOW YOU'RE BEST BUDS?!
FUEGO... VIC IS MY... SHE...
SHE IS THE ONLY PERSON WHO CAN CURE FROSTBITE!
WHO GIVES A FUCK?!
BOSS BURNS CAN DIE!
THIS WHOLE WORLD CAN DIE AS FAR AS I'M CONCERNED!
STARTING WITH HER!

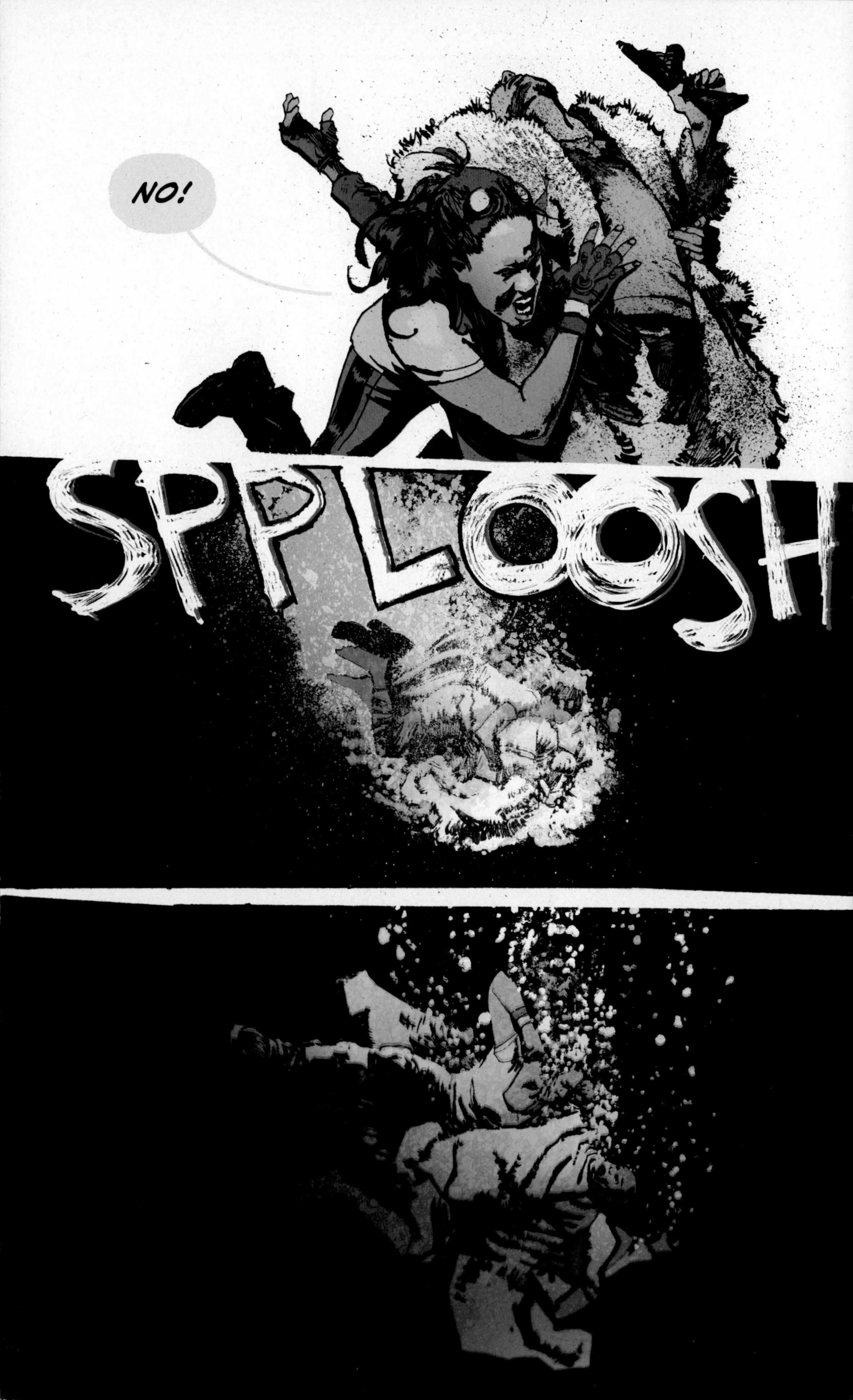
NO!
SPPLOOSH

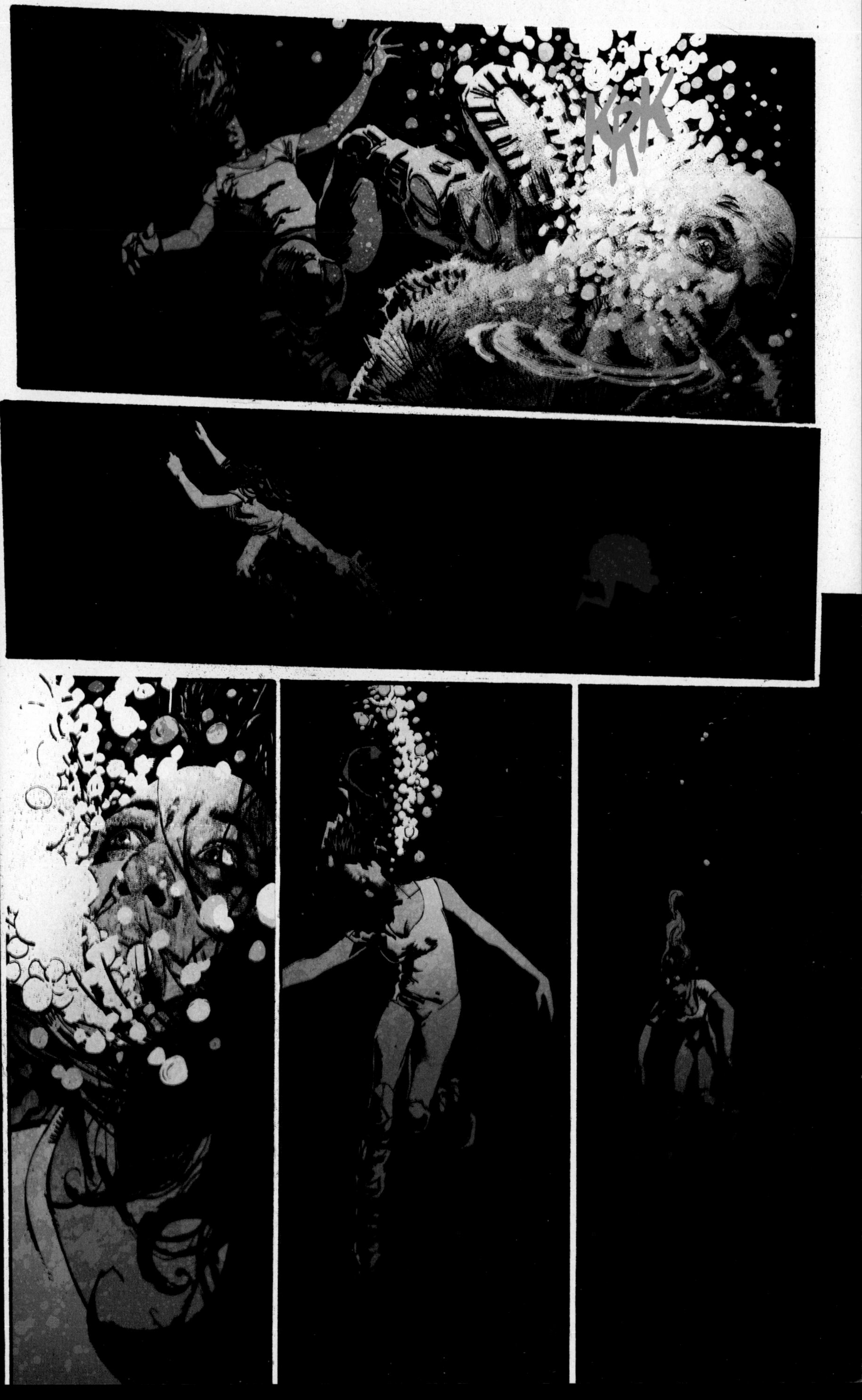
KRK

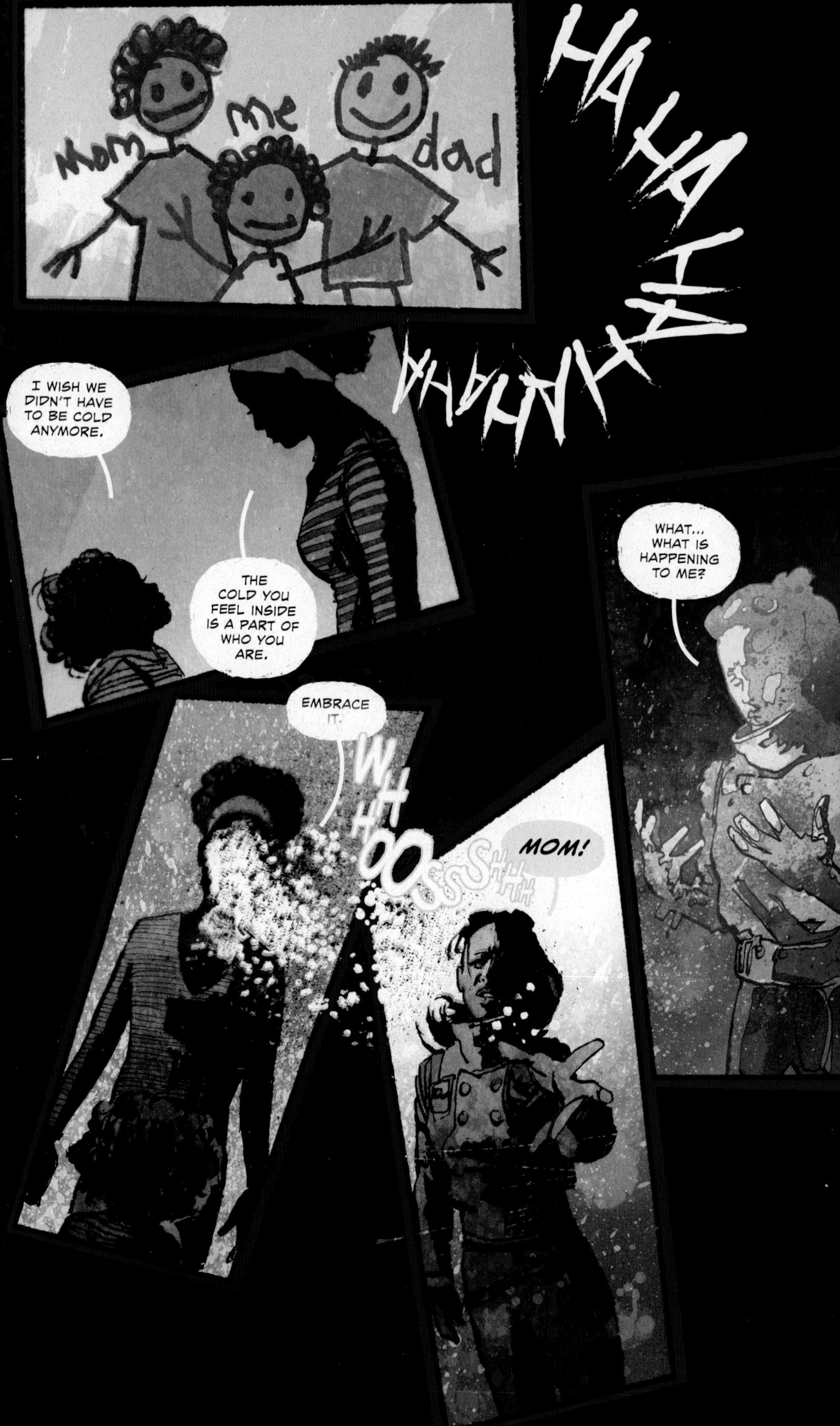
mom
me
dad
HAHAHAHAHAHAHA
I WISH WE DIDN'T HAVE TO BE COLD ANYMORE.
THE COLD YOU FEEL INSIDE IS A PART OF WHO YOU ARE.
WHAT... WHAT IS HAPPENING TO ME?
EMBRACE IT.
WHHOOSSSHHH
MOM!

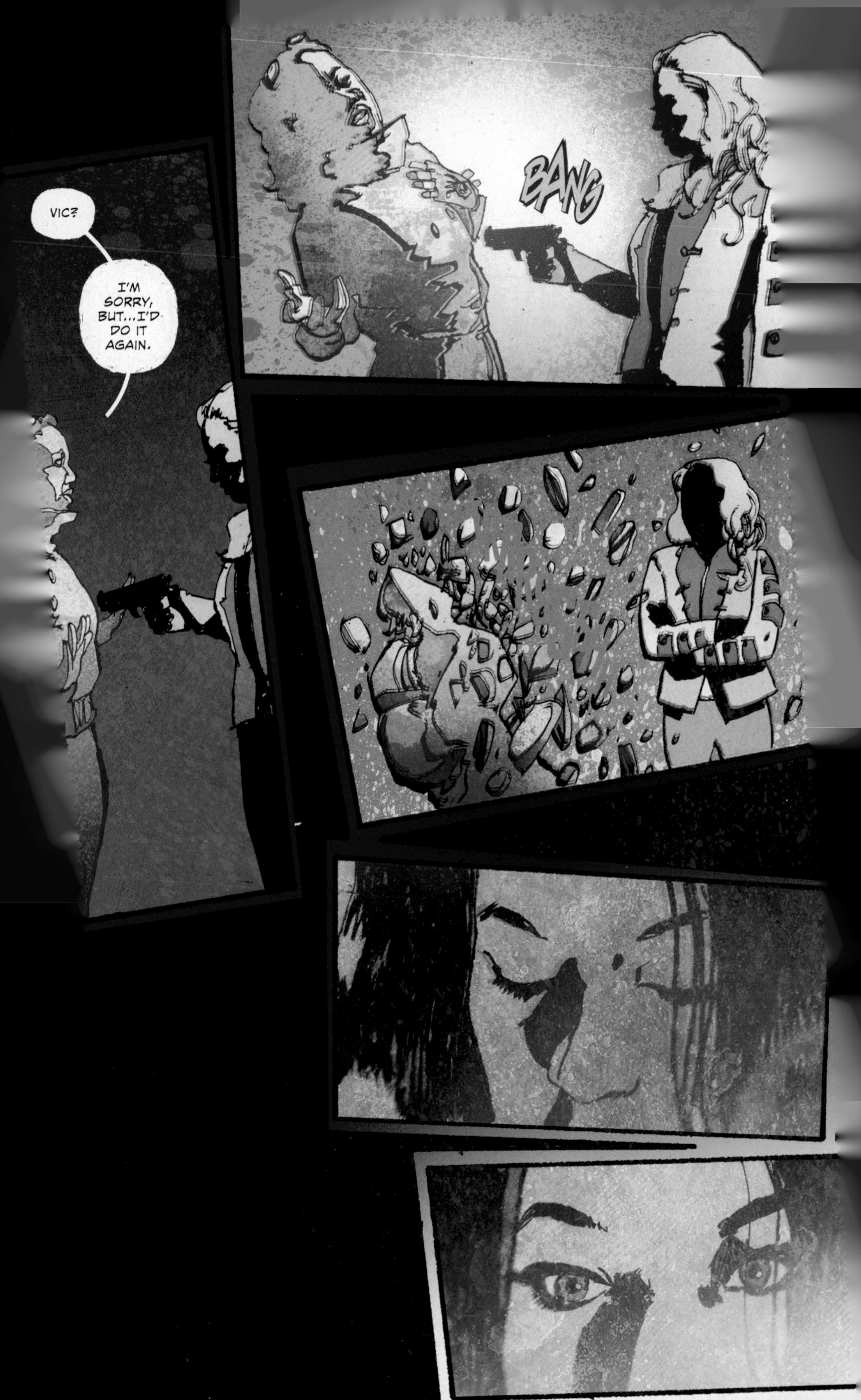
BANG
VIC?
I'M SORRY, BUT...I'D DO IT AGAIN.

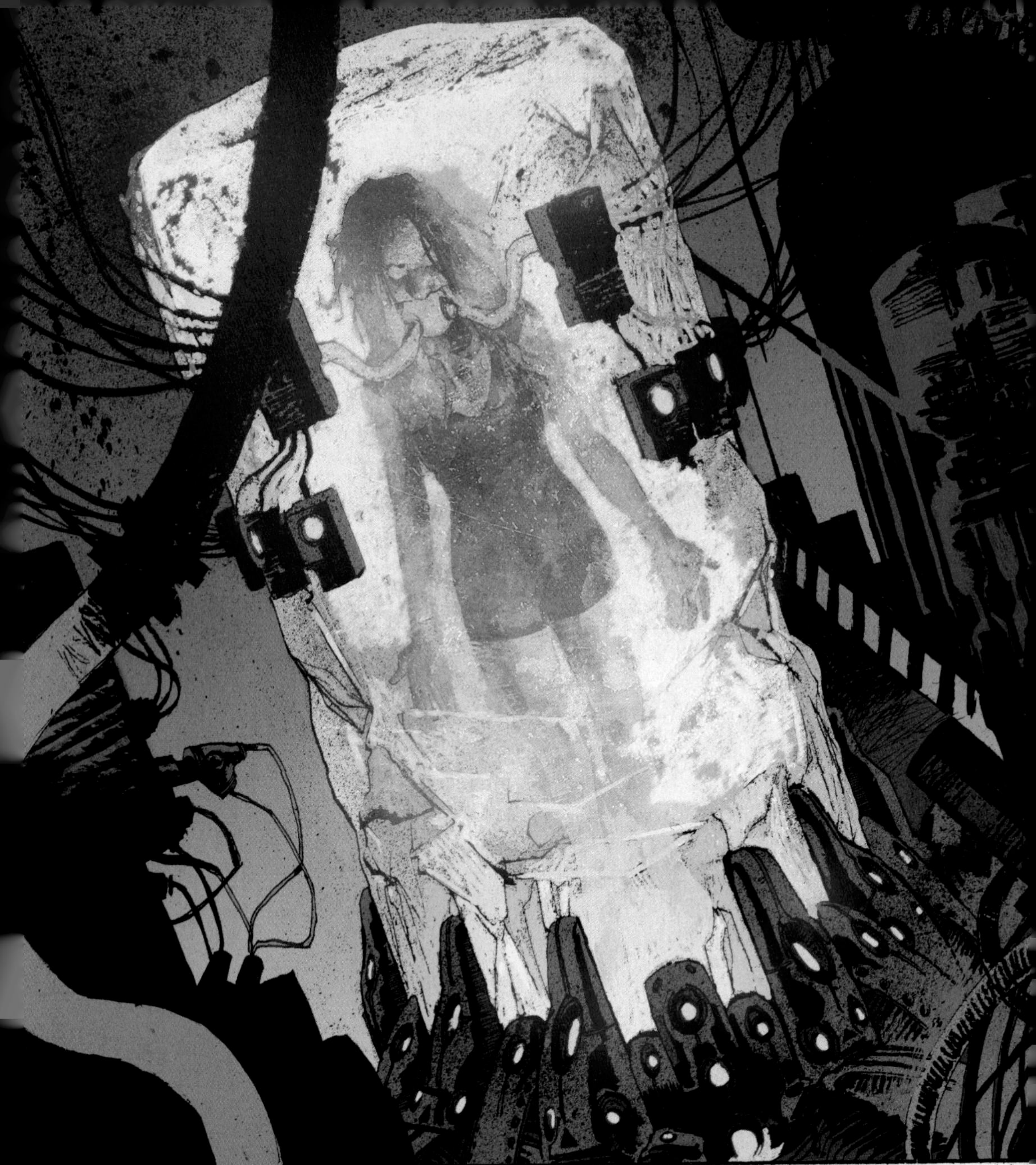

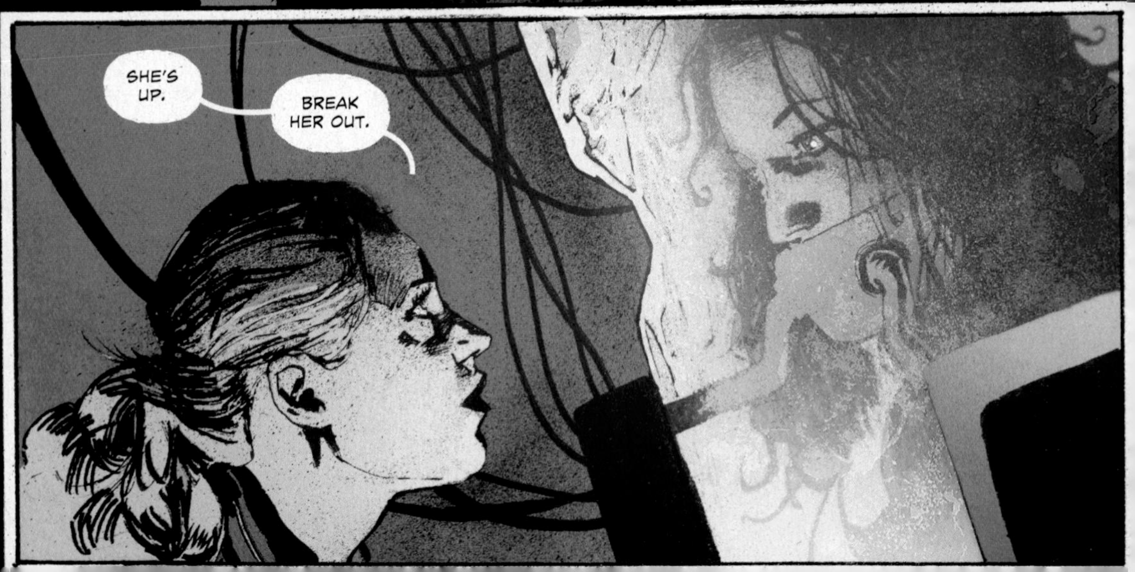
SHE'S UP.
BREAK HER OUT.

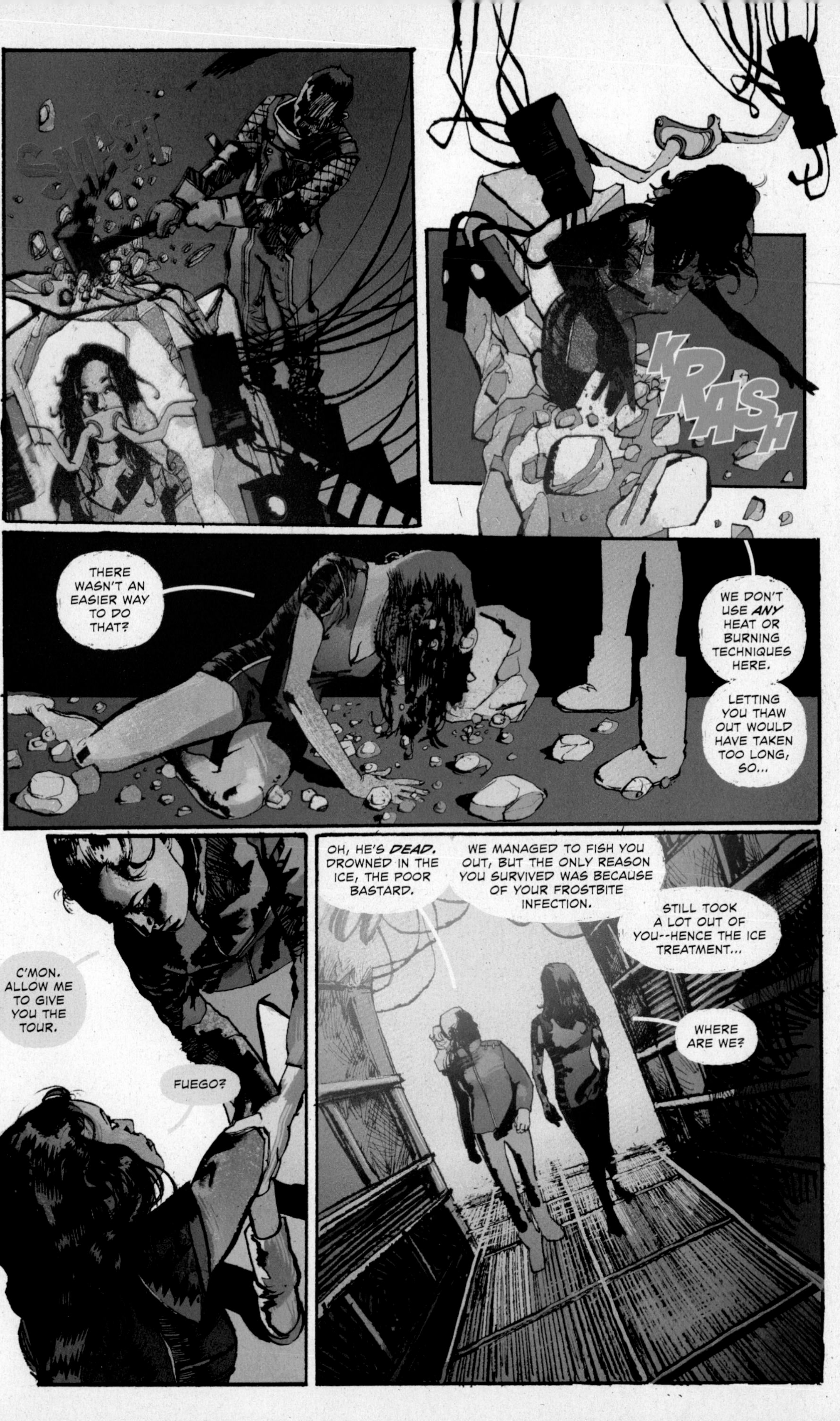
SMASH
KRASH
THERE WASN'T AN EASIER WAY TO DO THAT?
WE DON'T USE ANY HEAT OR BURNING TECHNIQUES HERE.
LETTING YOU THAW OUT WOULD HAVE TAKEN TOO LONG, SO...
C'MON. ALLOW ME TO GIVE YOU THE TOUR.
FUEGO?
OH, HE'S DEAD. DROWNED IN THE ICE, THE POOR BASTARD.
WE MANAGED TO FISH YOU OUT, BUT THE ONLY REASON YOU SURVIVED WAS BECAUSE OF YOUR FROSTBITE INFECTION.
STILL TOOK A LOT OUT OF YOU--HENCE THE ICE TREATMENT...
WHERE ARE WE?

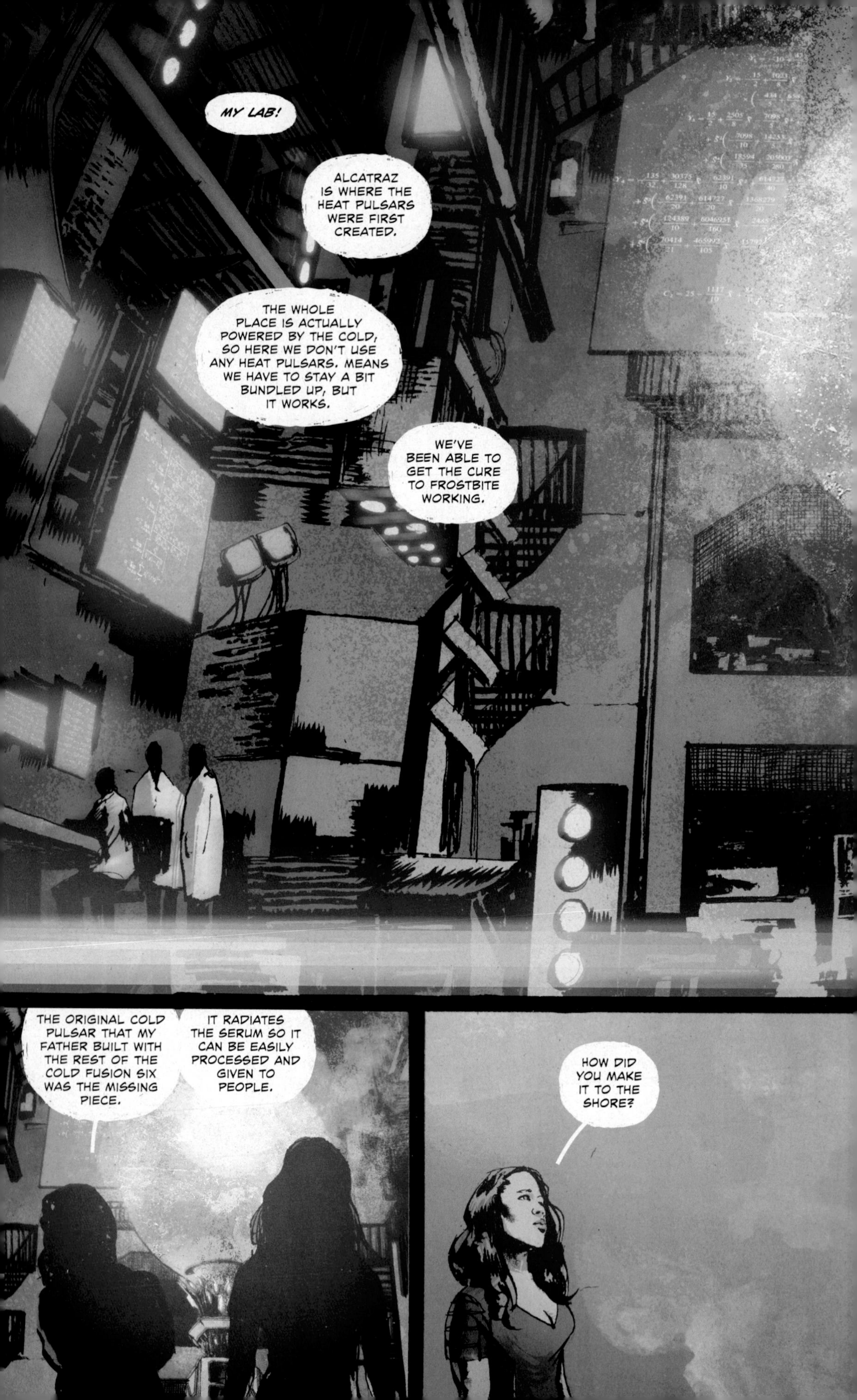
MY LAB!
ALCATRAZ IS WHERE THE HEAT PULSARS WERE FIRST CREATED.
THE WHOLE PLACE IS ACTUALLY POWERED BY THE COLD, SO HERE WE DON'T USE ANY HEAT PULSARS. MEANS WE HAVE TO STAY A BIT BUNDLED UP, BUT IT WORKS.
WE'VE BEEN ABLE TO GET THE CURE TO FROSTBITE WORKING.
THE ORIGINAL COLD PULSAR THAT MY FATHER BUILT WITH THE REST OF THE COLD FUSION SIX WAS THE MISSING PIECE.
IT RADIATES THE SERUM SO IT CAN BE EASILY PROCESSED AND GIVEN TO PEOPLE.
HOW DID YOU MAKE IT TO THE SHORE?

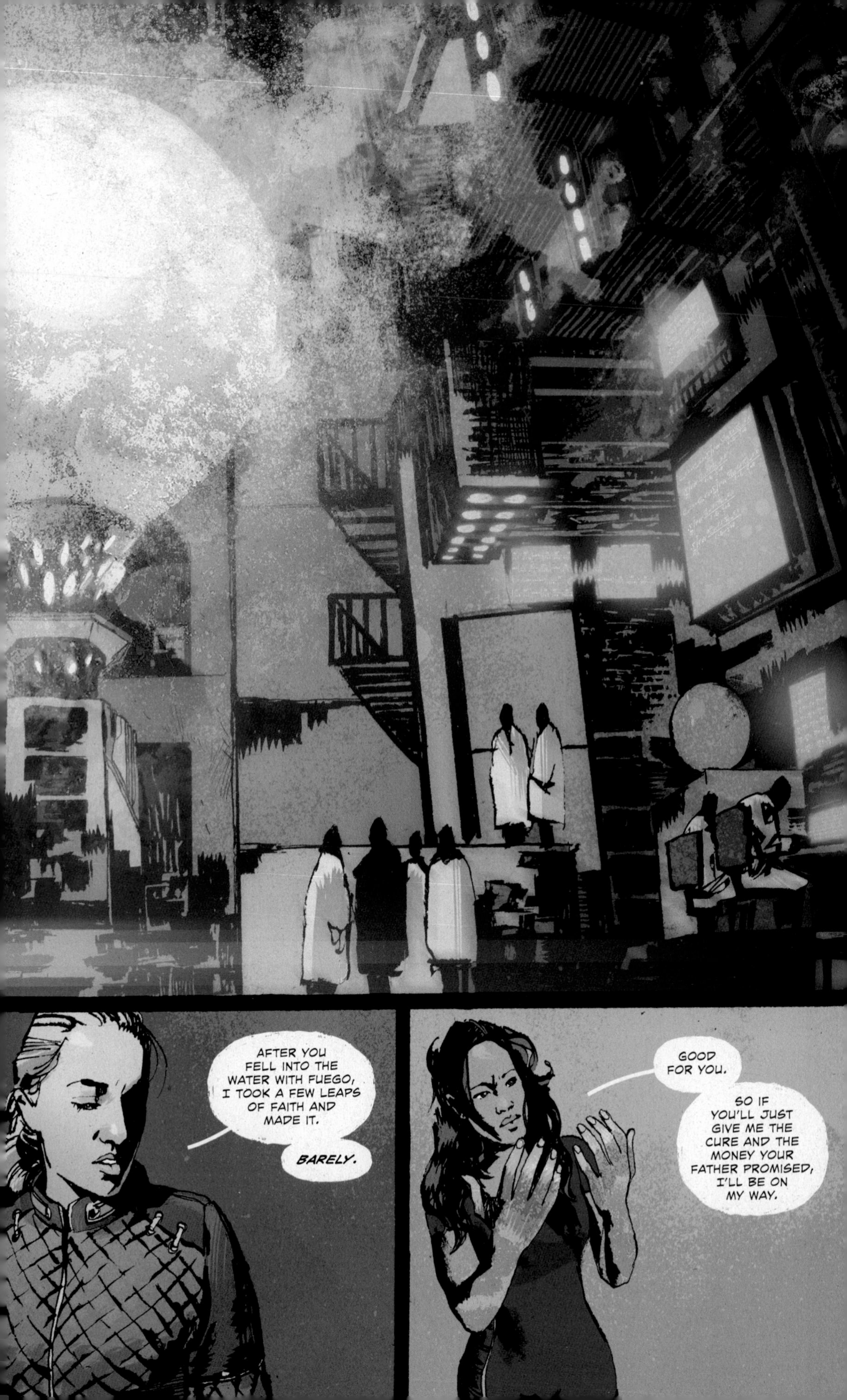
AFTER YOU FELL INTO THE WATER WITH FUEGO, I TOOK A FEW LEAPS OF FAITH AND MADE IT.
BARELY.
GOOD FOR YOU.
SO IF YOU'LL JUST GIVE ME THE CURE AND THE MONEY YOUR FATHER PROMISED, I'LL BE ON MY WAY.

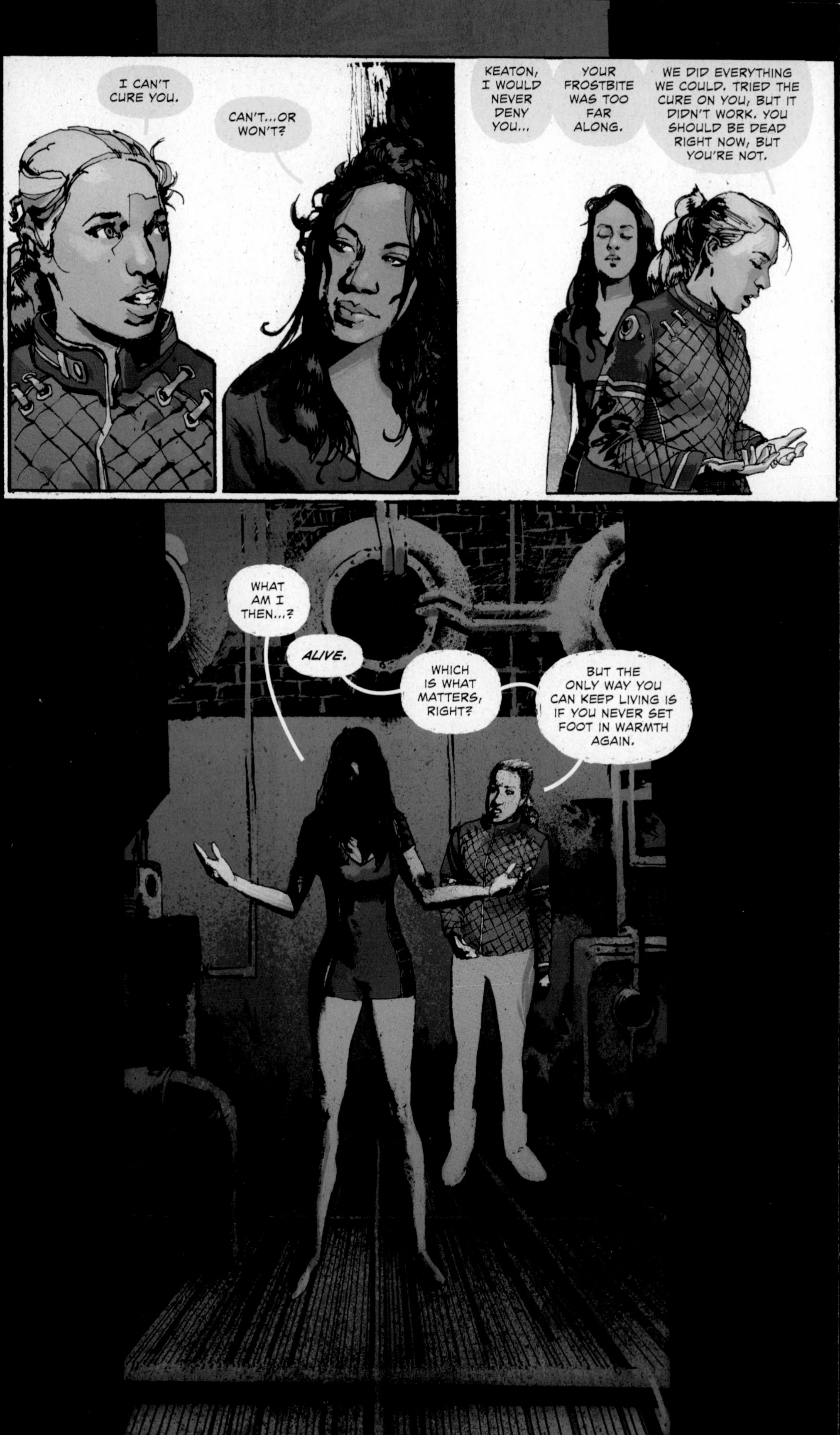
I CAN'T CURE YOU.
CAN'T...OR WON'T?
KEATON, I WOULD NEVER DENY YOU...
YOUR FROSTBITE WAS TOO FAR ALONG.
WE DID EVERYTHING WE COULD. TRIED THE CURE ON YOU, BUT IT DIDN'T WORK. YOU SHOULD BE DEAD RIGHT NOW, BUT YOU'RE NOT.
WHAT AM I THEN...?
*ALIVE.*
WHICH IS WHAT MATTERS, RIGHT?
BUT THE ONLY WAY YOU CAN KEEP LIVING IS IF YOU NEVER SET FOOT IN WARMTH AGAIN.

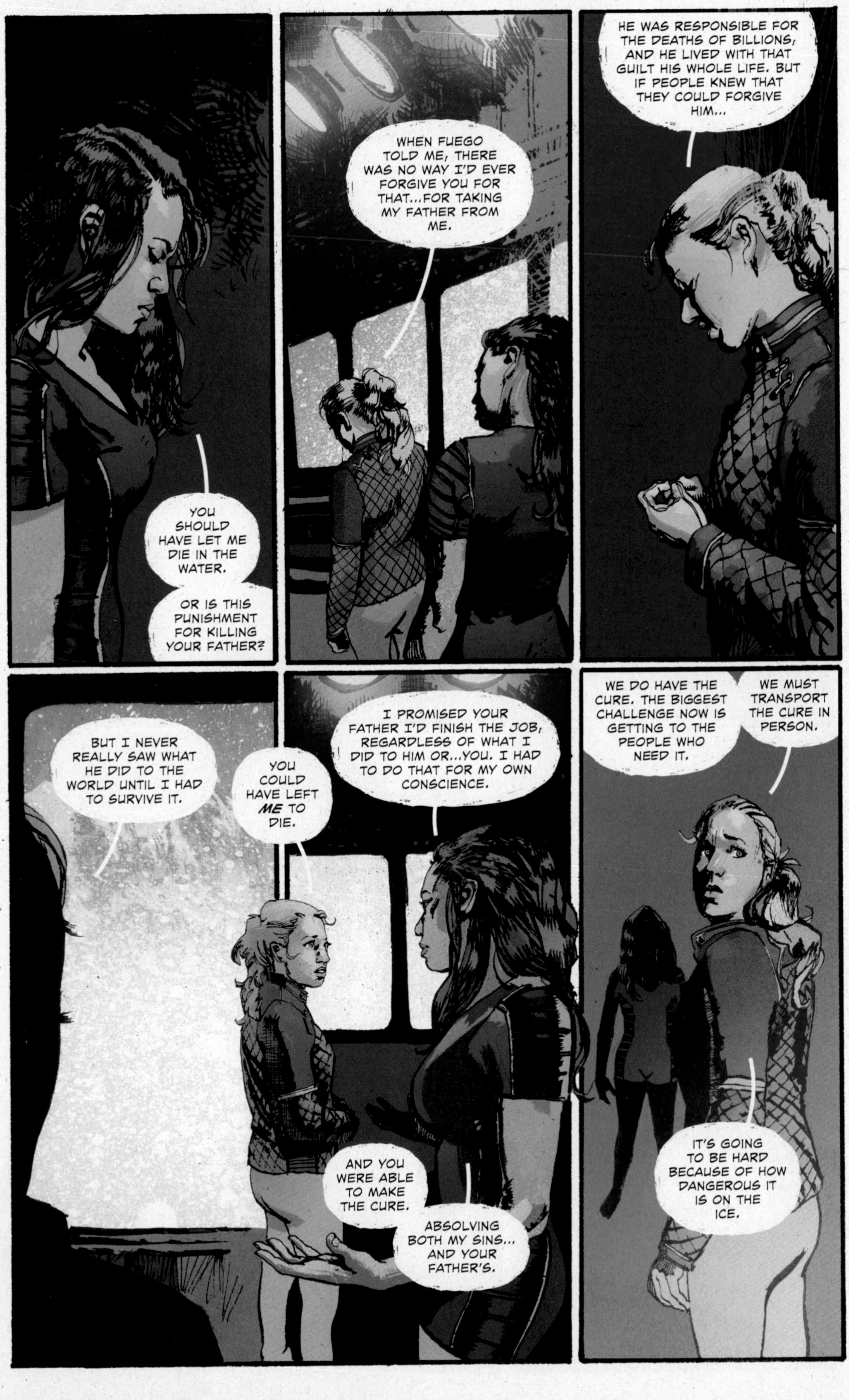
YOU SHOULD HAVE LET ME DIE IN THE WATER.
OR IS THIS PUNISHMENT FOR KILLING YOUR FATHER?
WHEN FUEGO TOLD ME, THERE WAS NO WAY I'D EVER FORGIVE YOU FOR THAT...FOR TAKING MY FATHER FROM ME.
HE WAS RESPONSIBLE FOR THE DEATHS OF BILLIONS, AND HE LIVED WITH THAT GUILT HIS WHOLE LIFE. BUT IF PEOPLE KNEW THAT THEY COULD FORGIVE HIM...
BUT I NEVER REALLY SAW WHAT HE DID TO THE WORLD UNTIL I HAD TO SURVIVE IT.
YOU COULD HAVE LEFT *ME* TO DIE.
I PROMISED YOUR FATHER I'D FINISH THE JOB, REGARDLESS OF WHAT I DID TO HIM OR...YOU. I HAD TO DO THAT FOR MY OWN CONSCIENCE.
AND YOU WERE ABLE TO MAKE THE CURE.
ABSOLVING BOTH MY SINS... AND YOUR FATHER'S.
WE DO HAVE THE CURE. THE BIGGEST CHALLENGE NOW IS GETTING TO THE PEOPLE WHO NEED IT.
WE MUST TRANSPORT THE CURE IN PERSON.
IT'S GOING TO BE HARD BECAUSE OF HOW DANGEROUS IT IS ON THE ICE.

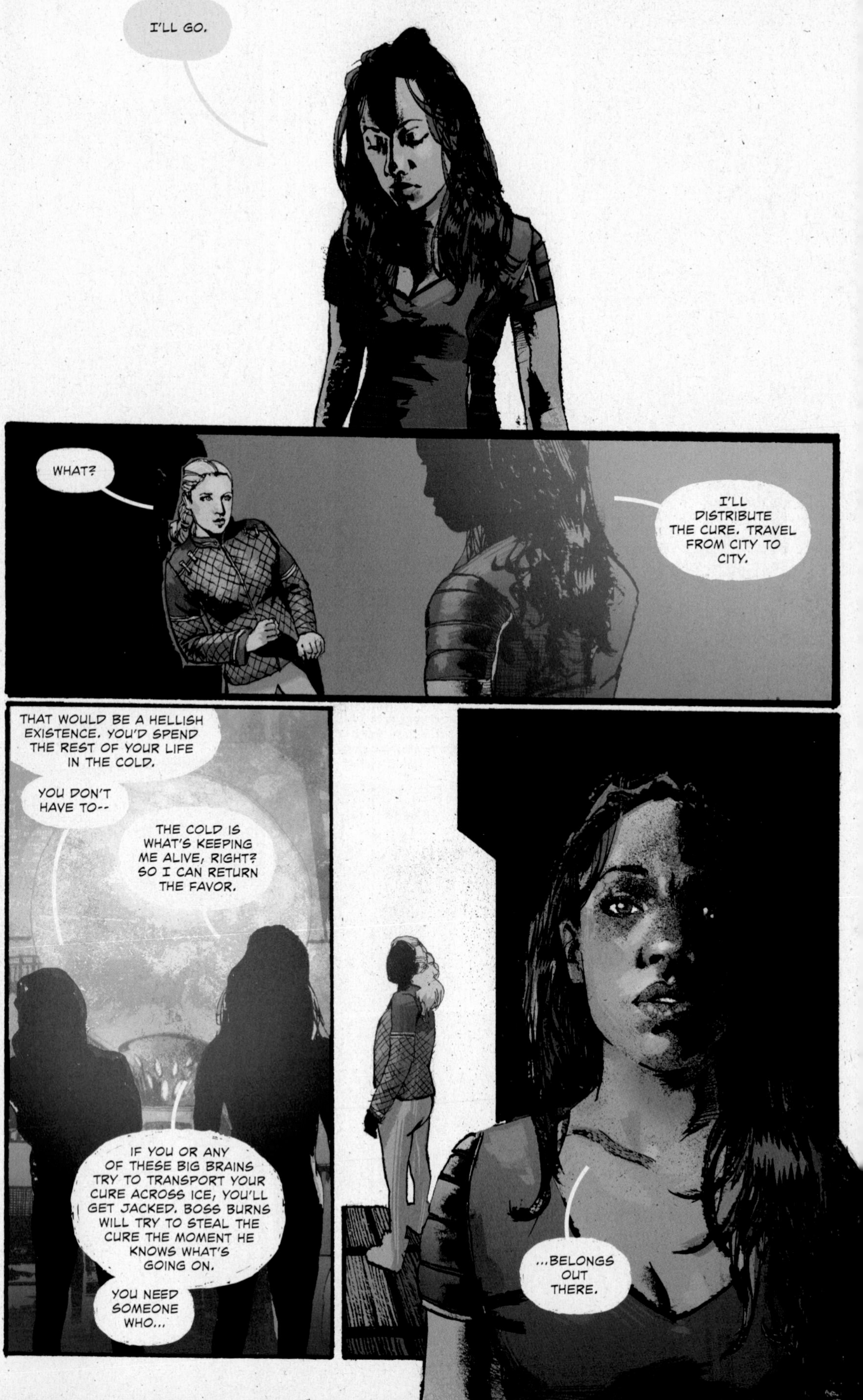

I'LL GO.
WHAT?
I'LL DISTRIBUTE THE CURE. TRAVEL FROM CITY TO CITY.
THAT WOULD BE A HELLISH EXISTENCE. YOU'D SPEND THE REST OF YOUR LIFE IN THE COLD.
YOU DON'T HAVE TO--
THE COLD IS WHAT'S KEEPING ME ALIVE, RIGHT? SO I CAN RETURN THE FAVOR.
IF YOU OR ANY OF THESE BIG BRAINS TRY TO TRANSPORT YOUR CURE ACROSS ICE, YOU'LL GET JACKED. BOSS BURNS WILL TRY TO STEAL THE CURE THE MOMENT HE KNOWS WHAT'S GOING ON.
YOU NEED SOMEONE WHO...
...BELONGS OUT THERE.

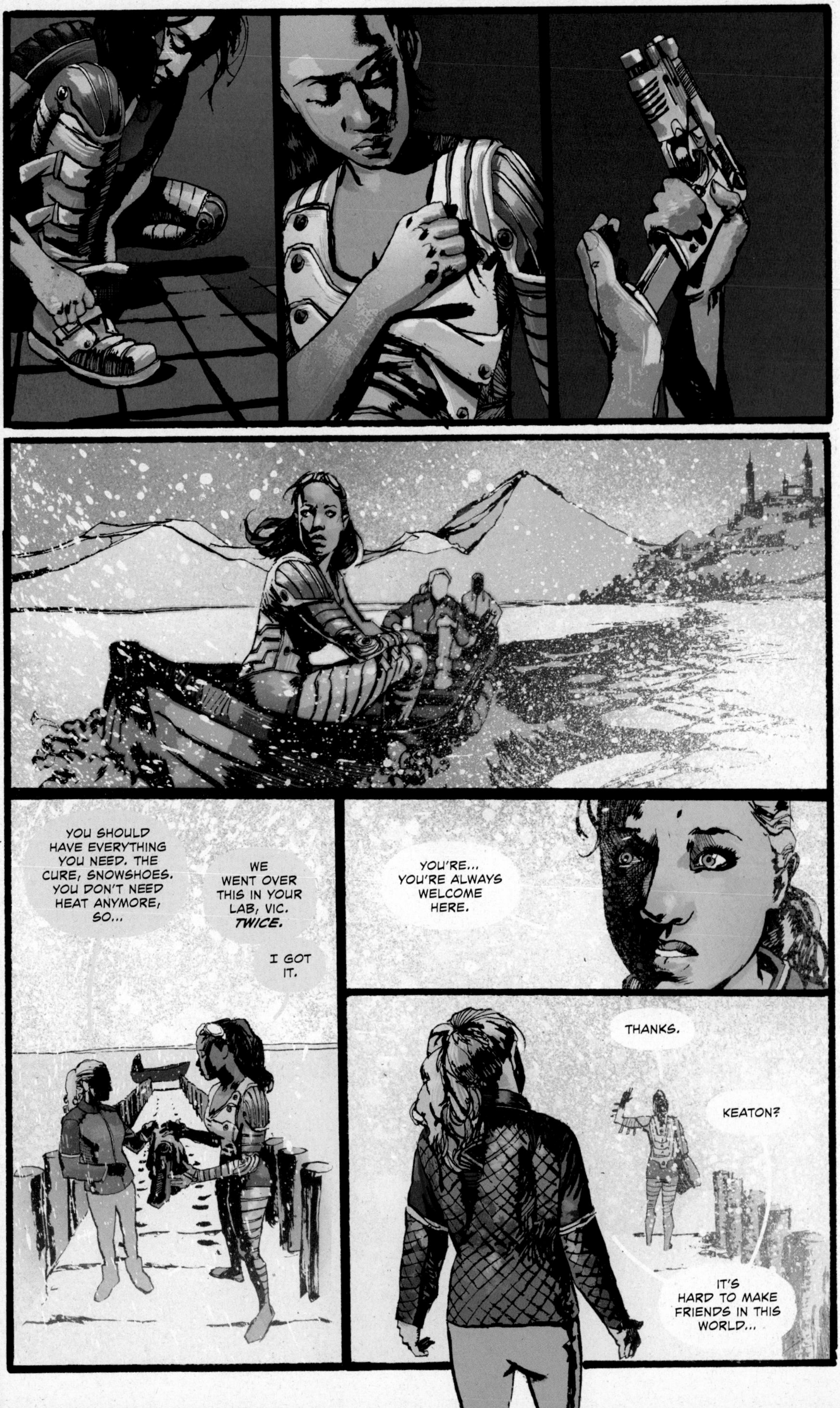
YOU SHOULD HAVE EVERYTHING YOU NEED. THE CURE, SNOWSHOES. YOU DON'T NEED HEAT ANYMORE, SO...
WE WENT OVER THIS IN YOUR LAB, VIC. *TWICE.*
I GOT IT.
YOU'RE... YOU'RE ALWAYS WELCOME HERE.
THANKS.
KEATON?
IT'S HARD TO MAKE FRIENDS IN THIS WORLD...

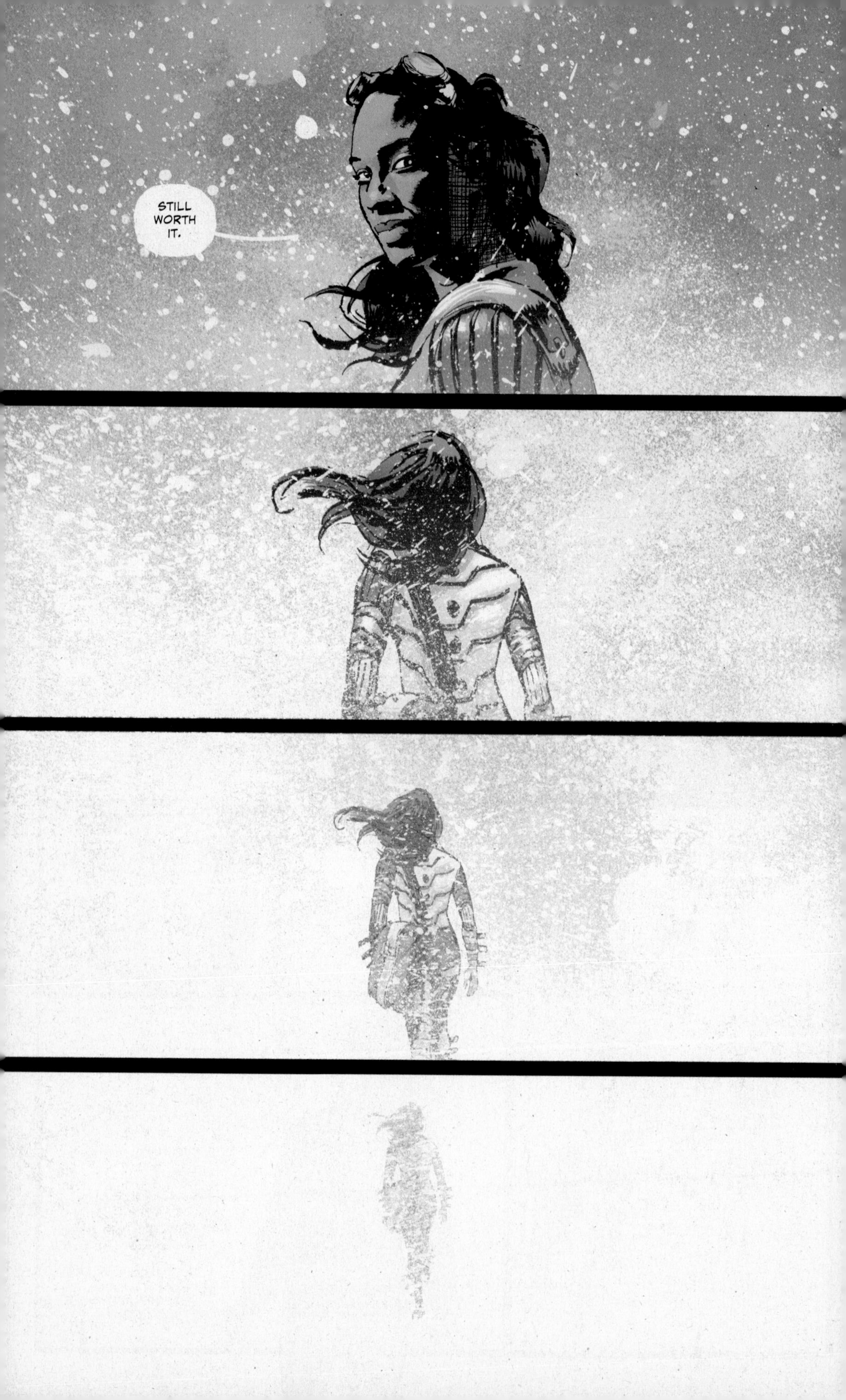
STILL WORTH IT.

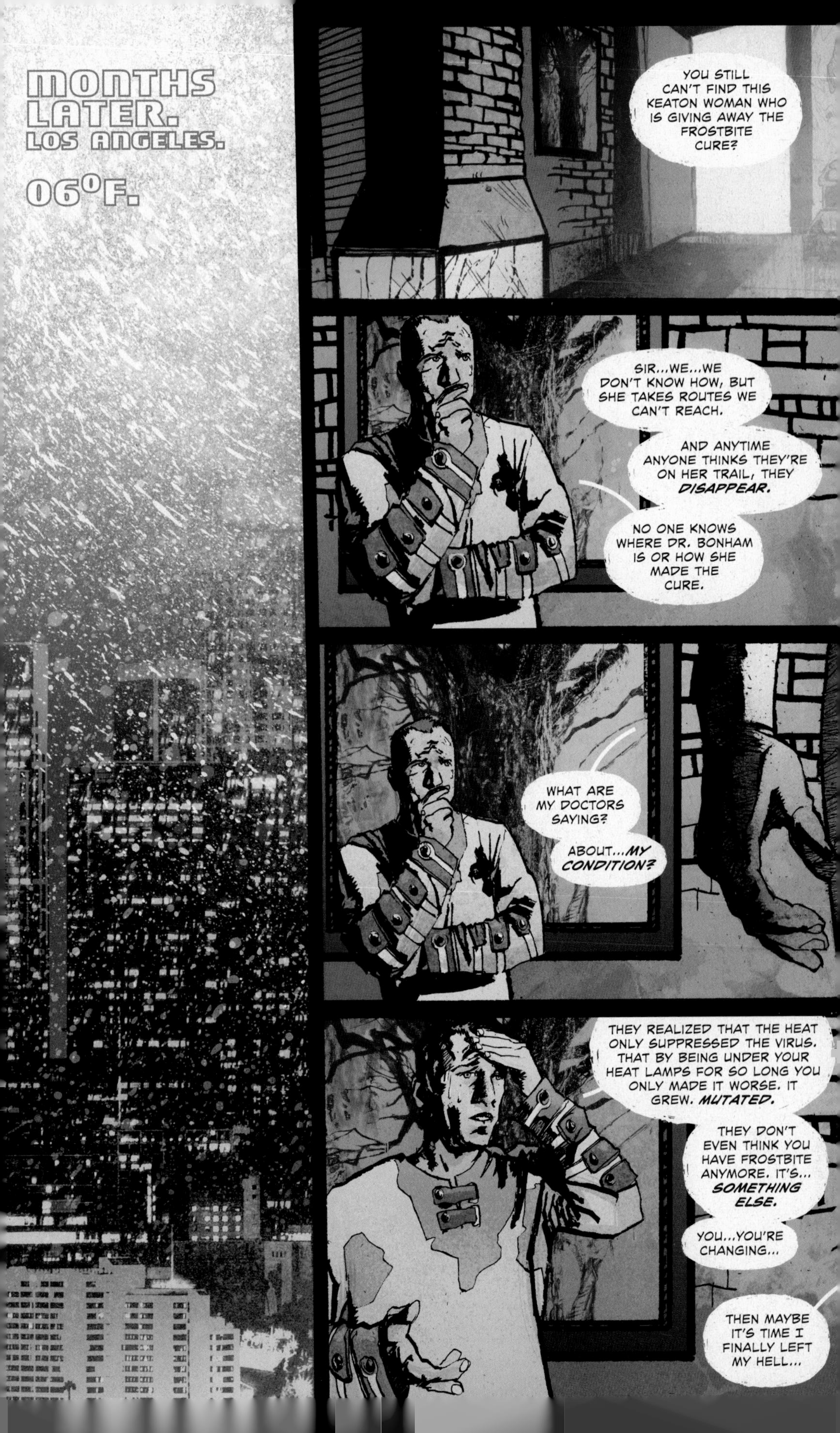
MONTHS LATER. LOS ANGELES.
06°F.
YOU STILL CAN'T FIND THIS KEATON WOMAN WHO IS GIVING AWAY THE FROSTBITE CURE?
SIR...WE...WE DON'T KNOW HOW, BUT SHE TAKES ROUTES WE CAN'T REACH.
AND ANYTIME ANYONE THINKS THEY'RE ON HER TRAIL, THEY DISAPPEAR.
NO ONE KNOWS WHERE DR. BONHAM IS OR HOW SHE MADE THE CURE.
WHAT ARE MY DOCTORS SAYING?
ABOUT...MY CONDITION?
THEY REALIZED THAT THE HEAT ONLY SUPPRESSED THE VIRUS. THAT BY BEING UNDER YOUR HEAT LAMPS FOR SO LONG YOU ONLY MADE IT WORSE. IT GREW. MUTATED.
THEY DON'T EVEN THINK YOU HAVE FROSTBITE ANYMORE. IT'S... SOMETHING ELSE.
YOU...YOU'RE CHANGING...
THEN MAYBE IT'S TIME I FINALLY LEFT MY HELL...

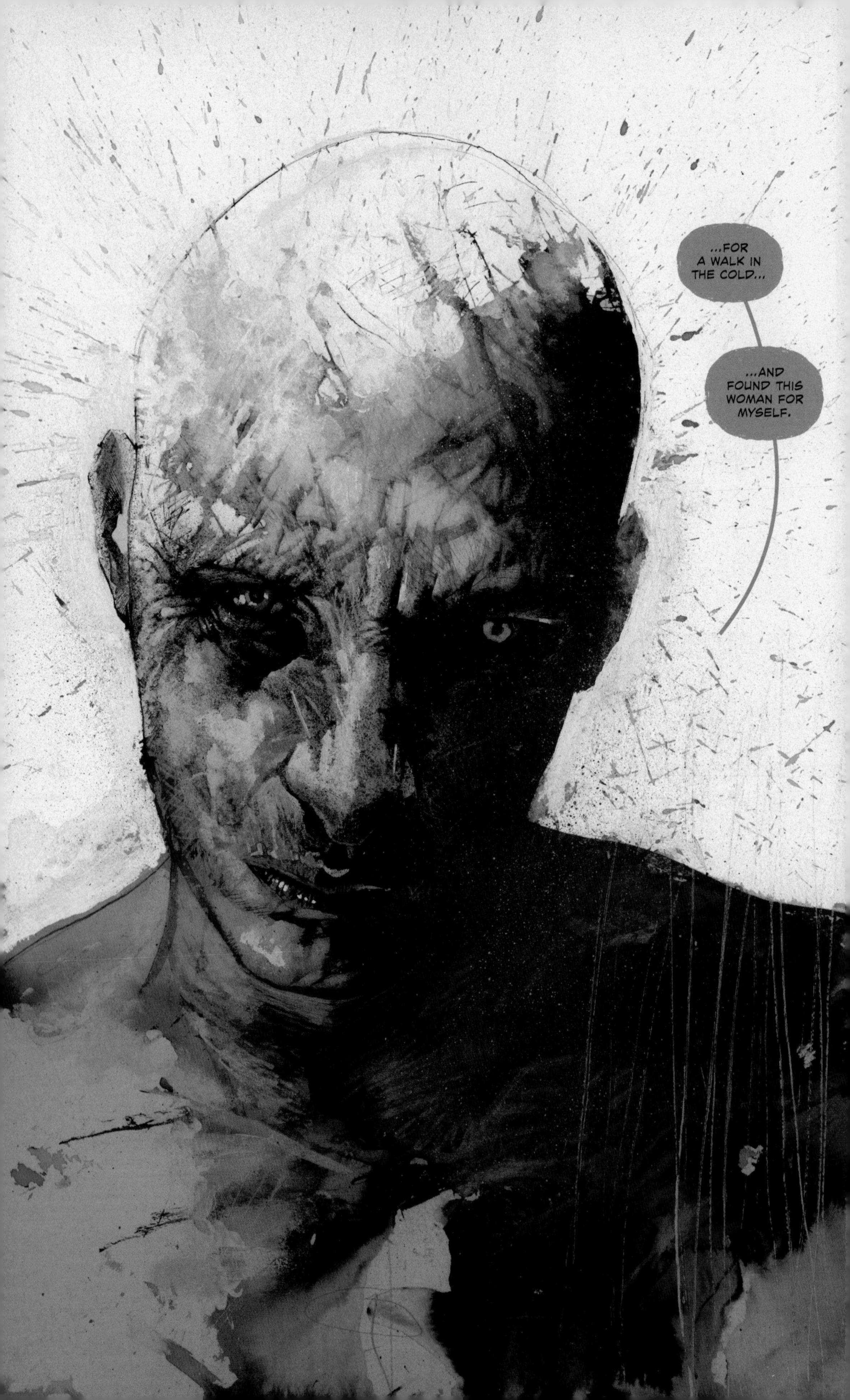
...FOR A WALK IN THE COLD...
...AND FOUND THIS WOMAN FOR MYSELF.

# COVER GALLERY

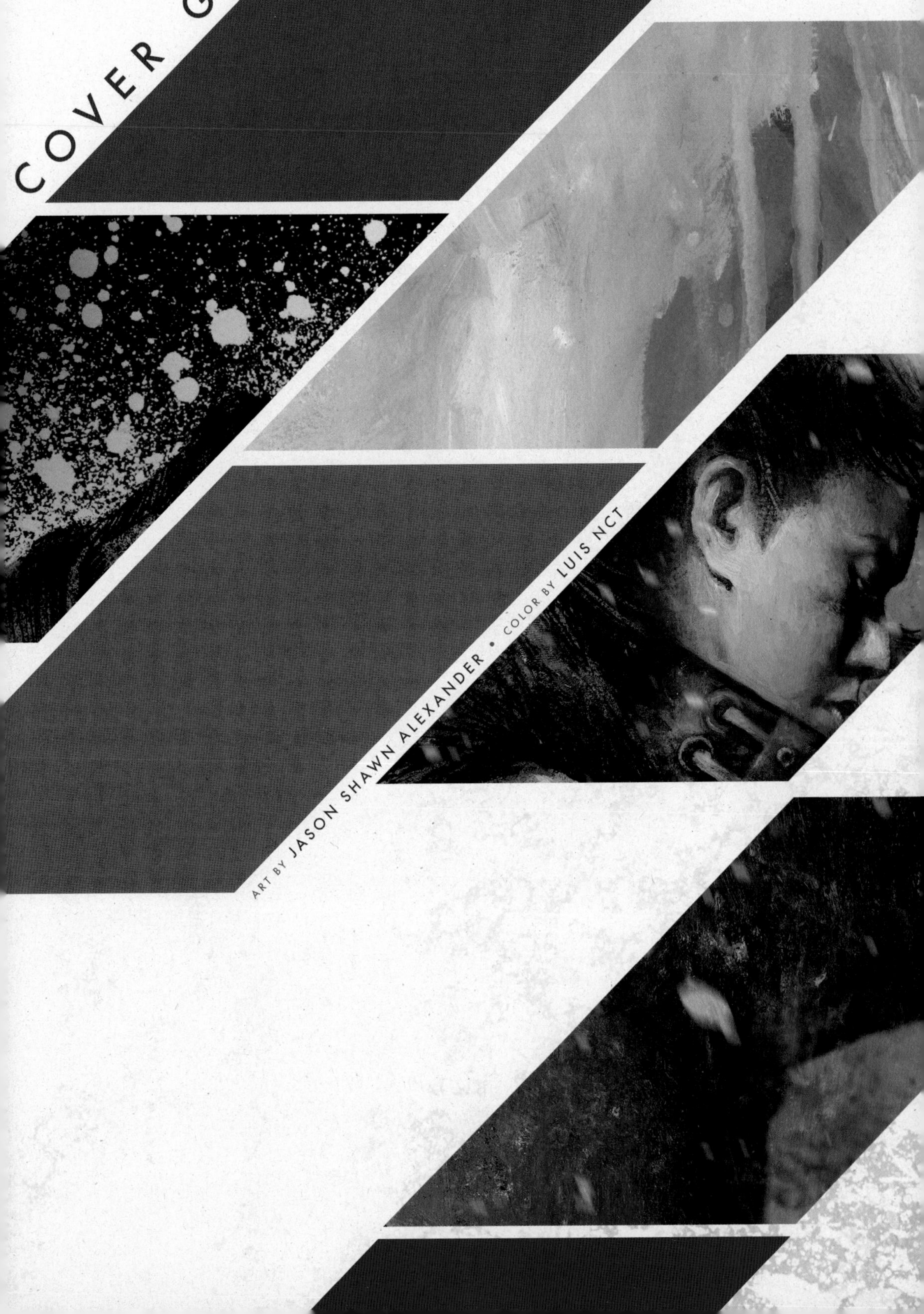

ART BY JASON SHAWN ALEXANDER • COLOR BY LUIS NCT

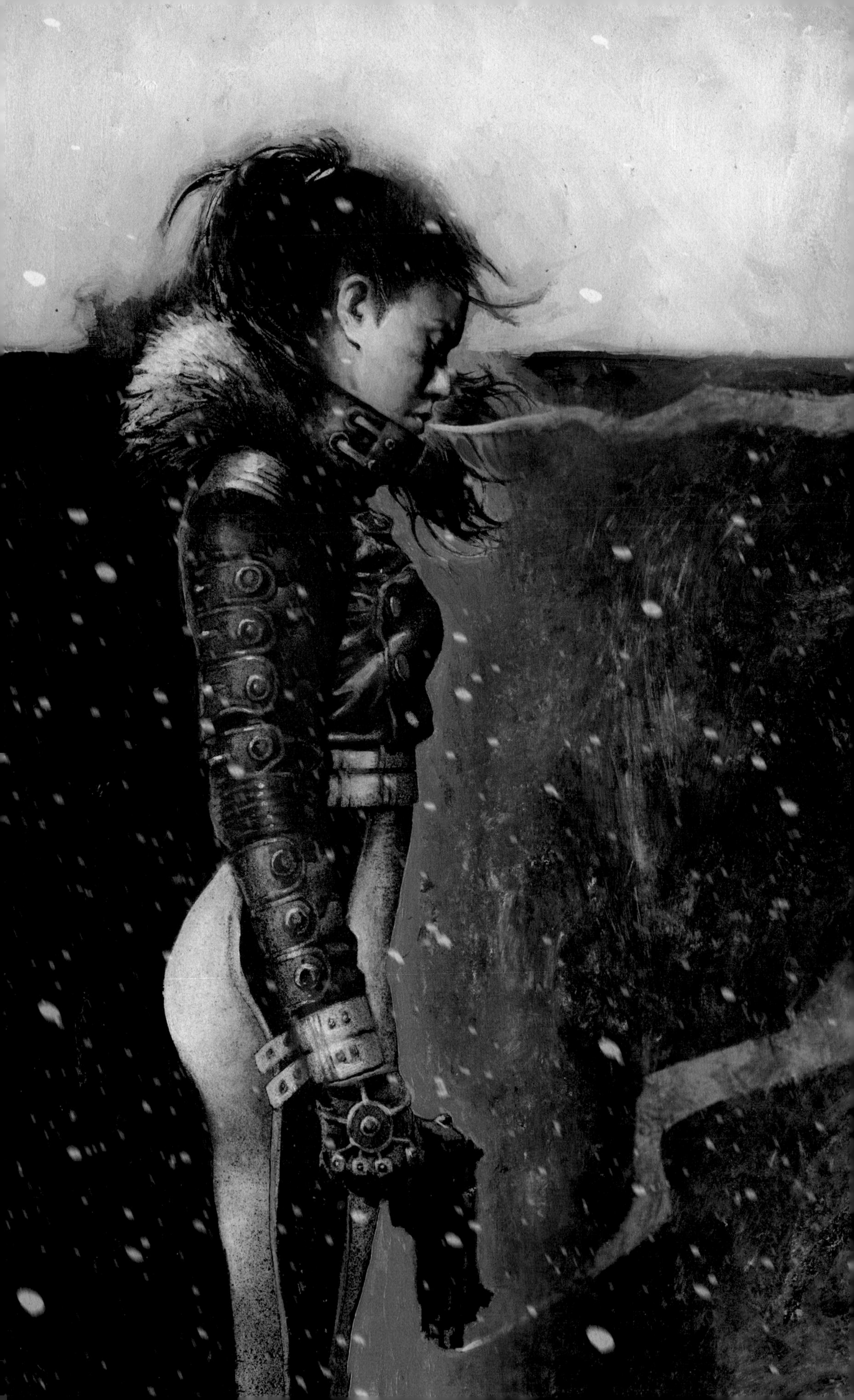

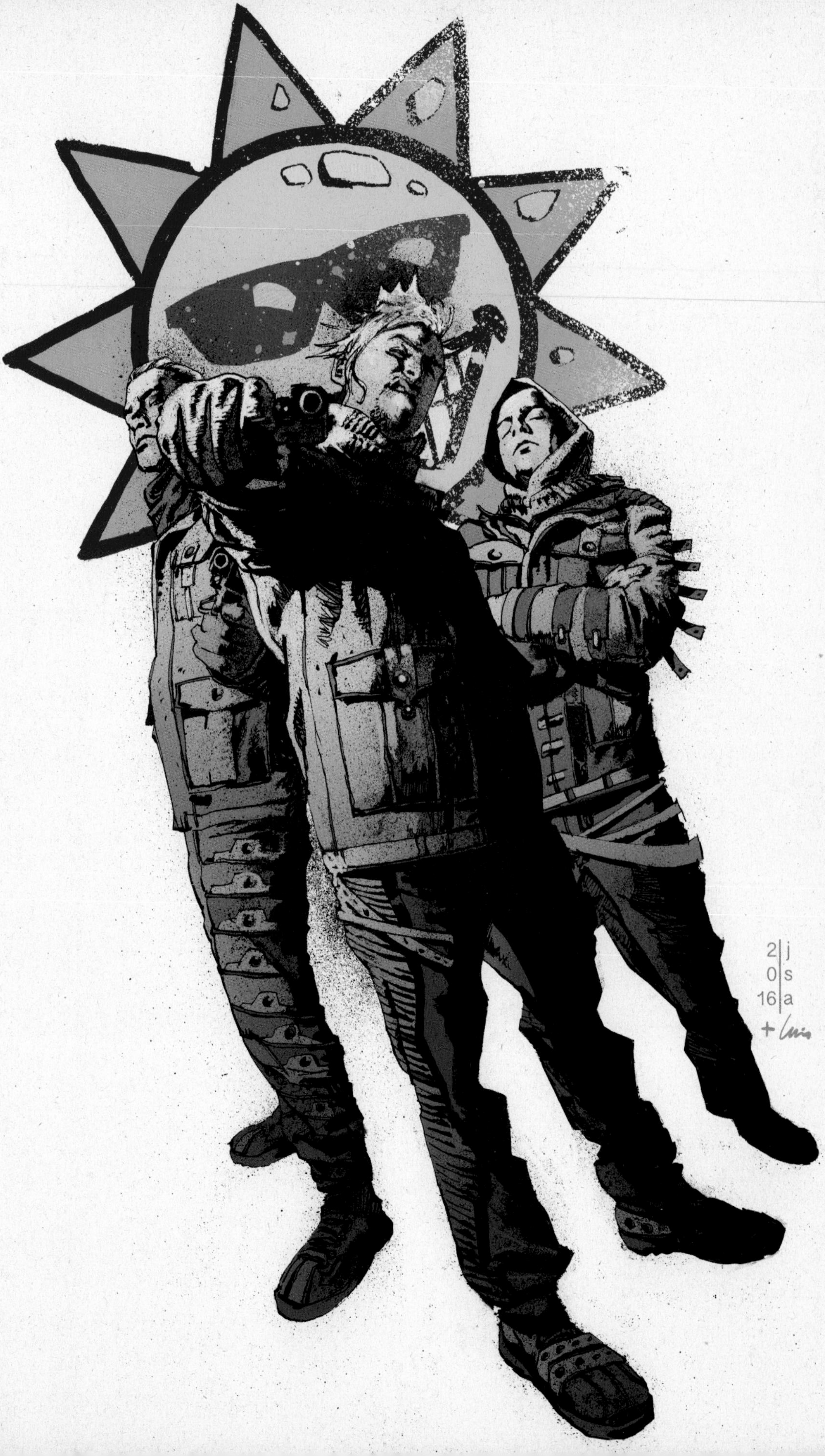
2 j
0 s
16 a

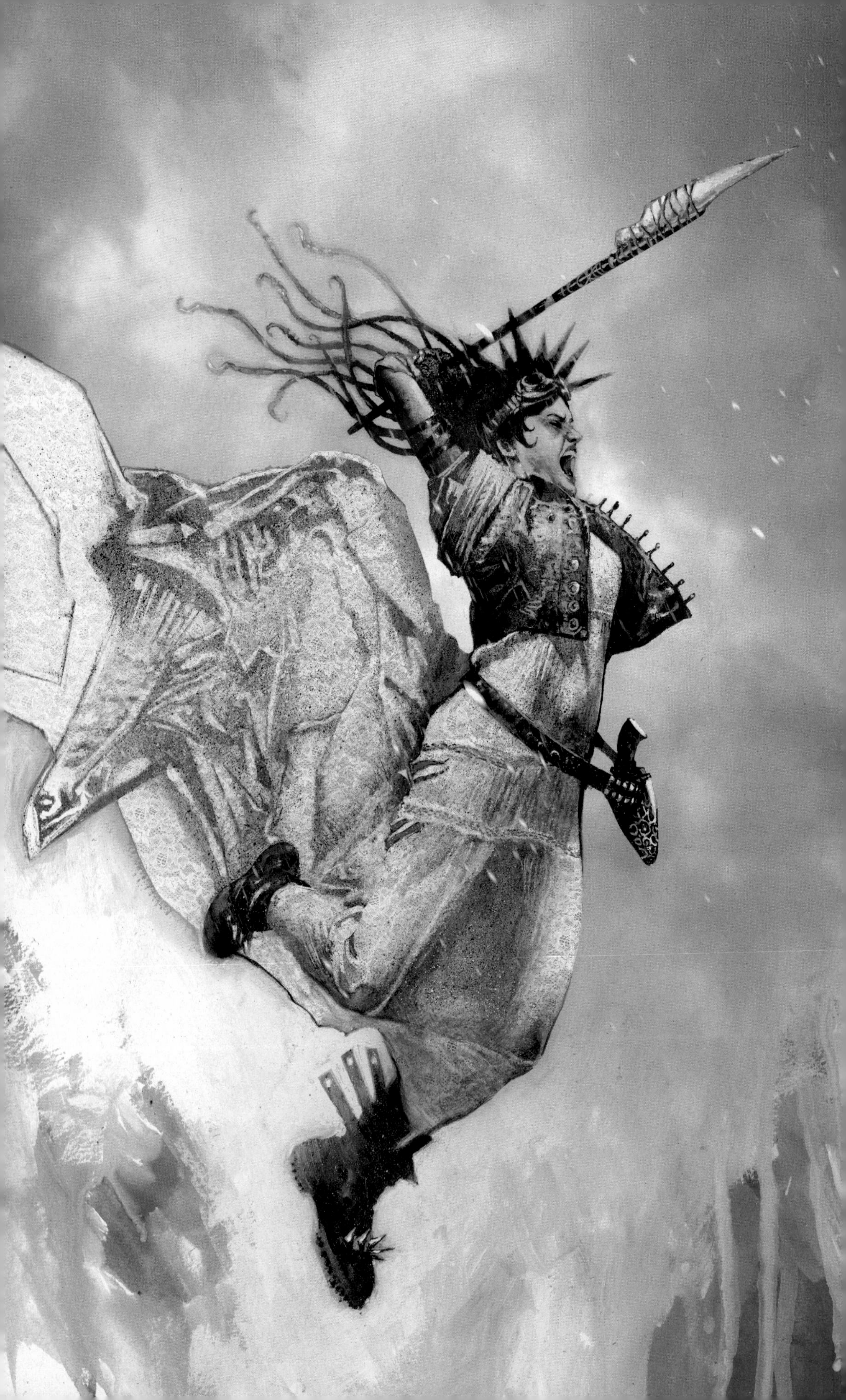

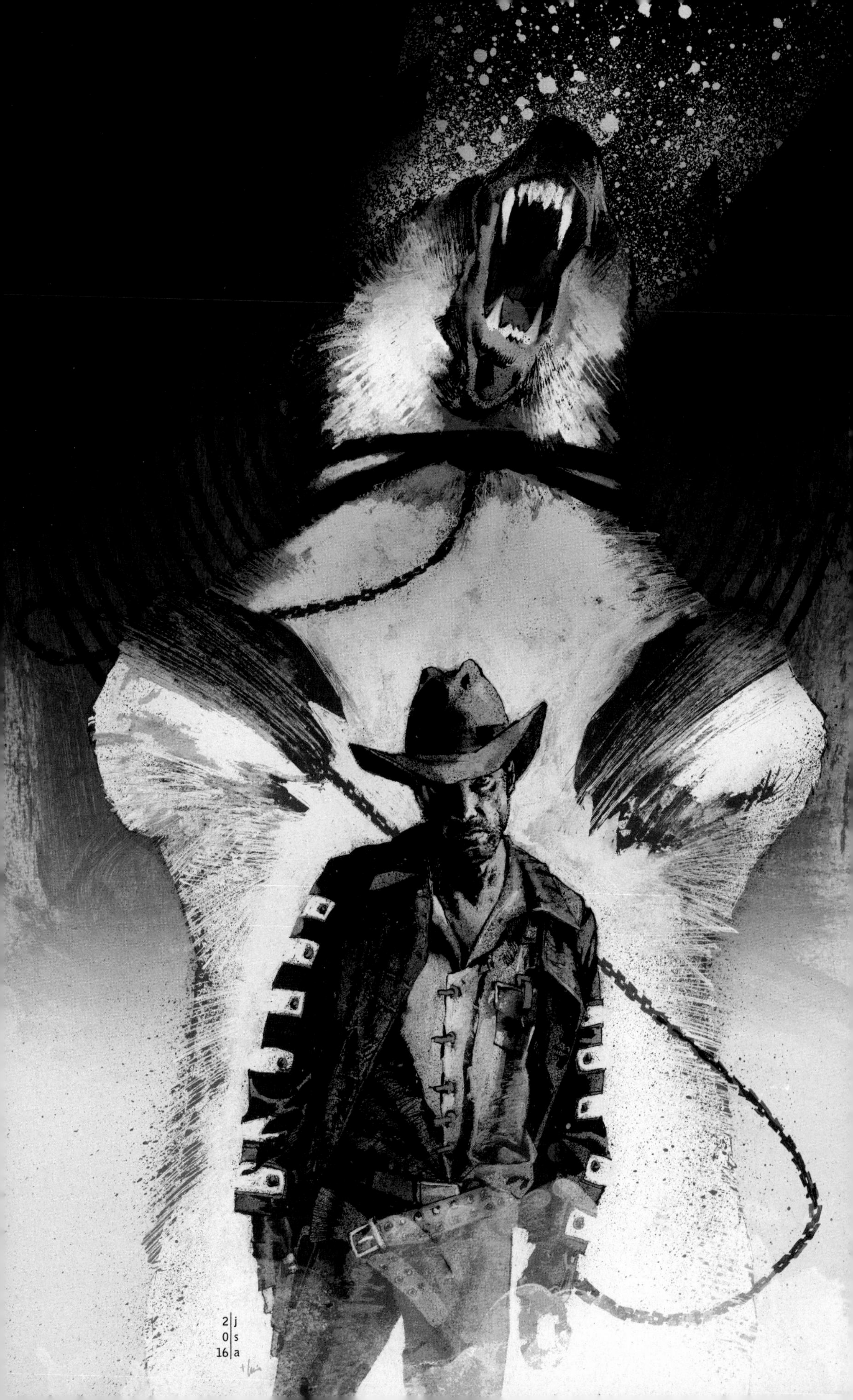
2 j
0 s
16 a

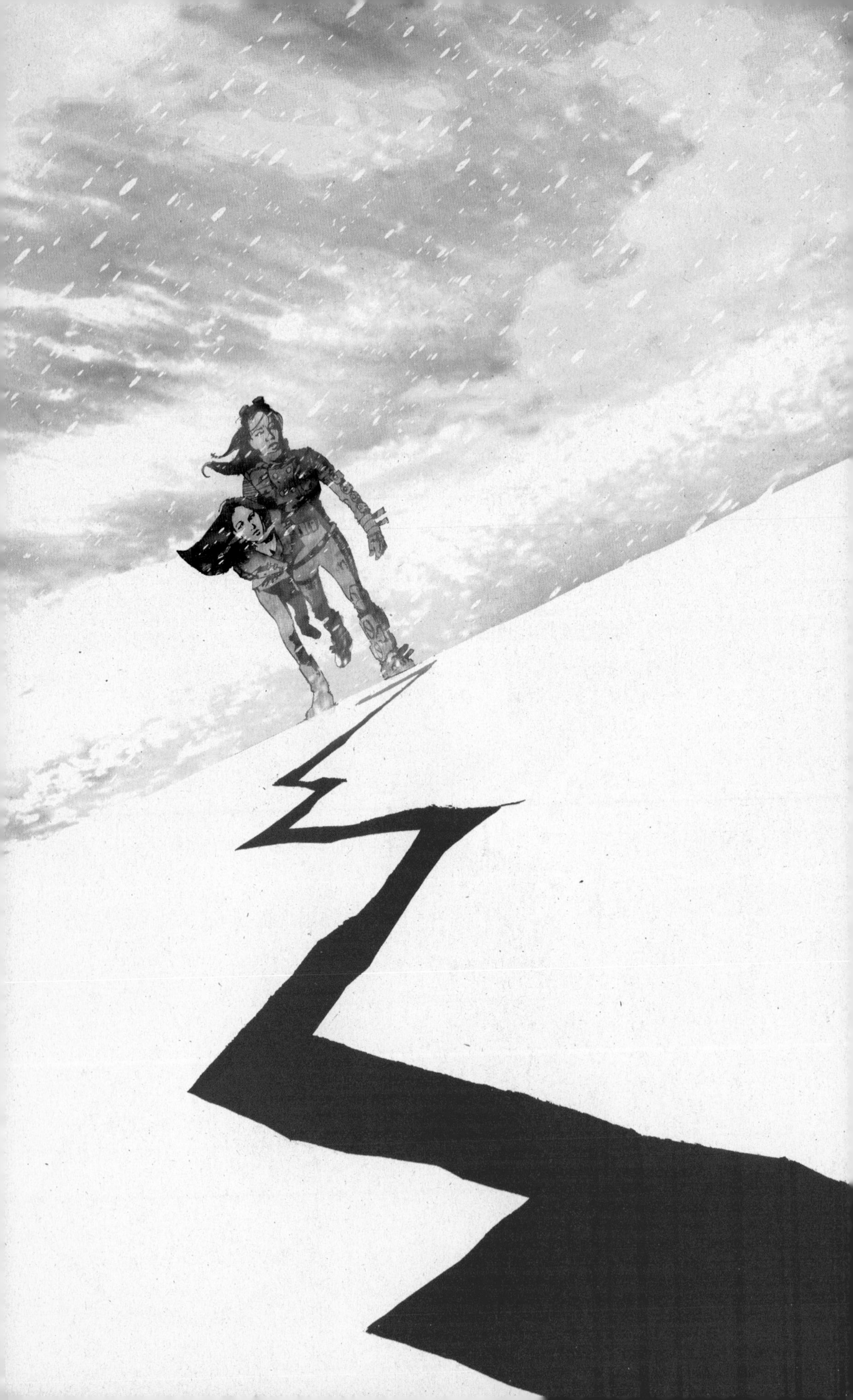

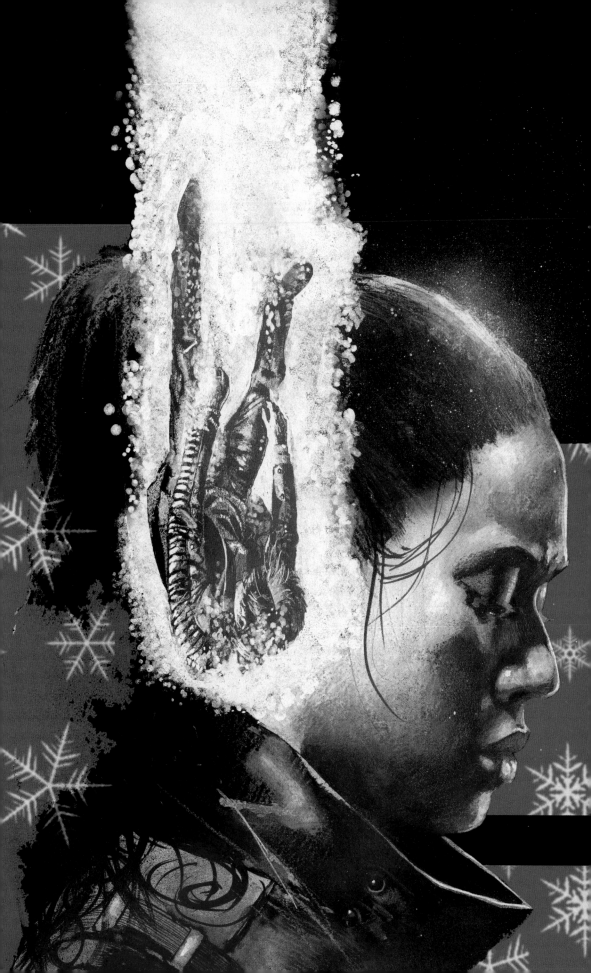